LIVE FOREVER &
FIX EVERYTHING

LIVE
FOREVER
& FIX
EVERYTHING

A Practical Plan for a Future
That Works for Everyone

JAMES BAKER

IMMORTALITY PRESS

LIVE FOREVER & FIX EVERYTHING
A Practical Plan for a Future That Works for Everyone

ISBN   978-1-5445-3396-4   *Hardcover*
           978-1-5445-3397-1   *Paperback*
           978-1-5445-3398-8   *Ebook*

CONTENTS

Introduction   ix

Chapter 1. Overview   **1**

Chapter 2. Problems   **9**

Chapter 3. Tools   **17**

Chapter 4. The City   **43**

Chapter 5. Relationships   **79**

Chapter 6. Empathy   **103**

Chapter 7. Immortality   **119**

Chapter 8. Health   **133**

Chapter 9. Money   **149**

Chapter 10. Inner Peace for Sale   **171**

Chapter 11. An Economy for a World That Works   **191**

Chapter 12. Right Now   **215**

Conclusion   **227**

Appendix 1. Assumptions for the City of Chapter 4   **245**

Appendix 2. Crypto   **269**

Appendix 3. Comparison of Currencies   **281**

Acknowledgments   **289**

Endnotes   **291**

Index   **297**

INTRODUCTION

The future of humanity can go one of three ways:

1. We annihilate ourselves and go extinct.
2. We continue to muddle along.
3. We learn to live forever and fix everything.

This is a book about option number three.

It is my vision of a positive path forward, which shows how we make a future in which today's global problems get solved. Along the way, we create a glorious new world for ourselves. My tastes are not universal. You may disagree or prefer a different path. That's okay. I describe a future with multiple aspects that fit together and reinforce each other. But the parts work independently too. And each part can be improved independently or replaced with something better. Everything in this book is based on technology we have today or technology we can reasonably expect soon. No new scientific breakthroughs are required.

Undoubtedly, the future will not turn out exactly as I describe. Maybe it shouldn't. Take what you like and feel free to reject the rest. Or better yet, use your skill and imagination to replace the parts you don't like with something better.

Before we move forward, I must acknowledge that I'm making several assumptions about you, the reader. I think you agree with me that business-as-usual is not the right path forward. I assume you know in your bones that better alternatives are possible. I'm assuming that you want a world that is more just, fair, secure, and sustainable. I'm going to guess that you are not an ascetic, renouncing worldly pleasures, but that you'd prefer a comfortable life for yourself and others.

While individual choices are important, collective action and public policy are also key. This book explores a future shaped by both individual and collective actions, with an emphasis on collective actions. Collective actions often flow from the introduction of new products and services—social media, for example. This book includes descriptions of new inventions that can foster meaningful collective action.

After you read this book, my hope is that you will see the world differently. Where you previously saw intractable problems, you will now see practical possibilities. Where you previously imagined problems to be tightly wound knots, impossible to detangle, now you will see solutions. Living in harmony with nature will no longer equate to giving up modern luxuries. Instead, you'll wonder why we have so little to show for our impact on the natural world. Addressing inequity will no longer mean giving up what you have for the benefit of others. Instead, you will see a world where you benefit because others have greater opportunities to contribute.

You will likely have ideas about how to improve my plan, or you may have concerns that call for further research. Ideally, that's how the future gets made: collaboratively. Today's common view of the future is often an internal conversation between vague hope and deadly inertia. I aim to provide you with your own clear and positive vision of the future. I hope, after you read this book, the conversation in your head becomes one between competing positive outcomes. Most of all, I hope that the future actually becomes something like what you are about to read.

In this book, you will visit a future that is possible in the next several decades. That means within your lifetime. We will discuss extending your lifetime, but even with conventional lifespans, this book is about a future with you in it. This is not a tale about some distant possibility. There is discussion of new technology, but technology is not the focus; human nature is. I describe actions we can take to maximize our genuine well-being. Of course, well-being means nothing if the world we live in becomes uninhabitable, so I also focus on ways we can improve our relationship with the natural world as well as with each other.

The world around us also includes technology, so I've accounted for that as well. Included in my vision are virtual reality, artificial intelligence, brain machines, and a futuristic city, but these things are probably coming anyway. The difference is that these technologies will work for you, not simply as parts of the larger economy. The economy will no longer be a giant machine with workers and consumers as minuscule parts. Instead, we will each be full-fledged owners of our situations.

I also describe ways we can organize a system not terribly unlike today's economy but designed to deliver the more ephemeral aspects of genuine well-being. Psychologist Abraham Maslow described a hierarchy of needs in which physical needs occupy one of five levels. The other four levels are safety, belonging, esteem, and self-actualization. Today's economy is optimized to deliver physical goods but doesn't do a good job addressing our needs on the other four levels. What if we had an economy that delivered on all five levels with the ease and reliability of ordering a pizza?

I can't quite promise that. Emotional well-being is both a matter of systems and a matter of developing ourselves internally. But there's a lot that systems can do to help. Longer lifespans give us time, motivation, and the energy to tackle big issues, plus a surprising psychological advantage. I'll describe all that and explain how we escape death.

Who am I? I'm a sixty-six-year-old self-taught engineer, inventor, and technology entrepreneur living in Seattle, Washington. Does this qualify me to invent the future? Maybe. As a child I liked to take things apart to see how they worked. That might be the best qualification I have. All human knowledge either comes from our animal instincts or because someone originally made it up. Much of what is made up is later proven wrong. But each time we make something up and prove it wrong, our overall understanding grows. Understanding what is possible and making the future better is what I'm interested in.

This book is one person's integrated plan for the near-term future. It is based on science we have and numbers that work. The plan is compelling because it delivers what I think people, including you, really want. The plan is not complete or perfect.

However, this book is not a prediction. I describe what is possible, not what is inevitable. Bad choices can continue to be made. Hopefully our bad choices will not lead to our annihilation and the end of the human experiment. I hope just having this one viable plan in print will help inspire us to make better choices.

It's important to explain that this book is not a story of a utopia. Utopia is an end-state, a destination. Rather, I aim to describe one set of possibilities for the next few decades. The longer-term future will hopefully take us far beyond what I describe in these pages. I've kept my focus on the next few decades because this is a critical period and deserves immediate attention. Your attention! I want you to see yourself in this future and experience this future for real.

As we start our journey, please remember that this is more of a roadmap than a step-by-step plan. Any plan of this scope requires flexibility in its execution. You will read descriptions of inventions and new technology that can be built with today's capabilities. Some of these inventions offer immediate commercial and societal benefits. But these are to be seen merely as examples or hints. Often it is easier for me to describe something specific to communicate a general idea. Specifics are also easier for you, the reader, to visualize. But when the plan gets put into practice all kinds of things can happen. Some of my specific examples will turn out to have obvious flaws: obvious when we try to write the software or build the physical items. That's the nature of inventing things. The fun is in creatively harnessing reality without losing the essence of our vision.

I will now take you on a trip for a few hours as you read this book; a trip into one vision of the future—a future that is entirely possible if we choose it. I hope it is a future you'd choose to live in with me.

CHAPTER 1

OVERVIEW

A BOOK ABOUT THE FUTURE STARTS WITH THE present. At present, we are seeing history unfold along an unsustainable path. However, many problems are easily fixed, especially with focused attention and active imaginations.

The truth is, most of our existing problems are predictable and avoidable. But that doesn't mean we will automatically recognize them and change our behavior in time to avoid their consequences. Bad stuff can always happen. People can and probably will make foolish choices. We can have senseless wars, famine, disease, and bad leaders. We can have misinformation that captures the public imagination. Inventions can have bad side effects that only become apparent later. Or inventions can have bad side effects that are obvious immediately and still become popular. Yet, all these problems are less of a threat than the threat of inaction. Inaction can occur because of simple inertia and existing habits, but also because of human psychology.

Human psychology sometimes values comparative advantage higher than absolute gain. Human psychology has a built-in sense of fairness and unfairness. Sometimes this sense of fairness gets over-activated and sees any advantage to another as a threat to self. Our challenge is to accept what is better for us even when others get more relative advantage. Others get more relative advantage mostly because they are starting from worse conditions. In other words, people are sometimes reluctant to give up their favored position relative to others even when everybody wins—a zero-sum mindset. But that makes the benefits no less compelling for those of us currently living in privilege. The limiting factor is perception, not reality—inertia, not incentives. Our biggest limitation is a lack of imagination, not love for the way things are.

Whether through inertia or as a result of other problems, one threat stands out from all the others. That threat is irreversible damage to the natural world. We don't currently know how close we are to a tipping point where, instead of continuing to mitigate our stress on the natural world, natural forces tip. When natural forces tip, nature starts undoing nature's past mitigations. We know that the climate includes nonlinear feedback loops for carbon dioxide that make tipping possible, but we don't know the level at which irreversible tipping occurs. At least, we don't know with enough certainty, and anyone who claims to know is at best making an educated guess. There are other natural mechanisms that can cause problems if we break them. We understand these mechanisms even less.

This warning of danger is not new information, but so far, the threat of annihilation has not been sufficient motivation for society to sufficiently change course. For sufficient motivation, we also need a future that is compelling in its own right—not a utopia with all the answers, not a theme park where we're isolated from the grittiness of real life, not a structured society unable to encompass the divergent interests of different people and groups, but a place you'd really want to live.

We each need a minimum level of peace, stability, wealth, and psychological health to consistently do what is in our own best interest. Is humanity ready? I don't know with certainty, but I think so and hope so. Many of the solutions available to us have always been physically possible. Our obstacles have been what is humanly possible.

At every turn, I champion imagination over sacrifice. What do I mean by this? Any big project takes both inspiration and perspiration. The perspiration part can either be mind-numbing drudgery or satisfying and meaningful action. Satisfying and meaningful action on a sustained basis is an utter joy. I describe a future in which most work will consist of satisfying and meaningful action. But before that day arrives, can the work of building that better future be satisfying? Yes! At least in part. Effort will be required, but think of effort as an occasional push, not what you do from the beginning. Effort is for when your car runs out of fuel ten feet before reaching the continental divide, not what you do from the start.

Think of this place of imagination as the place where altruism and self-interest converge. You want a better world because you want to live in a better world. This is a problem for those of us alive at this moment in history and living with privilege. Our preindustrial ancestors didn't enjoy a world capable of making enough physical goods to supply everyone's needs. Today we have the capacity to build, grow, and manufacture more than enough stuff for everyone. But we have not made similar strides toward the nonphysical aspects of well-being. Historians will look back on this period as the preindustrial age of emotional well-being, when only a select few lived fulfilled lives as human beings. What will it take to make a world where most of us are so privileged? Mostly imagination, some effort, some perspiration, but probably less than you think.

ALTRUISM

		No	Yes
SELF-INTEREST	**No**	Example: you engage in a drunken bar fight and end up hospitalized facing criminal charges.	Example: you give your life savings to charity, miss your rent payment, go hungry, get evicted, and become homeless.
	Yes	Example: you steal thousands of dollars from your employer and get away with it.	Example: through hard work, skill, and luck, you successfully invent a lucrative new lifesaving medicine.

Figure 1. Chart showing combinations of self-interest and altruism, with examples.

The examples I use are extreme, yet this grid is a useful way to look at civilization. Where do we put the invention of writing? Of agriculture? Smartphones? Your favorite joke? Where does your job go? How about your personal goals and caring for your family?

Let us move almost all human activity into the bottom right quadrant. Some of this is simply attitude-shift. There's satisfaction in knowing your efforts are leading us to a better future. Preparing for your own party is more fun than employment as a cafeteria worker, although many of the actions are identical.

In my plan for the future, I take the notion of urban density to its logical conclusion. Urban density is good for a number of reasons. Everything is closer and easier to reach. People in cities use less energy and fewer raw materials. A large nearby population supports services that would not be practical if fewer people could conveniently reach your location. The logical conclusion for density is a single giant city for the whole human population now and in the future. Is this practical? Would people want to live this way? Once most of humanity is conveniently close to almost everything, would you want to live in the second largest city? That would be like having access to the world's second largest computer network but not the internet. We can have many new services and conveniences of course, but what about the outdoors and nature? Can we all live in one city and each have a better experience of nature than we currently enjoy? What about the refreshing experience of wide-open spaces?

I'd like to think we can have the best of both cities and nature, so I imagined a plan that makes it so. I based the plan on calculations and numbers, but my assumptions could be off. We may need only half as much electrical energy, or twice as much. If so, the plan will need to flex. If we need twice as much energy, that means we will need a larger ring of solar panels around our city's core. But the plan still works. Likewise, with other assumptions. I provide my assumptions and numbers in Appendix 1 so interested readers can experiment with different assumptions. I left most of the numbers and calculations out of the text to make this book easier to read.

Victor Hugo is thought to have said, "Nothing is as powerful as an idea whose time has come." Although this is probably misattributed to him, it's a good saying and hopefully true. Is fixing the whole world now, with the tools we have, an idea whose time has come? Is it even possible? If so, the specifics are less important than the perception. This book describes one such use of the tools we have to create one example of a better world.

I describe a worldwide civilization centered in one physical place, one giant city. This city is easy to visualize, and building it is a good idea in reality. I hope this city would be high on your vacation list even if you're not ready to move there. Because it addresses the global problems of today, building this city is a compelling choice for us to make collectively. Because the city is a place you'd want to live, it is a compelling choice individually, too. Because the overall plan is both general and flexible, changes can be incorporated along the way. Changes can be incorporated forever, actually, just like the world we live in now, except the changes would be evaluated on the basis of making genuine improvements in your life versus today's world where the money system drives what happens in most people's lives.

How strange do you expect the future to be? The future will be different from today; that's a certainty. To a degree, we all create what we expect. If you generally expect the future to be different in positive ways and make your choices accordingly, you are a force for good. You are a more powerful force for good if your expectations are detailed and practical. Get used to the idea of a world that works (with specifics). This book contains one such set of specifics.

Einstein said, "We can't solve problems by using the same thinking we used when we created them." This is a book about solving problems with new thinking. But what are those problems?

CHAPTER 2

PROBLEMS

W E'RE GENERALLY FAMILIAR WITH THE interrelated nature of global problems and how they reinforce each other. Climate change causes flooding and crop failures, which further impoverish and make refugees of the farmers. The refugee farmers flee to a place they are unwelcome, causing political discord, which spills into violence and turns to war. Or pick another combination of events and another combination of problems. They are linked. That's the bad news.

The good news is that the solutions are even more interrelated. Education leads to productivity, which leads to wealth, which leads to better health, which leads to more innovation, better public services, and so on. Change in either direction has a compounding effect. The compounding effect, in a sense, is inherent and just happens. But it happens better if we understand the potential synergy and arrange our actions to take advantage of both the synergy and our understanding of it. It benefits countries to study their actions, collect accurate data, and share the data transparently. Our challenge is to collect and distribute data in a way that is useful to all and invasive to none. Chapter 5: "Relationships" discusses data and privacy in more detail. We will see how it is possible and desirable to thoroughly know what's going on.

I've sorted the world's problems into eight categories. Each category has multiple parts. Some familiar problems are not on this list because I consider them only as parts of bigger problems. For example, climate change falls under Problem #1: Damage to the Natural World. Population growth isn't on the list. That's because we will look at the harmful effects of overpopulation, not population itself; especially now that the rate of population growth has been cut in half (since 1966), creating cultures with many old people and few children. Refer to Figure 2.

Problem #1: Damage to the Natural World

Damage to the natural world includes hundreds of items, such as pollution, climate change, desertification, soil erosion, ocean acidification, deforestation, the Great Pacific Garbage Patch, tropospheric ozone, and hundreds of other specific items. Importantly, this category doesn't include the collapse of bee colonies, murder hornets in North America, or elephant poaching. Those are included under Problem #5: Relations between Humans and Other Species.

LIVE BIRTHS PER WOMAN 1900–2018

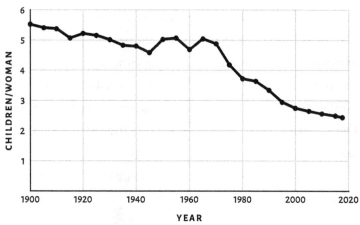

Figure 2. Live births per woman worldwide, 1900–2018. *Source: Our World in Data, a project of the Global Change Data Lab UK. The curve indicates five-year averages. 2018 is the most recent year for which data was available at print time.*

Problem #2: Injustice and Inequity

The category of injustice and inequity includes poverty (both relative and absolute), war, racism (and every other ism) in all its forms, crime, and the range of human nastiness from mass genocide to microaggressions.

Problem #3: Surveillance Capitalism, Loss of Privacy, Online Trolls

The problem of online trolls may not seem like it belongs on a list of global problems, but it does. Here's why: part of building a better world has to do with the ways we regard each other. To treat each other with well-deserved respect and admiration (when admiration is deserved), we need to be able to see each other's admirable traits, unfiltered. In the current online atmosphere, extremes are emphasized because the currency is outrage and continued engagement. If what pays was instead based on a more positive set of values, our online environments would be different. Online interactions would bring out a better and more exciting public self for those who want to express themselves online and a greater alliance between us all. How do we build a world where being a better person pays? Stay tuned.

Problem #4: Weak Personal Connections, Loneliness

Loneliness speaks to what, for many, is the dividing line between current reality and a richer, more satisfying life. If our efforts could pay us in satisfying and meaningful connections, many of us would opt for that kind of reward rather than more money. We can get much more efficient at aligning our desires, our efforts, and our results in this area. I'll describe a new way to measure value and compare it to today's economic system. Many of us are fortunate enough to have our physical needs for sustenance securely met. But our desire for positive interpersonal relations is not nearly so well met. We can fix that.

Problem #5: Relations between Humans and Other Species

Relations between species include animal cruelty, pathogens, mass extinction, and many other items. I propose that we change the way we interact with the natural world in a fundamental way, allowing much of the planet to return to the wild. But the choices about what constitutes "wild" will continue to be humanity's choice. At this stage, it would be negligent to simply abandon the parts of nature we've already changed. Some choices will be obvious, such as prioritizing wild elephants over more mosquitoes. Many decisions will be more contentious. What will our lasting impact on nature be? What is nature? What will nature become in the future?

Problem #6: Death

As you can guess from the title of this book, I'm against death. I'm against death for you and me. Technology is emerging to significantly extend your lifespan, and it is likely to emerge in time for many readers of this book. Not everyone will live forever; death will continue to be a possibility, just not inevitable. The future feels different when we no longer expect to inevitably age and die a grisly death.

Much of our motivation to ignore the current problems plaguing society can be categorized in one of two ways. The solutions either seem to require too much effort, or we see the effects of the problem as tolerable for now. We pass the real trouble on for the next generation to worry about. That approach changes when we expect to live to see the longer-term consequences of our actions. Until recently, we could all expect to die, but humanity would almost certainly go on. Soon the opposite will be true. The death of all humanity will be a bigger threat to our individual lives than aging. This creates a different mindset with new and better problems—problems that are both more challenging and more fun.

Problem #7: Disease

Curing death without addressing disease would be a cruel joke. Diseases are caused by any combination of these four things: infection, what we ingest, heredity, and physiological disease. Physiological disease includes deterioration over time. The four types of disease each require separate responses.

We avoid infectious disease by not getting infected. I don't mean to sound flippant, but to date, our greatest advance in public health is sanitation, especially keeping waste out of drinking water. Yet there is much more we can do to avoid contact with infectious agents.

What we ingest can nourish us, poison us, or leave us with a deficiency. Of course, the solution is to get enough of what keeps us healthy and nothing that makes us sick.

Diseases of heredity include genetic and nongenetic diseases such as psychiatric disorders. I don't have any particular insight into diseases of heredity except to note that DNA repair is beginning to emerge, and science is moving rapidly in this area.

Regarding physiological disease: wear and tear is different from aging, but ending aging will partially address physiological disease by effectively keeping our bodies at an age before symptoms begin. If you have a propensity for age-onset dementia but your body never ages beyond thirty-five, then dementia is mostly not a problem for you.

Problem #8: Limited Outlook, Despair, Withdrawal

This is partly a symptom of short lifetimes in a world of seemingly intractable problems. But like other moments in history, the previously impossible has become possible in a way that makes it compelling. A democratically-governed country, universal literacy, worldwide communications, worldwide transportation—each of these went through stages. First, they were impossible, then aspirational, then maybe-possible-with-hard-work, then each one happened, then not doing any one of them would seem insane.

But each advance took time until its moment occurred, and even then, the moment was only local. Democracy existed alongside aristocracy and still shares the planet with authoritarian rule. Literacy is still not the norm in some countries, especially for girls. Now the need is urgent and global. Can we really do this?

Until now, progress was a trend heading toward the unknown. Progress was seen as a journey, not a destination. Now we are close enough to see the destination, a point where everyone alive can live in cooperation with nature while enjoying conditions as good as today's first-world standards. At that stage, humanity gains a new sort of interrelatedness. Society's focus switches away from a scramble to survive and becomes something else.

I've categorized today's problems into eight items. My intention is to make it easy to keep track of what I'm addressing when I describe possible solutions. What have I left out? I'm not including matters that would be considered spiritual. I consider spirituality a personal area that is internal to the self, not a problem to be solved. But the focus of spirituality is not entirely separate. According to most belief systems, making a better world is a good thing and worthy of your attention.

One way to look at history is to look at what has disappeared. Slavery is the obvious example, but the vestiges of slavery live on, and work remains to correct the lingering effects of that injustice. But whatever happened to predation or duels? There was a time when being eaten by predators was a very real fear. And when was the last time you worried about being challenged to a duel to the death?

The future of the world is partially a self-fulfilling prophecy; we create our future based on what we think is possible. Making the future we want is no different. The difference now is that so much more is within our reach and simultaneously so much is at stake. This is why I think now is the time to consider the future from a viewpoint of what is physically possible, not based on outdated ideas of what is socially or politically acceptable.

CHAPTER 3

TOOLS

WHAT MANY DON'T CONSIDER WHEN THINK-
ing about the current state of our human experience
is that the future we want and deserve can be built
with the tools and techniques we have. Or tools and techniques
that we can reasonably expect to be available by the time we need
them. Or technology that doesn't yet exist but is straightforward
to create and doesn't require new science. Some of the things I
imagine for our future are readily understood. For example, I'll
describe new forms of currency and refer to Abraham Maslow's
hierarchy of needs. Some of the things I will describe are no less
real but not necessarily common knowledge. For example, I'll
describe reactive laminar airflow designs that make it possible to
share indoor space without sharing airborne pathogens.

But one tool, while eminently possible and real, is frustratingly confusing. I'm referring to cryptography, cryptology, and crypt-analysis. Don't worry about the individual words. For simplicity, I'll refer to all of this as "crypto." I'm referring to the technology that (hopefully) keeps your online banking information private. But also, I'm referring to a wide range of techniques that can help balance competing interests in powerful new ways.

Crypto can be frustratingly counterintuitive. It can do seemingly impossible things easily, but often can't do things that seem simple and obvious. Sometimes, this has the effect of making intelligent people feel stupid. Hopefully, I will describe crypto in a way that leaves you with a feel for what is and what is not possible. Think of this as cryptographic literacy. Most of us have a good feel for what electricity can and cannot do. We don't need to be electrical engineers to have a good feel for what is possible with electricity. Likewise with getting a good feel for what crypto can and cannot do. As you become familiar with some examples, you will get a feel for what you can expect from crypto.

I acknowledge that tools alone will not make a better world or make us better people. Work is required in addition to the tools. Hopefully this work can be mostly satisfying discovery, not meaningless toil. Context is key. What otherwise seems like toil becomes gratifying when the result is building a world that works. Routine tasks take on an element of joy. But in addition to the gratification of doing meaningful work, much of what the world needs can be just plain fun. This fun element is especially true for the ways that adapting to a better world both requires and enables us to be better people and more satisfied.

With that said, however, tools are critical for building our way toward a future that provides longevity, cooperation, and justice. The sixteen critical tools we will need in order to make this future possible are as follows.

Tool #1: Social Buy-In

The first tool I will discuss is social buy-in. This is especially important regarding the damage humans have inflicted, and continue to inflict, on the natural world. Social buy-in occurs not because the path looks easy; buy-in occurs when the goal is worthy and the actions look like they can succeed. So far, our efforts have been piecemeal and not robust enough. For example, if you care about climate change, you are told to drive a hybrid or electric car. Bothered by global poverty? Buy fair-trade coffee! Good choices, but not matched to the scale of the problems and therefore not by themselves inspiring.

What inspires people is a robust-enough plan, a plan that fits the scale of the problem. At some level, most of us know that we, as a society, are capable of acting at the required scale. And we understand that suitable specifics are both possible and known (by somebody). Many of us hold a sense of dread about the seeming sacrifices required. There is a temptation to not think about it and leave the work to future generations. Any level of work that leads to avoiding extinction can hardly be described as a sacrifice, but the point here is that creativity and imagination can directly replace sacrifice. We are not short on creativity or imagination.

Tool #2: Maslow's Hierarchy of Needs

According to Abraham Maslow, we have a hierarchy of needs.[1] At the most basic level, we have physical needs such as food, clothing, and shelter. Until those needs are met, other things don't much matter. But once we get enough at any one level, more of the same doesn't really make much difference.

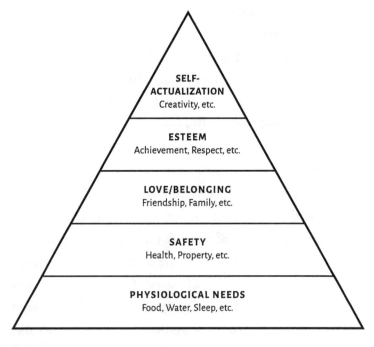

Figure 3. Maslow's hierarchy of needs, Maslow (1943).

For those of us fortunate enough to be secure in our physical needs, our interactions with others become more important than additional sustenance. I use Maslow's hierarchy as one of the tools because it is a useful way to list what matters to our emotional well-being. There is some controversy about the priority order of Maslow's four levels of nonphysical needs, but the order is not important to us. The point is to live a life where all these needs are fulfilled.

Tool #3: New Forms of Money and Measure

Part of human nature includes psychological defenses that worked exceptionally well at a pivotal moment in the past. Because of their success, those psychological defenses became a defining personality trait long after they served a useful purpose. Similarly, the price system was the best possible answer to the scarce resources that defined the world economy of the past. However, nonphysical goods and services are neither scarce nor actual resources. The price structure does not serve these needs.

Today, our economic system is focused on making and acquiring money. That may sound obvious or redundant, but economics can guide our choices in different directions. We must orient our economy toward the things that genuinely make life better for individuals, society, and the planet. We can create an economy that works not only by helping people receive what they most deeply want but also by enriching people who give to each other in imaginative ways. Why doesn't our economy value giving as much as receiving now? Because it doesn't pay. It doesn't pay under our current money system, but that system can change into one where imaginative giving pays in solid ways.

Tool #4: Brain Communication

This is a technology under development today and working in a primitive form but mostly below the radar and out of the news. More than the other tools listed here, brain communication is still not completely proven. The technology includes implanted microsensors to detect the actions of individual brain cells. The sensors connect to a transmitter, which connects to a computer so that the computer can detect activity from individual brain cells.

The user undergoes training to learn to signal the computer in a detailed and deliberate way. As an infant, how do you learn to move your fingers? It happens naturally by trial and error. Later, you may train your fingers again when you take up the piano, and you call it practice. Training yourself to communicate with signals from your brain will be similar, except instead of fingers, nothing physical moves.

Today's version of brain communication requires minimally invasive brain surgery. Most people don't jump for joy at the thought of brain surgery, minimally invasive or not. Hopefully, future versions will use external sensors, but early versions will prove the concept. The concept is that while our bodies have rich sensors for taking in information, we don't have rich ways to transmit information. We don't have comparably rich ways to express ourselves. For example, we have eyes that can see a whole picture in a flash. But we don't have projectors in our foreheads that can project video from our imaginations. The rapid output of rich information will vastly alter the human experience, especially how we treat each other.

Although it is still in early development stages, the signs are there. Empathy will be facilitated in a way almost indistinguishable from living the first-person experience of another person. Conversely, having an experience will no longer be just for yourself. Your inner experience will be shareable with others in vivid new ways.

Tool #5: Zone Pods

I coined the term "Zone Pod" to describe a small room that fools your brain into keeping you in the *flow* or in the *zone*. The zone is that state where your mind and body focus in a way that is relaxed yet energized. In the zone, you lose track of time, and hours later you look back and marvel at how productive you've been. Time spent in the zone is both productive and satisfying.

Maybe your zone is in the woods with birds chirping, or on a fast-moving train, or in a college library surrounded by students focused on their studies. The walls of a Zone Pod are large video screens; the sounds and air are adjustable to give you the feel of your desired location. A Zone Pod is not meant to be a convincing illusion. If you examine the walls, you will never mistake them for the trees of a forest. But with the air set to deliver the right mix of gases, ions, moisture, smells, temperature, pressure, and flow rate; with light that mimics the sun peeking through the leaves; and with the sounds of nature, your brain will accept the illusion well enough to help you stay in the zone.

Zone Pods are not meant to replace reality. The experience is meant to flexibly adapt the room where you spend some portion of your time. Compare a Zone Pod to a work cubicle. The flexibility of a Zone Pod allows you to be in the woods one minute and in a conference room or auditorium with other people a moment later. Zone Pods will not replace the real experience of being together in-person or as part of a group. But the experience inside one compares favorably to conferencing on a computer screen.

But there is a twist. In real life, interactions occur partially based on the physical characteristics of the bodies involved. Perhaps you don't offer your opinion because your colleagues seem too domineering. With a Zone Pod, you could discreetly adjust the illusion to show your domineering colleague as an eighteen-inch-tall version of themself. Now, the bombast seems almost cute and not at all intimidating.

Tool #6: Accordion-Construction

Think about your house. How many rooms does it have? How many people are in each room right now? If some of the rooms are currently unoccupied, your house is a candidate for accordion construction. Using mechanical devices, the unoccupied rooms squish to a fraction of their size until a split second before you enter. Then as you enter, each room is restored to the way you left it, including returning each object to the place you left it.

There are expensive cities where the cost of space makes accordion construction economical today. You will need new furniture, construction materials, appliances, and many other things, but it is worth the cost and effort to effectively have more space. More importantly, it is past time to reimagine those things anyway.

For accordion construction to work, we will need standards, easily configured interchangeable pieces, and enough distributed knowledge to make it work. Not unlike the early years of railroads, automobiles, or personal computers.

Tool #7: "Plumbing"

I say "plumbing" in quotes because I mean plumbing in a broader and more general way than the term is usually used, and I don't have a better name for this tool. Plumbing is what delivers the health benefits of sanitation as well as hot and cold running water. Sanitation safely removes dirty or contaminated water to a place where it is treated before returning the water to a natural system that further treats the water. Before plumbing, cities were terribly dangerous and unhealthy places to live. In nineteenth-century Manchester, England, over half of working-class children died before reaching their fifth birthday, mostly from infectious disease.[2] Then what happened? Sanitation! Plumbing separated the waste from the drinking water and reduced the spread of infectious disease, leading to the most effective public health advance in history.

But then we got vaccines and antibiotics. We stopped focusing on reducing the physical movements of bacteria, viruses, fungi, protozoa, prions, parasites, and allergens. I'll refer to these collectively as "pathogens." Additionally, a feature of our current plumbing is that it depends on nature to do a fair amount of the treatment of harmful waste. In the future, we will want to manage the whole process—and not just for water. We will want to treat the air we breathe, the surfaces we touch, and everything that goes in or comes out of our bodies. Eventually we will want to account for every molecule we touch, plus all the chemistry and biology that occurs in connection with our bodies.

It will be a long time before we understand nature and our bodies at the level of every molecule, but that's no reason not to build the infrastructure. Before we reach that molecular-level understanding, we can combine the best knowledge we have with a thorough tracking system to help us learn more. With attention to "plumbing," we can make a world where person-to-person infection is so rare that any case of contagion will be investigated with the thoroughness we now apply to plane crashes.

Part of health is avoiding pathogens, but part of health is immunity and healthy exposure to dirt. Exposure to dirt trains our immune systems. But today, our exposure is haphazard, leading to disease from some dirt and lack of immunity from the absence of other dirt. As we learn more, this will become more like a database problem based on a library of dirt and records of the immunological differences between individuals.

To reduce contagion due to respiratory viruses, air will be delivered in calculated flow patterns, usually vertically, between vents throughout the ceiling and vents in the floor. The air will be directed in a gently moving flow calculated to prevent turbulence and prevent airborne contagion. Today, some hospital operating rooms and laboratory hoods are designed to do this to a degree, but it is not practical for everyday construction. Or is it? If we build everything new, many things become possible. The air can be filtered of harmful pathogens and pollutants between each pass through an occupied space. With each pass, the air can be adjusted to the desired mix of gases, ions, moisture, smells, temperature, pressure, and flow rate.

Our bodies and brains evolved in air with a carbon dioxide level of about 280 parts per million. Today's air has about 410. Indoor air often has several times that level. Measurable cognitive impairment starts at about 1,000 parts per million. There's a lot we can do with air. We can start by better understanding just what constitutes the best air for us to breathe.

How about surfaces that scrub themselves between each touch? Or food that is grown with your individual body in mind and tracked from seed or egg to your plate? Your personal health and taste data can track the best ways to maximize your health, your pleasure, and your body's nutritional needs. The data will be kept private while helping further our general understanding of nutrition and health. I'm calling all of this plumbing: air, water, dirt, food, data, self-scrubbing surfaces—anything that has to do with the flow of substances, and also the behind-the-scenes mechanisms that do the mixing and separating.

Tool #8: Simulations

Neuroscience has shown us that decision-making may be surprisingly unconscious. Researchers have found that when you make a voluntary movement, brain sensors can detect activity noticeably before you move. This is not surprising; muscles take time to contract. But what is surprising is that the same brain sensors can detect activity before you decide to move. Or at least before you think you have decided to move.[3] Why is this important? Because we probably make many of our choices from a perspective that is partially outside of what we think of as conscious choice. We react and make choices directly from our expectations before we realize we've made a choice. No consciousness or deliberate planning is involved, even if it feels like we are making a choice. The effect of these built-in decisions can be obvious, such as bracing yourself for a fall. But sometimes the effect of these built-in expectations is partially or completely out of our awareness. We default to decisions we're not even aware of.

In the future, will it be possible to detect, observe, and alter the unconscious patterns that cause us to choose before we're aware of making a choice? Is ferreting out an unconscious pattern really as simple as detecting brain activity—something machines can help us with? If so, we can change our behavior and our circumstances in powerful ways. I'll state the effect on our lives in an overly broad way: we create or recreate circumstances we are used to, based on what we expect.

Some of us have more privilege than others, but the only privilege that is ultimately genuine is living abundantly in a just and equitable world. Unraveling the various isms (racism, sexism, etc.) requires both a change in circumstance plus a change in your inner landscape and the inner landscapes of others. Your inner landscape is built on expectations, which may have been shaped by a history of meanness, division, and exploitation (the opposite of privilege). Even if you and I woke up tomorrow morning in a world 100 percent free of all meanness, division, and exploitation, we would have an adjustment period before that reality fully sinks in. Our built-in sense of fairness operates over a long timeline. It takes time, conscious awareness, and repeated experience before our expectations adjust to a new reality.

That's where simulations come in. Although it is crucial to change circumstances on the ground, changing circumstances is not enough. Simulations allow us to experience a reality before that reality exists. Think of simulations as classrooms in an institute for altering your expectations. For a time, you live in a convincing-enough illusion, so that when you leave, you are used to the world you want. When you are used to a new set of circumstances, you naturally move toward creating that change. Gandhi is credited with saying: "Be the change you want to see in the world." It's easier if you've become accustomed to your changed world because you've been living in it for a while. Simulations allow you to tune the parts of your brain that decide before you realize you have decided.

Tool #9: Well-Being Bots

As part of your standard equipment in the future, you will have your own well-being bot. Well-being bots will become as ubiquitous as smartphones. A well-being bot is a software program. There will be multiple versions from multiple sources. You can choose one or more. The goal is to help each of us have better online experiences and real-life interpersonal experiences. Well-being bots help us connect in ways where we can comfortably be ourselves, experiment, occasionally make mistakes, and suffer minimal or no lasting negative consequences. Eventually, well-being bots will help us optimize the flow of influence through society so that each of us becomes a better and more satisfied person.

Today's technology companies have influence over users based on personal data, but the influence is not always in the user's best interest. Your well-being bot will be a repository of your personal information but won't necessarily reveal your identity or personal information to online platforms. Your well-being bot works for you and works solely in your best interest.

Well-being bots reverse the relationship between sellers and buyers regarding personal data. Instead of being influenced by unseen algorithms, you are shown the logic that goes into predicting what you might like. The algorithms work for you and with your help. Algorithms predict how satisfied you are likely to be with any potential purchase or online experience, and the algorithms explain why. You can view this prediction before engaging in a transaction. Sellers are given good information about what people want, but only anonymously and in aggregate. Well-being bots collaborate with other well-being bots behind the scenes to simultaneously maintain your personal privacy while providing the benefits of today's and tomorrow's online platforms.

But more important than purchases or selecting products is improving human relationships. This is where well-being bots truly shine. Your well-being bot looks at what you want in your life, what influences lead people like you to find what you want, and how to optimize everything that is available to you, including which people to interact with and in what ways. Algorithms are good at using clear-cut criteria to optimize choices. Well-being bots help you align internally to select your criteria.

Tool #10: Two Approaches to Life Extension

Immortality has recently jumped from the fringes into the mainstream of scientific and commercial planning at labs and pharmaceutical companies around the world. There are several reasons why, but one key concept is that of escape velocity. Escape velocity is the point when longevity increases faster than aging occurs. According to UN statistics, in 1950, the average life expectancy was 45.7 years. By the year 2010, the number was seventy years. In the sixty years between 1950 and 2010, average life expectancy increased over twenty-four years.

Twenty-four years of increased longevity over sixty years of history brings us to 40 percent of escape velocity. To achieve escape velocity, we must increase that rate 2.5 times. We will need to apply the increase not only to average life expectancy but also to maximum lifespan. Can we increase our rate of progress 2.5 times? In almost every human endeavor, we eventually do. The important question is: can we make that progress soon enough for you and me? Then we will need to sustain progress at the same or a faster rate. Eventually, escape velocity will be achieved. When we do achieve escape velocity, we will probably look back and see that we could have done it earlier.

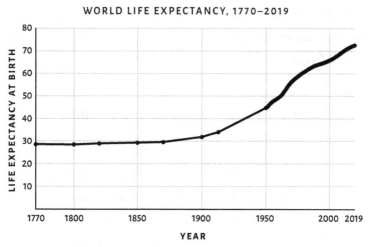

WORLD LIFE EXPECTANCY, 1770–2019

Figure 4. World Life Expectancy.
This chart shows worldwide life expectancy during the years 1770–2019. Data for years prior to 1950 is not granular enough to calculate escape velocity. *Data source: Our World in Data based on estimates by James C. Riley, Clio Infra, and the United Nations Population Division. For regional and global-level data pre-1950, data from a study by Riley, which draws from over 700 sources to estimate life expectancy at birth from 1800 to 2001.*

Escape velocity is the background we need to understand both ongoing approaches to life extension. The first approach is called

Strategies for Engineered Negligible Senescence (SENS) and is associated with Dr. Aubrey de Grey, a brilliant researcher who discovered that aging can be stalled by intervening in as few as seven biological mechanisms. He has already proposed strategies for addressing each of the seven mechanisms.

The second approach to life extension has to do with DNA and the instructions for development encoded into our DNA. Those instructions cause us to develop from fertilized egg to (hopefully) healthy adult, increasing in fitness all along the way. That is a very neat trick! But the same instructions keep running, which is how we transition from healthy adults to infirmed elderly people. As our cells continue to run their development programs, our bodies eventually become unable to support continued living. At some point, we will learn to modify DNA's instructions so that after we become healthy adults, we can turn off the mechanism that causes our cells to develop. We will learn to modify the DNA of healthy adults, not just unborn future generations.

Tool #11: Immortality Thinking

The certainty of death leads to one way of thinking. The prospect of immortality leads to a different way of thinking. Just because immortality may be possible doesn't make it a good idea. What makes immortality a good idea is immortality thinking. You've heard the expression: *live each day as if it's your last.* That attitude leads you to focus and appreciate the profundity of each moment. So does the prospect of immortality, and for the same reasons.

Your actions matter right now because you won't escape the consequences. Short-term thinking is out. Long-term planning makes more sense when you expect to live through the ramifications and impacts of your choices.

Tool #12: Define Our Way to an Expanded Economy

What if I told you that crime, pollution, illness, and traffic-congestion are all good for the economy? You would probably think I'm mistaken, but according to some ways of measuring economic output, each of those items counts as a positive.

It matters how we measure. There was a time when the only wealth that counted was food, or land, or cows, or gold. Now, it's money. Or is it credit? Or data? The point is that the definition of wealth changes and the right changes can lead to better living. Newly defined wealth at first doesn't seem quite real, then the newly defined wealth becomes the definition of what's real. This will happen again as our way of measuring wealth shifts from today's money system into a system for serving deeper human needs and desires. We will value new things in the future, and the way we measure wealth will shift the ways that we make decisions.

Tool #13: Ubiquitous Bandwidth

Many of the tools we will use to make our future better depend on connectivity, the ability to send information quickly from place to place. Today, we treat the infrastructure that carries our information as a premium product with tiers of service subject to prices determined by what buyers are willing and able to pay. But technology has changed. Capacity has increased while prices have fallen. In our city, basic fairness is served by treating bandwidth as a public good, like today's highway system. Except unlike highways, we can build enough wired and wireless capacity to never slow down at rush hour. Unlike highways, cables take up very little space, and unlike cars, signals use very little energy. What makes this work is that the amount of bandwidth a human body can use is finite.

We have mechanical ways of presenting information to our senses, such as video screens and speakers. Our senses can take in a certain finite amount of information. The technologies we use can be made better, but there's no point in rendering video in microscopic detail updated thousands of times per second.

That would be beyond what our eyes can perceive. This sets a natural limit on how much bandwidth a human body can take in. It makes sense to provide at least this much bandwidth to each person. The bandwidth allows each person to connect with any other person or machine.

This is not an unreasonable or difficult goal. Just as previous generations built highways and electrical grids with future generations in mind, we can do likewise, except those future generations will include us. The idea is to give each person an experience of enough bandwidth, where "enough" means available 24/7 in as much quantity as our senses can absorb. Then, add some additional bandwidth for better devices in the future and to compensate for possible delays by buffering ahead. A pair of optical fibers per person should do the trick.

Tool #14: Abundance

The last couple of tools I've outlined have hinted at the general notion of abundance. I'd like to expand on this notion of abundance to manufactured goods in general. In the future, we will think of ownership in terms of goods (physical things) but also in terms of manufacturing capacity. The world has an abundance of manufacturing capacity, and we are quite good at making more. But many of the items manufactured today are not what people most want. Many goods lose value, not because they wear out but because they are no longer in fashion or they become obsolete when a better version becomes available.

Goods require manufacturing capacity, raw or recycled materials, and functional design. Up until today, we mostly create goods to be used as they were originally built. In the future, when it's time for a replacement, the materials will be disassembled and remade into something new. We will mostly recycle the same pool of materials by simply shuffling big parts around or by recycling items down to their different chemical elements. Today, most recycling is closer to the latter. In the future, a registry will keep track of product designs and the products will be designed with recycling in mind.

This continuous building and rebuilding makes more sense with big things such as buildings. There will come a time when houses are manufactured in factories, mostly by robots, then delivered to a location, which may change from time to time. Between moves, or really at any time, you could send your house out for a makeover and get it back within a few hours. The house will be less a fixed structure than a flexible collection of reconfigurable pieces. Instead of owning real estate consisting of land and fixed buildings, you will own a collection of materials, rights to a design, and the rights to a certain amount of space.

When the world's manufacturing capacity can quickly make almost anything you want, abundance comes not from having more stuff but from more accurately knowing what you want. This is largely true for the wealthy today. The wealthy can buy almost any consumer item that is for sale, but their selection is limited to a small range of what humanity is capable of producing. Given an accurate way to measure our deepest satisfaction (or not), we can each decide what matters to us. Being honest with ourselves will become a more important factor in wealth than mere holdings. Using data to measure honest self-reflection will give us each a level of internal accountability to choose what we really want and avoid what would fail to satisfy our healthy desires.

Can we afford universal abundance? We'll dig into that question in detail, but the answer is a qualified yes. People can be net generators of wealth, and today most wealth already comes from people, not raw materials. Nature is still key and 100 percent necessary, but a good relationship with nature creates more wealth than a policy of maximum exploitation.

Tool #15: The Nature of Work

An improved social compact will change the nature of employment and work. Working will become more about making a genuine contribution than about earning a paycheck. Some work will consist of using brain communication to supply enriching and fun experiences for others, almost as a byproduct of having those experiences yourself. Today, work that involves a sense of mission and zeal is rare. Why will it become common? Two reasons: because it is satisfying and because it will pay. These two reasons become one reason when we start using a new form of currency that accurately reflects satisfaction.

What is more satisfying than being compensated well for doing what you love? Will everyone find something they love to do that also makes a contribution? Probably not. Some will not find work so satisfying that is it preferable to leisure, but most people will. An industry will develop to help those seeking greater satisfaction through creativity or through some other form of expression. Education will include a more personal element to help students focus on their inner drives and callings, not just where the student can fit into a job.

I mention the nature of work as one of our tools because the innovation that comes from a desire to contribute is different than just working for income. Work focused on improving the world focuses on different things, more meaningful things, and things that don't currently exist. Also, the motivation to grow through education and find meaningful work is greater if you plan to live for centuries. The world is better served by people who are grounded in their own autonomy and work each day because they care, not just because they are being paid.

Tool #16: Cryptographic Literacy

I saved this tool for last because it is, for many, the most counterintuitive. We're used to a common-sense understanding of how reality works. If I shout to you across a crowded room, others in the room can tell I am shouting and hear what I say. To be safe from crime, we need to give up some of our privacy. Money needs a central authority to issue currency, maintain order, and enforce rules against counterfeiting. Those are rules of common sense. But with crypto, rules can be renegotiated.

When the implications of crypto become widely understood, when there is widespread cryptographic literacy, we can expect to see changes in how society functions, especially the role of governments. Using crypto, there are many opportunities to make society better by replacing officialdom with information. We can engineer safer interactions because the systems will be more transparent, and today's seemingly conflicting interests no longer need to conflict. Society, in general, can afford to be more trusting with good cryptographic design in our institutions. It is not necessary for most of us to understand the inner workings of crypto, but it is essential that enough of us grasp the principles and implications. As with electricity, it is not important to know how it works if you know who to call when it fails.

In his book *Homo Deus*,[+] author Yuval Noah Harari attributes much of the success of the human race to our ability to create intersubjective reality, a kind of reality that exists because we agree that it exists. Examples include corporations, money, language, and law. Harari compares a corporation that builds cars to the cars themselves. If, beginning tomorrow morning, no one remembered or believed in car corporations (as if car corporations had never existed), no cars would be made, and the car corporation would cease to exist. The car corporation exists in intersubjective reality.

Compare that to a car. The car exists not in intersubjective reality but in objective reality. Objective reality exists regardless of belief. If tomorrow morning, all thoughts and memories of cars were instantly erased from your mind and you found yourself standing in the path of a car moving at high speed, you will still be killed. Belief in cars makes no difference to objective reality.

Things that exist in intersubjective reality, such as corporations and money, are especially powerful when billions of people believe, act, and coordinate their actions according to the belief that intersubjective things are real. Intersubjective reality is so real that neither reason nor reality can impinge. If the CEO of our car corporation came in tomorrow morning with the sudden revelation that corporations are an illusion made of pure belief, the CEO would be immediately replaced, and the corporation would go on as before. Cars would continue to be built. Intersubjective reality is that powerful!

What does this have to do with crypto? Crypto allows us to rapidly create entirely new categories of products and services, but only if enough people understand the possibilities. The possibilities of crypto fall into what Harari calls intersubjective reality. It can only exist if enough of us understand and believe that it can exist and make intentional actions toward contributing to its creation.

This chapter describes the sixteen tools we will use to make a better world. None of these sixteen tools requires a scientific breakthrough or mastery of currently unknown techniques. How do we use these tools to address our current situation? Let's address our current situation, starting with the problem that most threatens our continued existence: our damage to the natural world.

CHAPTER 4

THE CITY

H OW DO WE SIMULTANEOUSLY LIVE WELL AND restore the natural world? In the future, almost all of humanity will live in a single city. The city takes the notion of urban density to its logical conclusion. It incorporates the best features of urban life, life in the country, in suburbs, exurbs, way out in the wilderness, and any other place you might like to live, with the possible exceptions of a hermit-cave or life at sea. The city is one giant structure with room for the earth's peak human population. I'm estimating that to be about 11 billion people.

The city is built in a rugged way to withstand a wide variety of possible conditions, such as storms and temperature extremes. It's comprised of modular parts that can be made, moved, and installed with minimal disruption to ongoing life. How much space will this require? About 1 percent of the earth's habitable land. To the degree that wilderness can be reestablished, much of the other 99 percent can be returned to the wild.

As I said in Chapter 1, the advantage of cities is proximity. Each city dweller can visit more people and places with minimal travel. Additionally, services and activities can conveniently serve more people. Specialized businesses and services make more sense in cities than more sparsely populated areas because they can have enough visitors and customers. You will be able to meet face-to-face with any of the city's other residents in less than twelve minutes. It will be feasible for you to visit any restaurant, school, museum, store, park, concert hall, or other establishment whenever you'd like. Plus, everyone lives in your time zone.

Density has some downsides too—crowding, noise, pollution, loss of privacy, fewer natural surroundings, traffic, costs, contagion, and crime. My goal is to mitigate each of these downsides to a level better than either urban or rural dwellers experience today. I think this is a practical goal, but it requires us to build almost everything from scratch. Sometimes the quickest way to reach a goal is to start over, and this is one of those times.

Think back to every manufactured item we had one hundred years ago, including all the clothing, machinery, vehicles, kitchen items, furniture, and everything else. Think back to the infrastructure we had one hundred years ago, such as industry, streets, harbors, and bridges. With the possible exception of buildings and artistic works, it would not seem all that daunting today for us to build that much stuff again.

Why am I using the example of one hundred years ago? We've gotten much better at building almost everything in the last one hundred years, and the trend continues. With further efficiency improvements, which I spell out in Chapter 11, we will upscale our capabilities in the next couple of decades comparable to the last one hundred years of progress. Replacing all of today's stuff over the next couple of decades will require about the same amount of work as it would take today to rebuild all the manufactured goods of our one-hundred-year-old civilization. I'm not saying this work is trivial; it is not. The cost of building everything from scratch is a lot of labor and a lot of materials. However, the benefit is a world that works for everyone. It is hard to imagine building all this, then looking back and thinking it wasn't worth the effort.

We will need to advance our manufacturing techniques and scale them up to a new level, but many of the things we have today do not need to be replaced in kind or with things requiring an equivalent amount of work. For example, think of a refrigerator. Today's refrigerator requires far fewer materials and labor hours than the icebox of one hundred years ago. Not to mention the many tons of ice required. As we replace today's stuff, we will use techniques that continue the trend toward automation, efficiency, and whole systems design. Robots are a big part of the future of manufacturing, robots that are flexible and scalable. Integrated information streams are also a big part of the picture. That means good alignment between what is needed and what is built.

Let's discuss what needs to be built for this city we're creating. The city would start with a single circular building 150 stories high with a diameter of sixty miles. This is where people live, work, and play. Surrounding the central building is a donut-shaped structure that extends another thirty miles all around, out to a diameter of 120 miles (thirty miles on each side of the sixty-mile circular building). The donut contains vertical farms. Surrounding the 120-mile-wide ring of vertical farms is a larger donut-shaped structure that extends out to a diameter of 600 miles. The outer donut is 240-miles wide and filled with solar energy collectors. Overall, our city is a center circle surrounded by two concentric rings.

Within a few hundred miles is a large, elevated body of water. This provides overnight hydroelectric energy storage. Solar power drives pumps, raising the water during the day, and at night, the falling water drives generators. Perhaps battery technology or fuel cells will advance to the point where this becomes unnecessary, but if not, stored hydro is a proven technology at scale today. Refer to Figure 5 for scale.

I've described circles and rings to make the area calculations straightforward, but the exact shape is not important. If the shape needs to be modified to fit natural geography, it will only minimally affect the design. Assume no rivers, coastlines, natural forests, or mountains. A desert near the equator would be suitable as we will be recycling our water and other materials. Minimal cloud cover is desirable, and my calculations for solar energy are based on lots of direct sunlight from high in the sky. If the city is built in an area with less overhead sunlight, the outer diameter will need to be bigger to accommodate more solar panels.

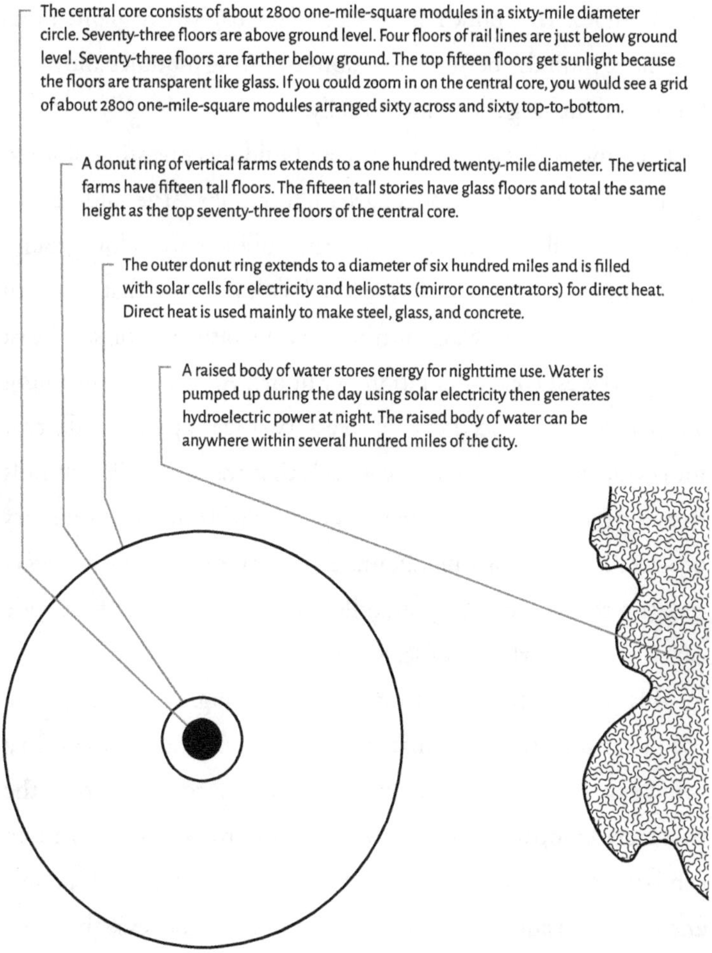

The central core consists of about 2800 one-mile-square modules in a sixty-mile diameter circle. Seventy-three floors are above ground level. Four floors of rail lines are just below ground level. Seventy-three floors are farther below ground. The top fifteen floors get sunlight because the floors are transparent like glass. If you could zoom in on the central core, you would see a grid of about 2800 one-mile-square modules arranged sixty across and sixty top-to-bottom.

A donut ring of vertical farms extends to a one hundred twenty-mile diameter. The vertical farms have fifteen tall floors. The fifteen tall stories have glass floors and total the same height as the top seventy-three floors of the central core.

The outer donut ring extends to a diameter of six hundred miles and is filled with solar cells for electricity and heliostats (mirror concentrators) for direct heat. Direct heat is used mainly to make steel, glass, and concrete.

A raised body of water stores energy for nighttime use. Water is pumped up during the day using solar electricity then generates hydroelectric power at night. The raised body of water can be anywhere within several hundred miles of the city.

Figure 5. Relative sizes of components of the city

Let's look at the sixty-mile-diameter circular building. This is the heart of the city where most human activity occurs. This where the 11 billion of us live, work, play, and interact. The circle consists of about 2,800 one-mile-square modules and a frame that holds the modules. The frame has rails along the top where giant cranes can move modules between locations by lifting modules above the frame and moving them horizontally.

Each module is a one-mile-square building consisting of up to 150 floors (fewer if the floors have high ceilings). The middle four floors hold rail lines. Floors below the rail lines are below ground level. The middle four floors are filled with rail lines that go north and south, east and west, northeast and southwest, or southeast and northwest (one orientation per floor). All the rails on a floor are parallel and spaced evenly, every two feet apart. Small, two-foot-wide, pizza-size cars have wheels that travel on adjacent rails. Passenger-size, four-foot-wide cars have wheels that ride on every other rail, straddling one rail under the middle of the car. Bigger cars (up to 120 feet wide) straddle more rails. The 120-foot-wide cars can carry a whole house. Refer to Figure 6.

This is where transportation gets interesting. Right now, we're used to sitting in a room that remains stationary and moving in a vehicle that was built for moving. In the city, rooms become the passenger compartments of vehicles and move. Almost any room can become a vehicle and move from place to place with people and objects inside. One example of a room that moves is the Zone Pod. Your Zone Pod temporarily becomes your car.

If you want to watch your surroundings while in motion, you can have your Zone Pod walls show what is happening just outside as you move. The effect is similar to a glass elevator, except your Zone Pod moves faster, farther, and in more directions. We're used to elevators, small rooms that move vertically under machine

The whole sixty-mile wide floor is covered with 150,000 or more straight, parallel tracks spaced apart at two-foot intervals every two feet. Not shown are mechanisms that pivot down from the ceiling to allow vehicles (with loads attached) to climb or descend to tracks oriented in a different direction on the next higher or next lower floor.

This larger car has wheels that straddle many tracks. Notice the tipping platform. This car can carry a building with people (not shown) inside. The platform is tipped to the right as the car accelerates to the right. The apparent pull of gravity inside the building is always straight down. Because all tracks are straight with no curves, there is no need to tip sideways to compensate for side-to-side G-forces.

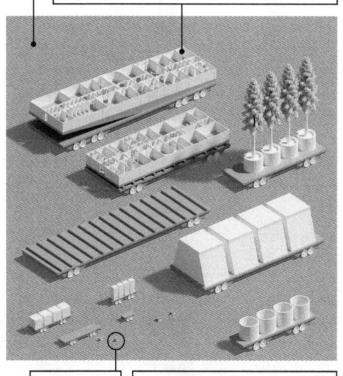

This two-foot square vehicle has wheels that ride on adjacent tracks.

Not shown: bigger vehicles for carrying loads up to 120 feet wide and 120 feet tall. Bigger vehicles can be temporarily formed from multiple intermediate-size vehicles as needed.

Figure 6. Vehicles of various widths showing tipping mechanisms and how wider vehicles straddle multiple tracks.[5] *Illustration by Ray C. Freeman III.*

control with people inside. In the city, rooms that become cars will be carried by powered wheeled platforms. Powered wheeled platforms will carry rooms of various sizes. Small (two-foot-square) powered wheeled platforms carry packages. Bigger powered wheeled platforms carry Zone Pods. Multiple powered wheeled platforms can work together to carry bigger rooms and anything large that needs to be moved.

Rooms of various sizes move both vertically, like elevators, and horizontally. Small rooms can move horizontally at up to 300 miles per hour and tilt up to fifteen degrees so that gravity always seems to pull straight down. You can meet face-to-face with any other person in the city in less than twelve minutes without leaving your room or spilling your drink. For preplanned events, you can move bigger rooms more slowly. You could wake up next to your morning destination thanks to the silent movement of your bedroom while you slept.

Not all of the 150 stories will have natural sunlight simultaneously, but the top fifteen stories will. That's because the top fourteen stories have floors and ceilings made of one-way transparent material such as glass. Looking down, at each level you see what appears to be a conventional floor. Looking up, you see the sky. From the top floor your sky view is clear. Fourteen floors down, the sunlight peeks through gaps where no one above is blocking the sun. The glass has LCD-like technology to block the view of people above from those below, providing privacy. Privacy circles slowly follow individuals as they move around, and some additional circles (decoy circles) move too, making it impossible to follow someone's movements from below. From below, it feels like you're under a leaf canopy with sunlight wafting through, as if the dots were big tree leaves. The walls between rooms are also glass with LCD technology, and the spaces between occupied rooms usually contain plants. The plants collect sunlight, cleanse the air, provide ambiance, and sometimes provide dinner.

But the trick that makes this all work is accordion construction. Rooms expand and squish accordion-style. When a space is vacant, it squishes. Having a party? Expand your home to multiple times its normal size for the occasion. Going out? Your home squishes to almost nothing. Your workplace squishes after work hours. Automation moves and folds the furniture. Mechanical arms move stuff out of the way, then put it back where you left it. Your twenty-room house usually has only one or two rooms at any given moment. When you walk from one room to another, the room you enter expands in real-time, ready for you by the time you enter the doorway. Rooms expand quickly enough to give you the sense that all your rooms permanently exist. When you leave a room, it squishes.

I'm basing the requirements for living space on an assumption that each person gets about 2,000 square feet of space. Some of that 2,000-square-foot area is used for machinery and squished rooms that are not in current use, so only about half of that, or 1,000 square feet per person, is open space. That's 1,000 square feet for habitation, working, and storing frequently used items. But that 1,000-square-foot figure is an average. Spaces expand and contract in the course of a normal day. Today, most of the rooms you occupy are 1,000 square feet per person or smaller. Rooms become bigger when you need more space.

When you need a larger room, someone else will need to be using less than 1,000 square feet at that moment, so the accordion function of rooms can respond and accommodate both people's needs simultaneously. And this accordion-style collaborative use of space extends beyond just rooms. Buildings within the city will also expand. In fact, entire zones will be built to squish and expand. Offices, schools, stadiums, and restaurants are only occupied certain hours of each week. No need for them to take up space when they're not in use. And since space itself is not the limiting factor, we can build special-purpose venues for occasional activities. When people gather in a public venue, their empty homes squish, allowing space for the venue. Refer to Figures 7 and 8.

One important implication of accordion construction involves elevators and their function. Today, each elevator car has a dedicated elevator shaft. In the city, shafts will open up between rooms as needed and squish or disappear after use. Instead of dedicated elevator cars, most rooms, including Zone Pods, can become elevator-cars and rail-cars. Rooms smaller than 120 feet tall (which would be almost all rooms) can become cars. By riding on a powered, wheeled platform, a room can move vertically from its current position to one of the four transportation floors, then horizontally to another position, and then up or down. So, you can be sitting in your room, and a few minutes later, you and your room can be somewhere else.

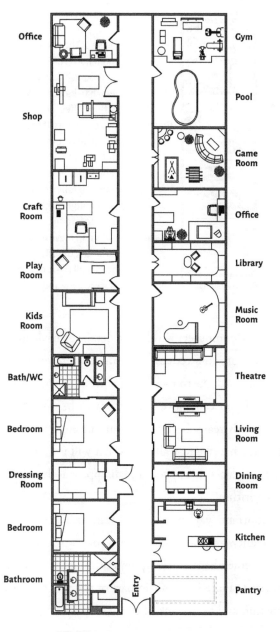

Office

Shop

Craft
Room

Play
Room

Kids
Room

Bath/WC

Bedroom

Dressing
Room

Bedroom

Bathroom

Entry

Gym

Pool

Game
Room

Office

Library

Music
Room

Theatre

Living
Room

Dining
Room

Kitchen

Pantry

Figure 7. This sprawling twenty-room house occupies about 6,000 square feet and currently has two occupants, one in the kitchen and one in the home office on the right.

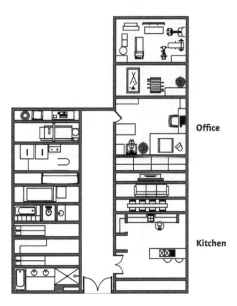

Figure 8. The twenty-room house of Figure 7 can squish down to less than half the size with no effect on the two occupants. If the occupants move to different rooms, those rooms immediately return to full size. With fast enough mechanical actuators to slide walls and move or flip furniture, the effect will be that all the rooms are always ready and waiting.

Office

Kitchen

Behind the scenes, computers handle the details of navigating and scheduling. You state your request in terms of where you want to be or with whom you'd like to meet. Moments later, you arrive. Why is life better if you can move your room to be anywhere within minutes? Is this really better than our current system of cars, trains, airplanes, bikes, and walking? What will it do to our sense of place to have places that appear and disappear at the whim of a computer's algorithm?

Place is an important way that humans (and other animals) relate to nature, reality, and each other. Have you ever forgotten something only to remember it again upon returning to the place you last remembered? Place is a built-in part of the way humans organize information and keep track of the world. We evolved in a natural world that appeared infinite and mysterious. In the city, we can reestablish place as vast, mysterious, and as real as our imaginations will allow.

How do we literally make space in the city? Despite our evolutionary history, in which we gained identity and belonging through our sense of place, that sense of place is ultimately a human construct. With the ability to construct environments virtually, we can make an almost infinite landscape.

That vast landscape, the virtual representation of place where people perceive reality, will be fixed and permanently unchanging. You can have as much space as you want for yourself and to share with others. Your space will be yours. You will keep the same neighbors unless someone chooses to move. Your territory can include portals that allow people to teleport from location to location, sometimes after a momentary delay.

Behind the scenes, while you perceive your portal opening, machinery is moving you to a new physical spot. The physical pieces of the city are flexible and fast-moving, while the virtual layout is fixed. The virtual layout is not constrained by physical limits. Like all things virtual, it can be created and modified at little or no cost. Vast virtual space comes at no cost without the penalty of longer travel times or greater energy use. Space becomes a canvas upon which you can design your piece of the world, all the while tapping into the deep-seated human (and animal) orientation to place.

Compare this to our current situation. Today, many of us spend the bulk of our time indoors where our surroundings give us little sense of belonging to a place. Today, our buildings are designed to provide an environment conducive to whatever it is we do inside and, if we're lucky, provide a view or some other cue to our place in our larger surroundings. Today, our use of space is a compromise between having the surroundings we desire versus the costs. Costs include both the dollars per square foot and the travel time to get from one place to another.

I've been using numbers here to describe the various features of the city and to give the reader a sense of scale. For example, the 1,000- and 2,000-square-foot per person numbers, the sixty-mile diameter, the 150 stories, and four transportation floors. Because I don't want to bog down the text with numbers and math, I've moved those assumptions and details to Appendix 1. I include enough information to make it possible for you to modify my assumptions and see what the effect is on other aspects of the city.

The point of this back-of-envelope engineering is to come up with a plan where everyone alive can live in physical conditions at least as desirable as today's first-world conditions. Earlier, I listed some of the downsides to high-density living, specifically: crowding, noise, pollution, loss of privacy, fewer natural surroundings, traffic, costs, and contagion. While these are very real concerns, we will have solutions for each of these that will make city living at least as good as most living situations available today.

Here's what I'm thinking:

Crowding describes the number of people per square mile, but it's also about the feeling of too much activity and not enough personal space. The sense of personal space is enhanced by quiet, without unwanted sensory input from others and their machines. Can we have luxurious parks, gardens, and views of sweeping vistas in the city? Some of this depends on how many people want to use physical places simultaneously. Occasionally, there will probably seem to be a crowd. But that's not unlike parks or even hiking trails today. Most of the time, there will be good options for getting outside and experiencing open space that is not purely virtual. Some of that "outside" will be under glass and some will be on the top floor, open to the sky. For those seeking a different nature experience, high-speed rail lines will allow rapid travel to unoccupied wilderness areas away from the city. Unlike today, when the distinction between inside and outside is clear, within the city, the distinction will be somewhat fluid.

Instead of crowding, each person will have a choice between many rooms and many virtual or physical outdoor places. People can gather in groups of various sizes or be alone. Much like the continuum between inside and outside, there will be a continuum between being alone and together with others. We have a sense of that today when we live in a house with others who are present although not necessarily in the same personal space.

The feeling of being crowded in an area is often magnified when our senses are bombarded. We will have mechanisms to control those effects. Mostly we will want to block out others' sounds, and for that, we will make most rooms with active noise cancellation to keep the interiors quiet. Active noise cancellation uses speakers to cancel sounds instead of creating sounds. Headphones with active noise cancellation are common and familiar. The same principle works on the larger scale of rooms.

Sometimes too much quiet is unpleasant because we can't orient ourselves to what is happening nearby. So, instead of orientation based on a cacophony of sounds from nearby activity, screens on the walls of your room might display what is going on nearby. The images show you the nearby activity, and you can control how much of it is relayed to you inside your room. Our familiar privacy technology will be used so that you do not see or hear what others do not want you to and vice versa.

Noise is sound we don't want, and the antidote is quiet. But there is also sound we do want. For that, we crank up the tunes! The same active noise–canceling technology can allow us to blast our chosen sound in our own space without affecting others.

More than just sounds, we can filter the visual distractions, smells, and other undesirable effects of crowding by physically blocking others' nearby actions from our senses.

You'll notice a theme. While in the past we had to achieve the right balance between togetherness and personal space by spreading out across the globe, now technology can make it happen while simultaneously maximizing density. This theme also applies to the other downsides of crowding: pollution, loss of privacy, fewer natural surroundings, traffic, costs, and contagion. Pollution is one area where the world has embraced this already. At one time, there was a saying that "dilution is the solution to pollution." In other words, space. Lots of space (or air or water or land) would take care of our pollution by spreading it out over a large area at such a low concentration that the pollution doesn't matter.

Fortunately, we wised up and realized that dilution is not the solution to pollution. The solution to pollution is to not pollute. For our future, I'd like to take this theme of not polluting even further. Technology as simple as plumbing and ducting can keep our air and water separate from our polluting waste. Since some of that polluting waste comes in the form of contagion carried by our bodies, we can arrange plumbing to filter and clean the air each time it has been exposed to a person.

Eventually, all of our interactions with materials can become a closed loop. We will reuse the same materials repeatedly, recycling them from waste into new products. As a society, we will take responsibility and maintain control over all our materials. Currently, we have a notion of "the environment" and the thought that we should take better care of the environment. I want to challenge the basic concept of "the environment."

The environment has come to mean the large pool of materials where we extract what we want and toss our waste. I propose that we plan to stop taking advantage of the natural world's ability to deal with our damage in this way. Instead, we will recirculate the same materials between our various uses in a closed loop that is based on our choices and our abilities to transform materials.

We don't currently have the knowledge or the technology to close the loop for many of our materials, but we can put the infrastructure in place now for use later when we know more. Mostly that means plumbing and storage. Until we understand how to recycle all of our materials, we will sequester and catalog the waste we cannot yet recycle. Later, we may find ways to benefit from our stored materials. Nature figured out closed-loop recycling eons ago, and we will too. Let's plan ahead for that day.

I mentioned laminar airflow among our tools. My idea is to arrange smooth, one-way vertical airflows in each room with little swirling or eddies. One person's exhale doesn't reach another person until the air has been removed through vents and cleansed. Most floor and ceiling areas are covered with vents. Sensors and valves adjust the flow of air moment-by-moment in response to the movements of people and things. If you cough or sneeze, a fast reactive system will blast a puff of air to deflect possible pathogens away from other people.

This is somewhat like the laminar-flow systems found today in some hospital operating rooms and biohazard or fume hoods. It would not be practical to add this type of air conditioning to existing buildings, but if we build from scratch, it becomes possible and practical.

Likewise with touch surfaces. Touch surfaces can have wipers, sterilizing lamps, and other mechanical means of reducing the exchange of pathogens. Sensors can keep track of surfaces that have been touched and not yet cleaned, while warning systems will alert you before you touch a possibly contaminated surface.

In terms of pollution, the idea is to accomplish what can be done with space by design instead. Keeping the population spread out is a poor answer for this problem. If we continue to depend on space to create isolation, we eventually run out of space or we fail to isolate ourselves from harmful pathogens. With technology and intentional design, the more isolation we want, the more we need to understand the situation and implement specific engineering solutions. Technology scales to match the size of the problem. Space doesn't scale in a similarly practical way.

Plumbing and materials-handling may be interesting to you or not. My point in including these details is to help you understand the mechanics of a city where everyone is well served by technology and aesthetic design. The future I imagine for all of us facilitates better lives. The future I imagine allows each of us to have enough.

What is enough? For most people in the West, our houses have enough running water capacity. If tomorrow morning your house suddenly became fitted with one hundred times its existing water capacity, enough to run several car washes and irrigate a large farm, most of us would not experience better living, not even a tiny bit. You already have enough running water capacity. That's the essence of enough. With enough, more of the same doesn't make life better. In the city, the plan is to offer enough space, energy, materials, and manufacturing capacity to each person. Of course, that requires the manufacture of a lot of items such as solar panels, robots, and components of the structure itself.

But in addition to necessary physical items, people currently accumulate items to fill psychological needs, such as status or signals that we belong to a group. In future chapters, I will address how the role of money, status, and physical stuff changes in a way that makes psychological well-being plentiful and excess stuff unnecessary. I'll describe how we get our psychological needs met in healthy ways with less need for material items.

Many of the things we build out of materials today will be built out of data, using virtual reality or augmented reality. The Zone Pods I described earlier for simulating face-to-face meetings and simulated clearings in the woods can also simulate luxurious surroundings. When your surroundings can be anything that pixels can generate, the value of status items changes. Status becomes about imagination, not budget.

Of course, we will still need many things in physical form. Some of these things will need to be manufactured in a way that is solid, and some can be assembled as needed and reassembled into something else between each use. For example, certain buildings can be stored in pieces and robotically reassembled when needed. The transportation system can keep some of your stuff stored in the lower levels of the city and deliver it within seconds, probably faster than you could find it in the back of your closet today.

Ownership is a key feature of making and having stuff. Owning a house is different than renting. Owning implies more responsibility and more freedom to do as you wish with your stuff. I'd like to promote a sense of super-ownership, amplifying what works from the ownership model and reducing the burdens of worry about loss, breakage, and upkeep. Owning will consist of owning the rights to the design of your items plus enough rights to use the infrastructure that builds and repairs stuff. The infrastructure incorporates all the capabilities of today's industrial economy, except more automated and at a larger scale.

The point of super-ownership is to transform the relationship between people and stuff from today's transactional relationship into an ongoing loving relationship between co-creators. What does it mean to have a loving relationship with stuff? What does it mean to co-create your stuff? At the least, it means having only stuff you love. Pride of ownership will become something different when everyone can have a virtually infinite amount of any physical thing. You can have virtually infinite stuff because your stuff can always get remade into something else. You cannot have infinite stuff all at the same time, but that would be inconvenient anyway. Where would you put it? How would you find the thing you want right now?

Do you have something you feel only so-so about? Improve it! That's where the co-creative part happens. Chances are, others can benefit from your thoughtful improvements. Continually improving our stuff doesn't work with manufactured items that are fixed in design and not easily modified. Today, most items are built this way. Today, we design items to be used as originally built until they break, wear out, or become obsolete, at which time they are discarded and maybe recycled.

In our future, manufactured items will be thought of as works in progress. Of course, they don't have to change if you love something the way it is. In a sense, this continuous-improvement cycle is a throwback to an earlier time when people had only a limited wardrobe, and as pieces of clothing wore out, those pieces became parts of a new outfit. Or more accurately, instead of old and new outfits, people wore evolving garments that morphed as sections were replaced, but the essence remained.

Eventually you will have a robot that weaves and sews a new outfit (or perhaps an old favorite) every time you open your closet.

It will be many years before this becomes more practical than a row of hangers, but that's the direction we will go.

Sometimes familiarity is more valuable than incremental improvement, and in these cases, you will have the option to have items of any vintage made and remade for you, including any wear patterns that make your stuff truly yours. Think of a musical instrument. What makes this all work is your ownership of, and rights to, a portion of the world's automated manufacturing infrastructure. Or maybe it is more accurate to call it a manufacturing and reconfiguring infrastructure. Although this sort of on-demand manufacturing may be many decades in the future, our city can be designed now with an eye toward this trend.

For some people, owning and improving the infrastructure itself will deliver the pride of ownership we can get from interacting with our creations. So, in addition to the evolving designs of specific items, you can expect the quality and methods by which your stuff is made to improve over time as well.

How will this manufacturing, design, and infrastructure be paid for? We will explore the economic system that makes this possible in more detail in later chapters, but for now I'll give a brief overview. I'll answer in two ways. First, I'll describe the mechanics, and second, I'll describe the incentives that encourage people to want to pay for the capabilities we need.

In terms of mechanics, it makes sense to separate the nature of the stuff we choose to manufacture from the field of manufacturing in general. We will want to make manufacturing capacity in generic ways, because this sort of standardization makes it straightforward to scale exponentially. Machines will make machines that make more machines. This is a gross oversimplification, but the principle is that expansion occurs through exponential growth, not only through the repeated application of innovation. We will want to continuously apply innovation too, but not as our only source of capacity increase. Nature very effectively used this principle of exponential growth (shaped by ongoing improvements) and turned an innovative arrangement of organic molecules into a worldwide biosphere.

What are the incentives that encourage people to invest in an infrastructure to serve the physical wants and needs of others? Our current money system rewards those who build infrastructure that serves the needs of owners and investors, not everybody else. But ultimately, we are all served by putting everyone in a position to continually improve everything. In later chapters, we will explore tiers of currency that represent different human values. People will want to further the capabilities we have for serving each other's physical needs, because this is an efficient way to put conventional wealth to work in service of a reward that will be more valuable to investors than today's money.

Our society-wide ownership of manufacturing capacity is similar to guaranteed minimum income, except instead of income, you would own a portion of the world's industrial capacity plus any designs that you create or buy the rights to. One currency of value here is useful and aesthetic design. Anyone can get stuff built, but not anyone can use your design unless you allow it. We are used to this sort of rights ownership with software, movies, music, and writing. What you receive in return for your creations can come in many forms. Maybe you just want to be appreciated, or maybe you want a more tangible form of reward. Some personal items will always need to be fully physical. Others can exist on a continuum between fully physical and fully virtual. For example, a vacation home can be assembled for seasonal use, then stored. While it is stored, the parts can be rented out for profit.

Now that we understand the form and function of the central area of the city where people live and work, let's go beyond to the surrounding areas. Around the central area is a ring of multistory vertical farms. The idea of the vertical farms is to grow delicious food and other vegetation, such as trees, medicinals, flowers, and plants to freshen the air. Plus the other things we will want to grow, such as animals, fungi, and microorganisms that live in soil. For reasons that will be explained in Chapter 8 and in keeping with the theme of taking responsibility for every molecule we touch, we will use more granularity than today's farming. Granularity, in this case, means growing things individually, each in a separate enclosed container.

Can we organize the lives of the organisms we grow for food on an individual basis? Is this a good idea? I think the answer to the first question is a qualified yes for the foreseeable future. But even if we don't quite get to the level of individual organisms, we can get close. Regarding the second question, yes, it is a good idea to grow organisms on an individual basis. It is a good idea for us to take over responsibility from nature for the life circumstances of individual plants and animals. This makes it possible to grow food just for you individually with attention to your health, your optimal diet, and your taste preferences. As we take increasing responsibility for the decisions formerly left to nature, we will learn useful new things.

Our fast transportation system will remove the need for large food storage and refrigeration systems. Food will be delivered directly to you from the vertical farms and will show up when you're ready to prepare a meal or eat. Plants will be grown in individual glass containers. Each larger plant will have a glass container to itself; smaller plants are grown several to a container. Each container has one or more plants, soil, water, nutrients, minerals, fungi, soil-microorganisms, and a system of sensors. The sensors keep tabs on the health of the plants in each container. Plant breeding is done intentionally. Insect-pollinated plants are pollinated by directing insects from plant to specific plant.

The glass containers range from a few cubic feet for small spices and vegetables to glass containers large enough for coconut trees. Coconut trees can grow one hundred feet tall. The vertical farm's top floors get the most sunlight, but sunlight filters down between the plants and through the glass floors. Each story of the vertical farms has a high ceiling, so that the height of the farms equals the overall height of all the central-core floors above the rail-line transportation floors. In other words, the fifteen stories of vertical farms are the same overall height as seventy-three stories of living area. Think in terms of twenty feet per floor in the central core, one hundred feet per floor in the vertical farms, and a roofline 1,500 feet above ground level for both.

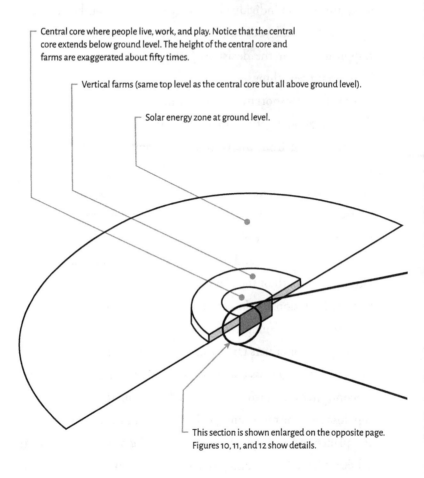

Central core where people live, work, and play. Notice that the central core extends below ground level. The height of the central core and farms are exaggerated about fifty times.

Vertical farms (same top level as the central core but all above ground level).

Solar energy zone at ground level.

This section is shown enlarged on the opposite page. Figures 10, 11, and 12 show details.

Figure 9A. View through the city as if it was sliced across the center.

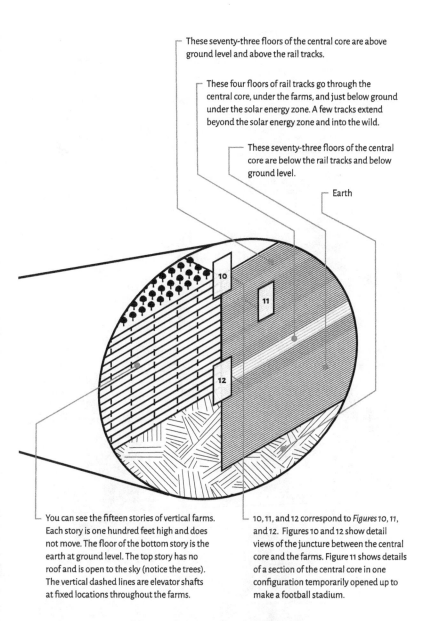

These seventy-three floors of the central core are above ground level and above the rail tracks.

These four floors of rail tracks go through the central core, under the farms, and just below ground under the solar energy zone. A few tracks extend beyond the solar energy zone and into the wild.

These seventy-three floors of the central core are below the rail tracks and below ground level.

Earth

You can see the fifteen stories of vertical farms. Each story is one hundred feet high and does not move. The floor of the bottom story is the earth at ground level. The top story has no roof and is open to the sky (notice the trees). The vertical dashed lines are elevator shafts at fixed locations throughout the farms.

10, 11, and 12 correspond to *Figures 10, 11, and 12*. Figures 10 and 12 show detail views of the juncture between the central core and the farms. Figure 11 shows details of a section of the central core in one configuration temporarily opened up to make a football stadium.

Figure 9B. Zoomed-in view showing a slice though the city.

OPPOSITE: *Figure 10*. Cutaway view of the city (corresponds to #10 in Figure 9B). The foreground shows sections of the support structure. The bottom left of Figure 10 shows glass farm floors (with trees). Just behind and to the right of the vertical support you can see the edge of the central core with closely spaced floors and gardens on top. The clear top floor allows you to peek down through the garden to floors below. In reality the glass floors are transparent one-way only. Looking down you see what appears to be a normal (nontransparent) floor. *Illustration by Ray C. Freeman III.*

PAGE 72: *Figure 11*. Cutaway view of a section configured for sports venue (corresponds to #11 in Figure 9B).
In this section of the central core some residential units have been moved and squished to create space for a sporting event. The spectators have brought their own comfortable theater rooms (and bathrooms) to the event. *Illustration by Ray C. Freeman III.*

PAGE 73: *Figure 12*. Cutaway view showing the four floors of vehicle tracks (corresponds to #12 in Figure 9B).
Juncture between the central core and the farm areas at ground level. The four levels of rails can be seen going in four directions. Notice the rail cars of different sizes, some carrying trees. *Illustration by Ray C. Freeman III.*

Some of the rail lines from the transportation floors extend outside the central core of the city, under the ring of vertical farms and beyond, past the solar panels, and into the wild.

Robots, with the help of people, tend the plants and shuffle glass containers from floor to floor, so each plant gets enough sunlight. The individual glass containers keep plant contagion and unintentional breeding to a minimum. Each plant is tracked from seed to plate, so any foodborne health problems can be traced back to the source.

For freshness, smaller plants are transported live in their containers to your kitchen or to a food preparation place. That food preparation place could be a restaurant where your meal is prepared from ingredients grown just for you. Or you could have your food prepared at a robotized facility that does inspection, cleaning, and food preparation to your taste. Those of us who enjoy preparing meals conventionally will do so in our kitchens, except there is little need for our kitchens to be limited in features or space since the whole kitchen squishes away between uses.

Plants in the glass wall area between occupied rooms can serve as decoration or ambiance in addition to food. Since your plants are grown just for you, the glass plant containers can be open to your living space. You share your air with next week's meals. In addition to food and decorative plants, you can mix in other plants for aroma and freshness.

For many people, food includes products from mammals, fish, birds, and insects. In time, it may become practical to grow meat in cultures, skipping the steps of raising and slaughtering sentient creatures. Without the need to raise animals for meat, we will need far fewer domesticated animals, few enough that the bottom floor of the fifteen-story vertical farms will suffice. In addition to meat, animals supply us with non-food materials such as leather, wool, and certain life-saving drugs, so it is unlikely the world will completely cease raising and slaughtering animals, but it is likely that we will reduce the number of domestic animals we raise.

The bottom farm floor is the only farm floor that is not glass. I'm calling it a floor, but it is more like the ground. The bottom "floor" is actually a layer of soil. Rail lines run below the soil, so you can think of it as farmland with a subway system underneath. Elevator shafts penetrate the soil and connect the farm floors to the rail lines. Unlike other elevator shafts, these elevator shafts don't squish or move between uses.

The thing to remember about the city is that it is a place for most of humanity that includes the best of what urban dwelling has to offer. Urban dwelling offers convenient access to other people, rich cultural life, and plentiful services. Plus, the city will offer a better, more intimate connection to the natural world and a clearer sense of place than people who live in either cities or rural areas experience today. Inside the city, health will be supported by fresh air, water, and food. Sources of fresh air and water are routed separately and deliberately for each person. The exchange of fluids and pathogens will be monitored and managed at every point where people cross paths. Crypto will allow us to eventually track every encounter and possible exchange of matter between individuals in a way that preserves individual privacy. But mostly, the city is designed to be a platform for other ways that life can be improved, especially in terms of interpersonal relationships.

The city is designed to deliver luxury in a way we are not used to. Part of humanity's evolution involves what past generations would have considered unimaginable luxuries. Access to hot and cold running water, light at the flick of a switch, instant knowledge about what's happening around the world, cures and treatments for deadly diseases, the likelihood that most of our children will survive into adulthood, the realistic expectation that most adults will live into old age; the list goes on.

Would people of centuries ago recognize themselves in today's world? If our ancestors were instantly teleported to the here and now, we can imagine introducing them to the wonders of today, but would they welcome the change? After initial disorientation, I'd like to think they would. Similarly, I'd like to think of us welcoming life in the city I have described.

The biggest advantage of quickly building the city is not new luxuries, although I think they would be welcome and fun. The biggest advantage of quickly building the city is our continued survival. Survival into the future is not a mere luxury. The damage we have inflicted on the natural world threatens our niche, and the survival of humans and many other species. We don't know to what extent our actions have already caused irreparable damage to nature. We also don't know exactly at what point we are doomed. But we do know that without a change in our behavior, it is just a matter of time until we are doomed to perish. Hopefully, we still have time. Discontinuing our destruction over most of the earth's surface is an achievable goal. How much risk is acceptable? How much do we care if the human experiment continues? How much are we burdened right now by the dread of knowing our current course of action may be causing our demise?

Life in the city will hopefully be interesting and compelling in a way that enough people will want to give it a try. At this moment, the city is only a rough plan, a plan for all of humanity and for nature. To be viable, it will require a significant investment of money, time, and imagination. Some small fraction of the city needs to be physically built for people to experience life there first-hand. Will that firsthand experience be compelling? Would you want to experiment with living there for a while? Until we know how compelling life in the city really is, the rest of the city can simply be lines on a map. After some of us start experiencing life in the city, we will know a lot more.

Living in new and different circumstances will be illuminating, but the material world alone is not enough. Now imagine people in the future looking back and teleporting their ancestors (us) to their present world. What will seem most compelling is not the physical city, but the nature of the human relationships taking place there.

CHAPTER 5

RELATIONSHIPS

T HE CITY IS A GOOD PLATFORM FOR LIVING
together as a species, but for those of us with sufficient food,
clothing, and shelter, what we care about has more to do
with our interactions with other people. The five levels in Maslow's
hierarchy of needs are physical, safety, belonging, esteem, and
self-actualization. Four of Maslow's five levels have to do with relationships (safety, belonging, esteem, and self-actualization). What
kind of relationships? Let's say safe, fair, healthy, deep, exciting, and
fun. Why will we prioritize service to others over self-aggrandize-
ment, synergy over revenge, respect and cooperation over domina-
tion? How do we become our best selves in relation to others?

Let's start with what we know. Emotionally healthy people
have better relationships. How do people arrive at emotional
health? Part of that is by having better relationships. Since we all

interact with a range of other people, a lot of our emotional health depends on who has the most influence on us.

But others' influence only nudges us in one direction or another. It's what we do inside that determines who we become. We know of moral giants who suffered horrendous circumstances. We know of monsters who had every privilege. We become good people because we choose to become good people. We choose to become good people because becoming a good person is possible and satisfying. Becoming our best selves is the result of inner work, yet having good relationships helps.

This chapter about satisfying relationships focuses on two things: directing influence and honest internal feedback. In other words, influence between people and the way we each influence ourselves. Technology plays a part in both. Today's technology directs influence and feedback as the side effects of other goals. Usually, those goals have to do with accumulating money and power.

What our new future includes is technology built to facilitate better relationships. Will technology that favors better relationships take hold in a world organized around money and power? I will address that in later chapters. Bottom line: yes, technology that favors better relationships will prevail. How will technology lead to better relationships in a world of money and power? As will be explained in Chapters 9 and 10, we will extend our money system to measure the meaningful stuff of relationships.

Inner change is hard and can be slow. Under the best circumstances and with the best technology, your pace of change will be dictated by how quickly you shift your deeply held expectations.

With the right environment, you can more easily shift those expectations in response to your deliberate choices. Good actors do this to embody a character for a role. Most of us can think of periods of rapid shift when we joined new institutions, such as school, the military, or a challenging new job. The difference now is that the role is to be our most positive, empowered, liberated, authentic selves. We have each experienced only the one set of circumstances that led us to become who we are. How might we be different now if we had experienced a different set of formative circumstances?

We see how powerful circumstances can be (in a negative way) with acute trauma. One traumatic event can have a huge lasting effect. There are ways to recover from the lasting influence of acute trauma, and similarly, we can shift from the influence of our past experiences. Even good experiences can be limiting. The key here is to make exploring new inner realms safe, economical, exhilarating, frequent, and fun.

Here is where the simulation tools are critical. Simulations are artificial worlds made of both people and things, including machines, for the purpose of learning at a deep level: learning at the level of our reflexes and built-in expectations. New technology is not necessarily required. We've had the capacity to alter deeply held expectations for generations. Counseling and therapy help people change. Plays and movies regularly create alternate realities in which we can empathize and understand the position and feelings of others. Politicians role-play their best answers before important debates. Method actors get into roles by living their characters in a variety of settings. The only technologies needed are excellent actors, sets, a loose script, and practice.

Yet, powerfully reexperiencing formative moments from the past has not been practical for the average person. We accept cultural limitations as if human expectations seldom change. In the future, ordinary people wanting to change their circumstances will have the practical means and social support to alter deeply held internal expectations. The additional technologies of crypto, virtual reality, wellbeing bots, and artificial intelligence will help make it powerful, private, safe, and affordable.

The technology will allow multiple people to simultaneously experiment with alternate interpersonal scenarios in a way that makes the risk of mistakes negligible. Imagine if you had grown up under different circumstances. In a simulation of those different circumstances, it becomes safe to experiment with expressions and personas that might be unfamiliar at first. But ultimately, your new expressions become a better fit than your current habits; a better fit than the patterns you adopted from your actual environment. We will each be able to experiment with as many different scenarios as we'd like. Spend a few days in a simulation where you can safely embody one or more trial versions of yourself.

You will be surrounded by others who understand you deeply, are great actors, and play exactly the characters you need. In real life, you remain anonymous. Many of the actors will be nonhuman machines. If you don't like who you became in today's trial version of yourself, you can erase all traces and start over tomorrow. No one will remember anything you choose to erase. Most of them are computers, and the few who are human won't know your identity. Eventually, you will have explored your inner range and found your best self. Others will have done likewise. Relationships between realized people are naturally satisfying but can be further improved over time if we are surrounded by those with the best influence.

Before I describe a world full of relationships between realized people, I want to dwell on the world as it presently operates under surveillance capitalism. Surveillance capitalism is the process of commodifying personal data with the core purpose of profit-making. Since personal data can be commodified, personal data has become one of the most valuable resources on Earth. Profit is not the only core purpose. Sometimes the purpose is to influence votes or promote a point of view, or to discourage one action while encouraging another. Or simply to take time and attention in a way that becomes habit-forming. One metric of value under surveillance capitalism is engagement (time spent); another is response to advertisements.

As a system for organizing influence, surveillance capitalism influences multiple individuals to behave in repeatable ways. Surveillance capitalism encourages behavior for the benefit of others (usually hidden), using data that the target is not privy to. Luckily, until now, the messages have been largely distinct, cacophonous, and mutually interfering. Left to proceed along the current path, this pattern will change.

Today, customer intelligence (surveillance data) is held in separate silos by separate organizations for separate purposes. Many of those purposes involve selling you something. Today, those messages are uncoordinated and somewhat cancel each other out. This is about to change in a way that will further empower surveillance capitalism and disempower individuals.

Search engines follow your interests. Email providers harvest the contents of your personal communications. Streaming movie and music services know your entertainment tastes. Credit agencies know how you use money. Retailers know what you buy. Wireless providers know your physical movements from GPS. DNA reveals your biology, health, and family relations. Official records tell the story of births, deaths, marriage, divorce, bankruptcy, criminal history, and legal disputes. Social networks know not only who you know, but the nature of your relationships. Soon you can add to that facial recognition with mood analysis, pulse, respiration, pheromones, brainwaves, digestive chemistry, and more.

With the current trajectory, this data will be merged, and your dossier fed to an artificially intelligent detective with all the time and patience in the world. Why is this so? Because from the point of view of two holders of surveillance data, there's mutual benefit to sharing. Unless both data holders compete in exactly the same space, they both benefit from the exchange. Also, the mechanics of sharing in an equitable way is becoming easier—equitable between the holders of surveillance data, that is. Sharing is not so equitable to you, the subject of the data. There's a saying regarding social media: "Unless you're paying, you're not the customer; you're the product." Who gets to see your data? The artificially intelligent detective and its owners, maybe others, but not you.

Why is this bad? There's the obvious loss of privacy, but it's worse than that. Indirectly, there's a loss of agency, of not being fully in charge, because others know deeply personal things about you in a way you cannot see. You may choose to inhibit yourself to not be surveilled and recorded, or your inhibition may be more unconscious. You may be reluctant to take risks when mistakes immediately become part of your permanent record. For all the reasons that political surveillance states are not creative hotbeds, capitalist surveillance doesn't foster artistry and imagination either. Not to mention all the meaningful work not being done while skilled people spend their working hours focused on ways to get more of your personal data.

Add to that the focus on comparative ranking on social media, even between people who like each other, or the preening, the fear of missing out, and the tendency to amplify the most extreme positions in lieu of a more nuanced connection. There is an unspoken belief that somehow these downsides are corollaries to technological progress with a resignation to the inevitable human costs. What else is wrong in the current online world? I haven't mentioned ransomware, spam, phishing, identity theft, data theft, doxing, or other obvious problems because these don't have upside corollaries. They are simply problems that would best be eliminated. We can build technology to fix all of this. Crypto is a key part of that technology.

Excesses of capitalism are not new. The earliest advertising we know of dates from the eleventh century BCE in China. At the time, music and dialogue (poetry) were used to sell candy.

Similarly, purchasing and accumulating stuff to display status is nothing new. Selling stuff for that goal is equally old. Today's online world is dominated by commercial entities with the goal of making money. The flow of much online information is shaped to maximize engagement (time spent) and sales via advertisements.

This is the way we're heading under surveillance capitalism. The way we're heading is clearly not an ideal environment for fostering better relationships. What would an ideal environment for fostering better relationships look like instead?

Princeton scientists Angus Deaton and Daniel Kahneman published research in 2010 showing that happiness is the result of the fulfillment of two abstract psychological states: emotional well-being and life evaluation, plus an income of at least $75,000 a year.[6] The surprise is that while income above $75,000 increases life evaluation, additional income doesn't increase emotional well-being. Income lower than $75,000 a year corresponds to reduced life evaluation, reduced emotional well-being, and reduced happiness.

This research comports well with our discussion of Maslow's hierarchy. The $75,000 covers physical needs and some security. Then, other things become more important than an abundance of the stuff that money easily buys. But what if we could simultaneously satisfy our physical needs more efficiently while satisfying our relational needs for emotional well-being in an efficient and structured way? I'm convinced that we can do just that. How do we satisfy our nonphysical needs in an efficient and structured way? We create the equivalent of goods and services to promote safety, belonging, esteem, and self-actualization. Let's take each in turn.

Safety means more than the absence of danger. The spectrum of safety extends to include a social environment where it is safe to express yourself. In a safe environment, you have no reason to fear destructive envy or criticism. You have plenty of inner safety to receive helpful feedback. You receive genuine appreciation when you give others your insightful and honest feedback.

Belonging means not only having people who will be cordial in your day-to-day interactions but being appreciated for the essence of who you are. And belonging includes being appreciated by those who know your truth.

Esteem means not only having status but deserving it and knowing you deserve it. You see the unvarnished truth about yourself and know that it is good.

Self-actualization spans the range from working at a job you love to becoming a fully realized being. The ultimate essence of self-actualization is beyond the scope of this book, but for many, self-actualization takes the form of service. Self-actualization comes from contributing to others' safety, belonging, and well-deserved esteem.

Can technology transform the world from surveillance capitalism to an economy where we truly serve each other, a world where we spend most of our energy supporting the betterment of each other's inner and outer lives? No. That requires inner work. But technology can help—technology in the form of a better economic system.

Why don't we already have an economy that fulfills our healthy human desires? Isn't that the whole idea of Adam Smith's invisible hand and specialization? Short answer: the money system doesn't measure the right stuff. What gets measured gets emphasized. What gets emphasized is the stuff of physical needs and the demands of the money system itself. Some would say the distortions of the money system itself. Billionaires cannot buy safety of the deep, personal kind, or belonging, or sometimes even an honest opinion. There's a certain kind of esteem in the eyes of others that comes with being a billionaire, thus the difficulty a billionaire can have finding an honest opinion. But the esteem that billionaires receive for being billionaires is shallow compared to the esteem that is possible for all of us.

There was a time not long ago when the super-rich couldn't buy lifesaving antibiotics, today's world news, or a phone call. I hope that the inventions I'm about to describe descend the price curve as rapidly as antibiotics and telecommunications. Some inventions will descend the price curve quickly, and others will take more time because they will need to sell at high prices until we improve our methods and drive down costs through experience. I am hopeful in cases of both fast and slow price reductions. Regardless of the speed of the price reductions, we may be more limited by the pace at which we can shift ourselves internally to become better versions of ourselves.

How do we improve relationships? Let's start with personal data. Here is a path for how to organize personal data and a healthy alternative to surveillance capitalism. It depends on new technology based on crypto and new government policy. The beginnings of that government policy are already law in the European Union.

In this new system, as under the current system, your personal data about communications, entertainment, financial transactions, location, health, DNA, and other things will be merged into a comprehensive dossier. As under the current system, your dossier will be analyzed by a patient detective in the form of an artificially intelligent agent.

But there's a twist. In the future, the only person who gets to see your data is you! Your data will be held in your personal well-being bot, which you own and control. Your personal data will be held nowhere else and only shared in ways you choose to share it, usually anonymously.

You get to see your dossier. You see all your personal data. You see the predictive profile derived from the synthesis of your information. You see the predictions of algorithms, algorithms that predict what you will buy, read, watch, listen to, and who you will vote for and care about. You will be shown your likely susceptibility to various messages. You will be shown the reasons why each prediction is being made. You can agree or disagree. When you share honestly with your well-being bot, your data gets more accurate. More accurate data is more powerful and more predictive. Your well-being bot might point to potential purchases for things you wouldn't anticipate wanting, but it will also help you realize in advance if you're about to make a purchase you will likely regret. When you engage with others through social networks, your well-being bot will prioritize others' information—not based on selling you something, not based on provoking just enough outrage to keep you engaged, but based on furthering friendship, personal development, your emotional well-being, or whatever goals you choose.

Your well-being bot is software that belongs to you and serves only you. You can run it on your own device or in a cloud service. Multiple vendors will sell competing well-being bot software, and you can choose one or more. You give your well-being bot general instructions. Your well-being bot executes the details based on accurate data and understanding. The understanding is based on your data, but the understanding explains its reasoning.

Your well-being bot comes preset with general instructions by default. There's the obvious, "Get me the best price on purchases," but also the not-so-obvious, "Let me be influenced by others in ways that lead me to be a better, more satisfied person." Well-being bots collaborate with other well-being bots behind the scenes, using crypto to maintain your and others' privacy. You benefit from imaginative algorithms and big data, but unlike surveillance capitalism, the thinking behind the algorithms is transparent and you select the nature of the influence.

Well-being bots have the opposite goals from advertising. Advertising attempts to sell stuff to those who otherwise wouldn't buy it with the often false promise of improving the buyer's experience through consuming. Well-being bots collaborate to organize an economy where creating is prioritized over consuming (because creating is more rewarding) and where relationships are valued over transactions. Well-being bots collaborate to organize an economy where imaginative giving leads to better rewards than persuasive selling. The economics of this will be explained in later chapters. For now, I'll describe how your well-being bot works.

First, I will use examples involving familiar transactions to illustrate the mechanics of information sharing in a way that honors the intents of multiple parties. Then, I will describe how well-being bots use crypto to foster better relationships.

Let's imagine you want to choose a movie. The minute you notify your well-being bot, it loads the whole database of encoded knowledge about everyone's movie preferences and the algorithms that use this preference data—without personally identifying information. When your well-being bot rents your movie, it does so anonymously. You remain anonymous even if you pay for an account with the movie-streaming service. You watch the movie and tell your bot how much you enjoyed the movie (or not). Your report of your enjoyment goes toward selecting other movies in the future, and while your feedback adds to the overall knowledge pool, the fact that your preference is yours remains hidden from the streaming service and is only found inside your well-being bot.

From the streaming service's perspective, it is important that their accumulated preference knowledge (the data) and their recommendation wisdom (the algorithms) remain proprietary. You may just want to enjoy a movie, but others want to start competing movie-streaming services. It is the job of crypto to handle these competing demands. You get the full benefit of others' preference data, and the streaming service gets the benefit of your addition to the collective pool of knowledge about movie preferences. No personal information is exchanged.

Here is another example.

Under today's tax-reporting system, you reveal lots of personal data to taxing authorities. What if you could automatically pay your taxes anonymously, leaving no trace, but still prove that you paid what was due and on time? If you become subject to audit, you would still reveal only as much as necessary. The first and most important step of the audit would be to prove you paid, certified by the software company who made your well-being bot and possibly by your tax preparer. Only if this yes/no indication of your payment is not sufficient does the tax authority proceed to step two. Step two is where you reveal how much you paid. If that is not sufficient, step three reveals the date you paid. Step four reveals the basis line by line, but only until the basis for the audit is satisfied or an error is found—again, it's a job for crypto. No tax authority sees your personal data, such as income, unless there is a problem. This is a win for taxpayers who have a well-being bot to look after their interests (lowest taxes) and a win for tax authorities who can be confident that fair taxes are being paid.

I chose the example of taxes to reveal an important theme of the future. In our future, information and data will do what was previously managed by the roles of officialdom. The role of officialdom in this case is to enforce tax law and collect taxes. If we had perfect information about how much each citizen owes in taxes, we would need less official apparatus, there would be less risk of leaking of your personal information, and less work both preparing and reviewing tax returns. We won't achieve perfect information, but we can get close with technology enabled by crypto.

Crypto can also be leveraged to deter crime. Crime is deterred when there's a high likelihood that criminals will be caught. Imagine a video camera that records everything it sees but encrypts the recording. No single person or organization has the decryption key. The decryption key is made moment-by-moment based on who is visible in the video. Only if some supermajority (for example, 85 percent) of all the people in the video agrees can the video be decrypted. There's no way to determine who is in the video without decrypting the video and watching it. Yet there's no way to decrypt the video without agreement from 85 percent of the people in the video. So there is no way to coerce the people in the video because it is not possible to determine who would need to be coerced. If a horrific crime is reported in the news, people who were nearby will be moved to give up some privacy in order to identify the perpetrator. For garden-variety mischief, it will be hard to elicit a similar civic response from 85 percent of the population.

It is the math of crypto that prevents the video from being decrypted without permission. Neither the camera manufacturer nor the installer nor the entity that pays for the camera can override the encryption. Only a supermajority can decrypt the video, a supermajority of people who can't be identified without seeing the video. The only way to get the supermajority to agree is through a public appeal. These cameras can be ubiquitous, deterring violent crime, without invading anyone's privacy.

Our last example involving familiar transactions has to do with money. For this example, assume we will be using some sort of digital currency. In some countries, petty bribery of government officials (and not-so-petty bribery) is a common occurrence. People are resigned to an unofficial tax on the goods and services provided by government. What if we had a currency where each time money is transferred, the payer or the payer's well-being bot could flip an invisible switch to indicate that this money was taken by extortion? The recipient (in this case, our corrupt official) has no way to tell which money has flipped switches. But if a single transaction occurs where the preponderance of the money has switches flipped, then all the switch-flippers are put in contact with each other and told the details of the corrupt official's transaction. The people who were extorted are told the corrupt official's identity, where the money was spent, how much, and what for. The corrupt official is not warned, but all the extorted people are put in contact and empowered to act collectively.

These ideas are works in progress, illustrated here to give you a flavor of what is possible. Details remain to be worked out. In the camera example, how do supermajorities work when only two people are present? In the bribe-money example, when and how does the bribe-indicating switch get turned off? These questions can be answered. The point is that privacy is by design, enabled by crypto, and need not be managed by a trusted authority.

Some of the technology to make this work is tricky and mistakes are possible, rendering the protections flawed, but nothing here is beyond our abilities. Some of this requires government policy. Safe air travel is hard and requires government policy too. I don't think we will look back and see the development of services based on crypto as nearly that difficult.

I've been illustrating ways that crypto can help maintain privacy while delivering services we are familiar with. Now, I will describe how crypto can be used to foster better human relationships. In Maslow's hierarchy of needs, privacy has mostly to do with safety. But crypto and well-being bots apply to areas other than privacy. Now, I will describe some possible new services that are designed to foster better relationships based on belonging, esteem, and self-actualization.

Relationships where we are known, understood, and accepted by others promote both a satisfying sense of belonging and the better living that true belonging enables. But belonging works both ways. Belonging also involves extending ourselves to others who we like and trust, to indicate that they belong with us. Over time, we have evolved in the ways of building trust, and mostly this happens step-by-step as we get to know each other. We reveal ourselves by degree, one step at a time. When we sense welcome acceptance, we allow ourselves to be more open. Sometimes the reaction is less inviting, so we withdraw or choose another line of conversation. Over time, we grow to know and trust other individuals based on our experiences with them. We don't reveal everything at first because we rightly sense how some things might not be helpful to the relationship and we don't yet have reciprocal trust.

This graduated approach works in face-to-face, human-to-human interactions, and the same principle can apply if we build it into our technology. With crypto, there is no need to reveal information unnecessary to the current moment. The principle here is that crypto can help foster relationships using a trust-by-degree approach. Trust-by-degree may be the first crypto principle where we see widespread adoption of new services, because this is an easy place for the public to begin to see and understand the benefits. One benefit of having a well-being bot is to confirm the honesty of what you say without revealing more than is called for in the moment.

Today, we have a range of services provided by official entities, especially governments, where we trade a degree of our privacy for credibility and assurance backed by the official entity. Examples include identity documents (driver's license, passport), records of ownership (real estate), and rules for trading (stocks and bonds). The agreement is that we give up some privacy to governments and the governments agree to not use our personal data for other purposes. Then, governments agree to use their monopoly on force to discourage those who break the rules.

But there are problems with our current system. Government employees can make mistakes that compromise data. Fraud occurs because it is not hard to forge official documents, and there is a significant likelihood that criminals will not be caught. Here's where crypto comes in. Crypto allows us and our well-being bots to confirm truths with a high degree of confidence and little extraneous data. Do you have $14.99 and a US shipping address? That's all your online merchant needs to know—not your identity, not the shipping address (only that you have one). Do you qualify for this car loan? A lender can be assured well enough that you do without knowing so much as your name.

Why is this important? What difference does it make if the lender on your car loan knows your name? It probably doesn't, but there are cases where graduated trust is important. In an interpersonal exchange, this translates to "Can you deeply identify with my experience?" or "Can I trust you to help me decide what to do next?" Both parties need to be confident that the answers are true, but additional information may not be needed. The more macro-question may be, "Do I want to reveal myself to you?" We are not currently accustomed to being confident of others' truth or honesty, especially without a long period in which we get to know each other. We are not accustomed to feeling safe when we first extend ourselves in honest and personal ways. Crypto can enable a higher degree of personal trust than we are accustomed to, but only when the trust is warranted. (Appendix 2 explores crypto in more detail.)

Earlier, I mentioned a simulation experience designed to allow us to develop our personalities, not unlike an actor getting into a role. We can use realistic-enough video and audio from the same type of setting we use to simulate a workspace such as our Zone Pods.

The idea is that we would be digitized, surface-mapped, altered in a way to obscure identity and added into a rendering for others to observe and interact with from within their own Zone Pods. The script would be planned by a combination of human and computer intelligence. The goal is to experience an interpersonal environment designed to practice new ways of behaving. Perhaps you want to become more outspoken and assertive. You would plan the strategy with the computer intelligence of your well-being bot and together pick other players and their attributes. Then you would interact with a combination of others, some of whom are digitized real people and some purely computer simulations indistinguishable from real people.

Perhaps, at the beginning of a session, your well-being bot would simulate certain others at half their actual size to help free your brain from the power dynamic where you are less assertive. Real humans who work as actors would specialize in addressing certain situations and traits. Your well-being bot would be the only witness who knows your identity and remembers your history. You could rewind and erase that memory if you choose. You could erase that memory both to maintain your privacy and to have the safety that comes from really being able to start over. Now you get a second chance to make a first impression. Take as many runs at your situation as required while you become comfortable being your best self.

Each of us will practice addressing the aspects of ourselves that cause insecurity or unsatisfying behavior. Practice leads to improvement, which will lead to esteem and healthier interaction with each other. An important job would be that of skilled actors who gain real satisfaction from helping people in meaningful ways. The actors would take roles in your simulated reality and work with you as a coach or trainer, except your real identity would be masked and the actors work alongside other actors that are computer simulations. Computer intelligence using crypto would ensure your anonymity.

Simulations provide one way of using crypto and virtual reality to direct the flow of influence. Today, influence generally flows in reciprocal patterns, back and forth both ways between sender and receiver. Sandy Pentland, in his 2015 book *Social Physics*,[7] has measured the way influence spreads between people. He measured how people are influenced by exposure to others and by others' examples far more than by incentives. He uses the example of obesity, which he measured to be one of the most communicable conditions there is. If everyone at your table has a second slice of pizza, chances are you will too.

The science of nudges follows similar lines. Nudges are as simple as setting the default choice in an online or paper form. For example, "Your recommended retirement savings will be automatically deducted from each paycheck unless you check this box to cancel." Compare that to: "Fill in this blank with your desired monthly retirement deduction." New employees are up to twice as likely to save for retirement if the first wording is used.

We can apply that sort of logic to our own interactions and our own place in the community. Students taking standardized tests do better if they're sitting next to high test scorers (without cheating). Now, we can all sit next to the best students in the class. Everyone at our table will stop after one slice of pizza. We will all save for retirement without seeing it as deprivation.

But I want to emphasize more substantive ways we can adjust how influence can flow to our benefit. We have ways of measuring the deep well of satisfaction that comes from a life well-lived. There is a positive correlation between wealth, prominence, and satisfaction, but the correlation is weak. What has a strong influence on satisfaction is whom we associate with. Just the simple manipulation of enlarging certain people and shrinking others in virtual settings not only changes the power dynamic but the flow of influence. We can choose to be influenced by those we admire and minimize the pull from others. Or we can leave the details to our well-being bots. You could tell your well-being bot, "I want to be satisfied in life, and I'd like to be a better person." Or you could choose more specific goals. Your bot will decide whose influence is most likely to move you toward your goals and increase the influence of those who will help you make it happen.

Because well-being and influence can be measured, the task of distributing the flow of influence to maximize well-being is a straightforward task of optimization. Computers are well-suited for this kind of optimization task. The internal work of becoming self-actualized is harder but can be made easier when we accurately measure and report our inner levels of satisfaction. Honest self-reflection is key. Intelligent tools and the well-meaning work of others can help if we let them. We will be more likely to let them, even at the cost of a certain amount of pride, when we realize how thoroughly our incentives are aligned. Also, we are more likely to accept well-meaning influence from others when we can remain anonymous.

But self-actualization and choosing who to be surrounded by is not all about hanging out with giants. Certain others will always remain important to us regardless of our immediate satisfaction or whether their influence is beneficial to us right now. For example, our children, spouse, close friends, and other people we care about.

In these relationships, we can have our well-being bots emphasize the flow of influence to support our family or group. In other words, we will make personal sacrifices for those we love, just as we do today. The key factor is deciding for whom we live our lives. We each live for ourselves, but enriching the lives of others has rewards too. Those rewards already guide much of our behavior, but our current economic system treats those rewards as if they don't exist.

As a result, we don't have an efficient, organized system of measuring how well our actions benefit others. The basic point of having relationships is to mutually enrich each other's lives and well-being; otherwise, we'd be better off being hermits. There is much to be gained from establishing a structured system for maximizing each other's emotional well-being with as much attention as we currently devote to the economy of physical resources.

Assuming we have sufficient physical resources, most of what we care about involves our relationships with others. Our current technology, including the world of finance and economics, is structured around physical needs. People use the system we have to inefficiently address relationship needs. Status is an obvious example of a relationship need that can be addressed by the current money system, but only poorly.

We can now make new tools. With new tools, we can build an economic system designed to serve genuine human needs. We will explore the new economic system further in Chapter 11. But there's another technology on the horizon that could change the nature of human relationships in a more fundamental way.

CHAPTER 6

EMPATHY

O UR SENSES ALLOW US TO EXPERIENCE LIFE firsthand. From experience, we develop memories to guide future behavior. We can learn skills and teach them to each other. Human language allows us to indirectly incorporate others' firsthand experiences and others' learned skills into our personal knowledge. Some of these skills and some of this knowledge have been refined by millions of people over millennia. We have stories, poetry, books, movies, songs, art, sculpture, museums, and travel. But they only work because we have empathy: the ability to put ourselves in another person's position in our minds. Empathy is amazing, but less rich or potent than firsthand experience. We also have technology designed to deliver firsthand experiences to others. These technologies include amusement park rides, psychedelic drugs, religious awakenings, meditation, and even space travel.

But we don't have a way to share our first-person experiences with others directly. The brain machines I am about to describe cannot do that either, but the effect can come pretty close. Think of it like fully immersive virtual reality for all your senses. But you are the creator of the experience, not the recipient. You create worlds from your imagination with as much richness and detail as you choose to imagine. Others can experience these worlds with high levels of detail and realism.

Of course, the recipient has voluntary control over whether to let your world in and how much to accept. Your experiences can be recorded, saved, and cataloged so others can find your experiences later by seeking them out or simply through curiosity. The flip side is that anything you experience or imagine can become a treasure for the whole human tribe. You are no longer living each moment solely for yourself; your experiences and your imagination can become part of the vast human archive, an archive of possible lived experiences for millions or billions of others. Which creations of your imagination are worth sharing with others?

Experiences will become valuable items in the world economy. In some ways, this is already true. The market for experiences includes travel, entertainment, and education. The difference is that future experiences will be as rich as you or someone else can or choose to imagine. Those experiences will be created by people generating content with machines connected to their brains, content we don't have words to describe today, except maybe with the idea of telepathy.

What are these brain machines and how do they work? Before we go there, let's take a step back. The fundamental concept I am about to describe is so simple that it is maybe too obvious to see, like the proverbial water to a fish. First, some background.

In communications theory, every channel has a certain bandwidth. A telephone line has a bandwidth that can be expressed in bits per second. So do our eyes, our ears, and each of our other senses. So do the parts of our brain when they communicate with each other. Connecting your left and right brain hemispheres is the corpus callosum, a collection of about 500 million nerve fibers. A typical human brain has a bandwidth of several billion bits per second between the left and right hemispheres. That's about a million times the bandwidth of all our senses combined.[8]

Our bodies, and those of most animals, have lots of inbound bandwidth. Our eyes can process the light hitting nearly 100 million retinal photoreceptors. Our ears have about 25,000 nerve endings to send details to our brains about sounds. Our bodies are built to receive and process a lot of information quickly.

But we are not nearly as rich in outbound bandwidth from our brains. We have a few hundred muscle groups under voluntary control throughout our whole bodies. We can make sounds, but our voices can make only a portion of the sounds we can hear. We have no faculty for transmitting images like we are able to see images. Yet, in our imaginations, we can generate whole worlds with sounds, pictures, emotions, body feelings, and more.

Here's the part that is like water to a fish. If we had more outbound bandwidth, we'd automatically learn how to use it. Here's why. The more outbound bandwidth we have, the simpler it is to use. This is important, so I will say it a different way. High outbound bandwidth equals simplicity. I'll repeat that one more time for emphasis: *high outbound bandwidth equals simplicity*!

Why is more bandwidth simpler to use? Being able to see the big picture makes the whole clearer, just as a chart can communicate the trend in a series of numbers. The saying about blind men describing an elephant shows the difficulty of compiling information one piece at a time. It is easier to make sense of more information at once. We are built for that.

Spoken language uses words, and although we seem to have a built-in language instinct, spoken language takes years to learn. Even after years of dedicated practice, we know only a single spoken language, or at most, a handful of them. Spoken language, even including tone and nuance, is a lower bandwidth compared to the way our eyes can see. While vision is the highest-bandwidth sense we have, even our eyes cannot see with the full richness of our imaginations.

Yet, seeing and understanding reality through vision requires no years of study. Dogs and cats see and understand their surroundings through vision. Speakers of French or English or Khoisan can all understand the same visual images without training. If we could project pictures from imagination through lenses in our foreheads, we could communicate more easily than we do with words. This simplicity through information richness is the principle hiding in plain sight.

Early brain machines will probably need computer assistance to create images as fluidly and quickly as we can in our imaginations.

We don't necessarily visualize images with enough thoroughness to fill in every detail. But machines can fill in details using intelligent guesswork, and we can watch the image form on a screen with our eyes. Then we can correct any mistaken assumptions made by the machine until the resulting image is good enough.

This is not unlike creative expression of any sort. The creative process consists of two steps: create and adjust. Repeat the two steps until satisfied. Unlike speech, visual conversations can involve multiple simultaneous "speakers," even millions of them. And visual "conversations" can incorporate elements that have intelligence of their own.

What do I mean by elements of conversation with intelligence of their own? Engineers today build simulations of machines with elements that have intelligence of their own. For example, electronic circuits are built and tested as simulations before physical parts are connected. The simulations are not just to help us design physical machines. Sometimes the simulations *become* the working machines. An electronic circuit that exists only in simulated form, but works like a physical device, is just as useful.

I said that more outbound bandwidth equals simplicity and described this in terms of visual images. I used visual images as my example because visual images are familiar to us all, but vision is only one of our senses. We have our familiar senses, but there are many more possible senses with brain machines. We can learn to communicate using vision, sounds, taste, touch, and smell, but the exciting part comes when we invent new senses. These new senses need not have any corresponding physical reality. These new senses only need to exist in imagination. To be a sense, these new senses only need to make "sense." I'll explain using examples.

I am about to describe a sense that is just as real as touch or your sense of gravity but not to a human. Some birds and fish can sense magnetic fields. Homing pigeons use this sense of magnetic fields to navigate using the earth's magnetism. As humans, we have no direct way of knowing what magnetism feels like to a homing pigeon, but we can imagine it. Imagine being able to feel magnetic north as easily as you can feel which way is down due to gravity. I imagine a sort of pulling that always faces the same direction, no matter if I twist or rotate. You may imagine something different. As you imagine how a homing pigeon feels magnetism, you created a new sense in your imagination. That sense you created in your imagination "makes sense" to you. In your imaginary sense, the input would be the earth's magnetism.

But imagine that, instead of magnetism, there was no physical input. Instead, imagine the input you sense is the product of another person's imagination. The sender communicates by creating something in their imagination and chooses to transmit that creation to you. You may not immediately know how to make sense of your sender's imagined creation. But with repetition and multiple examples, a pattern will emerge. Not all brain communications will use new senses. We can use familiar patterns such as sounds and pictures separately or in combination with new senses. We can use easy-to-grasp patterns such as my imagined pull for magnetic north, which may or may not mirror the experience of a homing pigeon. Or we can create rich, new "senses" for the purpose of communicating deeper and more nuanced inner states, inner states that facilitate deeper empathy. For example, you could communicate a full-bodied sense of what it is like to be you.

Our new senses don't have to correlate with any external or real physical properties. A new sense can be created expressly to communicate an inner experience. Those of us who have inner experiences beyond the normal human range may need to design new senses to make our inner worlds available to others. The stuff of unusual inner worlds (complete with new senses) can be valuable, possibly quite valuable.

So, how do these brain machines work? Today's early lab models require brain surgery to implant tiny electrodes that each listen to a few synapses. Machines read the electrodes and the machines detect patterns, but the machine learning of patterns is not a one-way street. The user learns to create meaningful patterns through training. The training can be thought of as biofeedback similar to the way people learn to relax or wiggle their ears with a mirror using formerly involuntary muscles. Or think of it as trial and error not unlike the way we learn to operate our bodies as infants and children.

As infants, we learn to wiggle our fingers through experimentation. Later, when we learn to type or take up the piano, with practice we learn to wiggle our fingers with more precision. We move, then we detect the way we moved. We move again. We learn from repetition and variation. Our brains send signals to our muscles. Our senses detect the finger movement and signal our brains. Practice. Observe. Repeat.

To add new outbound bandwidth under voluntary control will involve some combination of brain sensors, machine intelligence, feedback we can perceive (such as a video screen), training, and possibly psychoactive drugs. Today's brain machines require surgery, and the implanted electrodes may not last. Although the surgery has been compared to walk-in eye surgery for correcting nearsighted vision, it is likely the technology will be more popular when we can sense individual synapses remotely through our skulls without brain surgery.

Drugs may be required because we may need to simulate earlier developmental stages when our nerves were "noisier." With noisy nerves, there is activity to shape through learning, even without a deliberate choice to initiate activity. Before neuron pruning, infants may start learning to move a muscle after an involuntary twitch that gets things started. We may have lost the ability to deliberately initiate new kinds of brain activity, but we can observe and learn to shape involuntary "noise." Then, once we get familiar with our new brain activity, we will be able to initiate brain activity in voluntary patterns without the noise.

We've discussed machine intelligence for detecting synapse patterns and elements with intelligence of their own. Machines will fill in the details as we create imaginary visual images. But there are more powerful ways to incorporate machine intelligence in the communications channel. Machines can do many things better than our brains. Machines can compute, remember, sense the physical world, organize knowledge, remember facts, translate between human languages, and project the implications of certain courses of action far better than our unassisted brains.

Can a $10 thumb drive hold more knowledge than a PhD education? Maybe. That may not be a helpful question, but the point is that we can combine the advantages of both brains and machines. The machines don't need to be physically inside our heads. The key is to have a high-bandwidth outbound connection from our brains to the machines. We already have high-bandwidth connections in the inbound direction through our senses.

Machines have already taken the place of human brains for some things such as performing computations. But using machines for memory can offer us more benefit than computation. With a fast connection to machine memory, we can keep a running log of almost every thought we have. Our brains are much better at having ideas than storing memories. Machines can do some of the rote parts of logical thinking, too. Some thoughts can spawn processes that play out the implications of those thoughts. With more outbound bandwidth, we will be able to use machine memory and machine intelligence in a way that feels like experiencing our own consciousness. Except with the benefits of better memory and certain forms of higher intelligence.

We will generate ideas and our machines will project the possible consequences. Machines will find the necessary facts and perform calculations. Machines will store each mental thread so we can return to a previous point and jump off in a different direction, except we are connected at the speed of imagination versus the speed of talking or a keyboard. Think of this like a movie set where you are more the director than combination stagehand, camera operator, set builder, actors, and crew.

Machines can handle those details unless you choose to jump in and adjust something.

Those simulated actors, set builders, and crew (creations of your mind) can have (simulated) lives of their own that interact in ways that lead to multiple possible results. Each result is private, free of cost, and without lasting consequence. So you can choose which of your thoughts-brought-to life to keep and which to discard. Could some of them become valuable lessons or entertainment for others? Compared to today's person-to-person interactions, you can have more freedom to experiment and a safe environment for a wide range of expression. In Chapter 5, I mentioned training to alter your expectations and reset your sense of what is normal. With brain machines, the actions of your autonomous virtual characters can help you decide which possible aspects of yourself to pursue (or not).

There are ways people would like to interact that would be desirable by both parties (or all parties) but don't happen. Social mores get in the way, or the risk of embarrassment prevents people from expressing themselves or initiating communication. We can develop ways to open deeper, more intimate human relationships based on ideas, interests, and desires not often expressed today. This requires a level of trust and safety that is currently not common.

Your well-being bot using crypto can help with this. As you express your inner state through a brain machine, you can set your permissions so that only certain people can see what you express of your inner world. You can set your permissions so that your communication is visible only to those who have expressed states similar to yours. Even then, you could remain anonymous except in one realm: the inner state you wish to share. Later, you may choose to share more of yourself if you find you have more in common. Or not. Choose who you communicate with and your sources of influence from those who earn your respect. For many of us, learning to earn and maintain others' respect while fully expressing ourselves will require practice. The trick is to honestly express a wide range of thoughts and feelings without alienating others, not to build an overly "nice" or saccharine persona.

Learning is key, and learning will be one of the key differentiators between humans and machines, whether the scenario I describe regarding brain machines comes to pass or not. Training a human doctor takes years of graduate study, a residency, and lots of hard work. Training two human doctors takes twice as much work in total. Training a machine doctor takes a certain amount of work, possibly much more work than training a human doctor. But training a second machine doctor is as simple as copying and pasting information from one machine to another. This ease of replication is likely to substantially separate human and machine intelligence, no matter how much we incorporate machine thinking into our own experience.

Yet despite the learning advantages of machines, human learning has a unique advantage. Each new human learner can learn more and better than the teacher. That's because human learning is motivated. Why do you want to know? Curiosity and other human motivations bring our interest, creativity, and imaginations to the contents of our learning. Will computers be able to do this? That remains to be seen. For now, humans have the advantage.

Learning will be different for humans in substantive ways once we have the technology to allow us the experience of operating with knowledge and skills before we personally have that knowledge or master those skills. Compare learning to fly an airplane with speaking a few words in a foreign language. First-time pilots get to fly the plane with an instructor to take charge, as necessary. But the student pilot is immersed in the whole experience and actually flies the plane until the instructor takes over.

Speaking new words in a foreign language for the first time is just not as immersive or memorable as flying a plane. But perhaps it could be. Perhaps we can mimic the experience of fully using new knowledge before we master the knowledge. Perhaps we could experience ourselves speaking a new language before we know the words. Like the training wheels on a bike, we can use machines to keep us learning quickly on the steep part of the learning curve when we otherwise might fall over.

We learn in several ways. We learn from our own experience or from other people directly. We learn from other people indirectly through books and videos. We learn from intuition every time we make stuff up. With things we make up, we usually need to apply further thought and possibly observation, research, or experiments to generate knowledge that is solid. The theory of relativity exists because Einstein made it up, then checked it out and made refinements. Some of those refinements required Einstein to get help from others. The same process applies to almost all of the collective knowledge of humanity.

Outbound bandwidth on the same order of magnitude as our bodies' eyes and ears will allow us (with the help of machines) to expand the pipeline of knowledge from intuition to confirmation. That pipeline might go through multiple adjustments on the way to truth, but that pipeline is what leads us to the practical application of our knowledge.

There may be a precedent for higher-bandwidth outbound communication in nature. Whales may already have higher-bandwidth outbound communication than we do. What I am about to describe is speculation and may not comport with reality. But whether this comports with reality or not, it is a useful thought experiment.

Whales use sonar to "see" underwater, based on reflected sounds—reflections of sounds that the whales themselves emit. Perhaps whales can emit not only sounds to generate reflections but sounds corresponding to the reflections themselves. The reflections indicate aspects of an underwater scene. Like rays of light that indicate pictures to our eyes, the sounds represent an image of something the whale has "seen" or imagined.

The implication is that instead of a symbolic language with words, whales project very literal images that other whales can "see" as if they were real underwater scenes. We use about one hundred orofacial, laryngeal, pharyngeal, and respiratory muscles to produce speech. Some whales have thousands of muscles that flex their melon, the squishy head-bump that shapes and focuses a whale's sound waves. Maybe they can operate those muscles to shape sound waves quickly and independently enough to transmit more information than us, information that other whales can understand just as easily as "looking around" with their sonar. Complex and immersive communication occurs between whales, yet no words are required.

This chapter on brain machines describes the most speculative or sci-fi aspect of my vision for the future. It is hard to predict when effective brain machines will become available and acceptable to the public, but there is nothing I know of that stands in the way. No fundamental scientific discoveries are required. There seems to be adequate funding. All that's needed is a modicum of luck, competent execution, and relatively few years.

I think the bigger problem may be for us, the public, to get our heads around this one, even those of us in the scientific and tech-aware public. The key is understanding the pivotal role of increased outbound bandwidth, especially the notion that having more outbound bandwidth equals simpler language. Could dogs and cats create virtual worlds from their imaginations? Probably. Would we be able to understand the virtual world of a dog's imagination? I think so, at least somewhat.

The previous chapter discussed satisfying relationships. This chapter describes brain machines in the context of increased empathy. The chapters have something in common. The world enabled by the technologies I describe doesn't align very well with the foibles of today's society. The benefits I describe fit better in a society of individuals more mature, autonomous, at peace with their inner demons, and marshaling more of their inner resources than today's society. Will we become that society?

I am confident that the answer is yes. Why am I confident? This is sort of reverse logic, but I'm convinced we will become that society because the advantages are so compelling.

History is replete with examples of human institutions that changed individuals, institutions that would not exist or succeed by happenstance. International corporations coordinate the work of thousands of people toward common goals—not because thousands of people share those goals but because people get paid to act in a certain collaborative way. Some employees are paid more because their collaboration more powerfully influences corporate performance. Why did this lead to corporations? Because for complicated tasks, a thousand people organized into a corporation can outcompete a thousand people working independently; in other words, because the advantages are compelling.

Corporations pay people in money. In Chapter 11, I will describe a currency more suited to organizing people into structures fit for a wiser, more mature society. But the compelling benefits of a wiser, more mature society have been apparent for eons, and so far, we have not formed that wise and mature society. We need a more immediate impetus to make the leap, and that impetus is immortality. Immortality is the focus of the next chapter.

Living longer fits with a wiser and more mature society. Immortality is both cause and effect. On the one hand, more years can lead to more emotional maturity, more learning, and more self-development. On the other hand, there's motivation.

Attaining inner peace and becoming an old soul is worth the effort when you expect to enjoy the benefits for centuries to come. We will watch our physical stuff wear out while our relationships and inner resources grow in richness over time.

CHAPTER 7

IMMORTALITY

WHY DO WE AGE AND DIE? THERE ARE SEV-
eral reasons, and several can be right at the same
time. For any effect, there are proximate causes and
more general causes. For example, an officer stops and questions a
driver about speeding. The driver decides to tell the officer, "Must
be the new shoes. Thick leather pushing down on the accelerator
more forcefully than I'm used to!" While technically true, thick
shoe leather is a proximate cause. The more general cause has to do
with the bank robbery our driver just committed.

Aging has many proximate causes, sometimes more than one
for each type of cell in our bodies. But our focus here is on a
more general cause of aging. The most useful way to think about
the general cause of aging probably has to do with developmental inertia. Development takes us from fertilized egg to adult

through a series of steps, each of which improves our evolutionary fitness and chance of reproductive success. Natural selection shapes our genetics by selecting members of each generation who do well at every stage—every stage up to and including replacing ourselves with healthy offspring who are ready to survive on their own.

Nature doesn't select among those elders whose offspring are already thriving; it selects among the already-thriving offspring. Meanwhile, our bodies' developmental mechanisms continue to operate even though the results are harmful. The unit of evolutionary success is the species, not the individual. From evolution's point of view, individuals are replaceable parts of the human species. Nature's winning strategy is to reliably replace individuals in the service of species survival. Our bodies use the same replacement-parts strategy with some of our cells. This individuals-as-replaceable-parts strategy no longer serves us. Human survival and the restoration of nature are now better served by the long-term survival of individual humans.

Not all organisms age. Not all organisms develop in a way that makes them less fit with age. For example, the hydra, a small sea creature, doesn't appear to age at all. It could be said that bacteria are immortal. Although most bacteria die because of conditions, bacteria that continue to live eventually split, each one becoming two bacteria. One parent bacterium becomes two daughter bacteria. Every bacterium alive today is a descendent of bacterium number one and carries a part of that first bacterium in organizational structure, even though all the bacteria's molecules have been replaced many times. There has never been a death in the direct lineage of any bacteria alive today.

Spores are another example of organisms that don't necessarily age. When spores dry, they cease living and go into suspended animation. If a dry spore comes into contact with water, the spore becomes reanimated and alive again, even if thousands of years have passed. As an interesting side note, some dry spores can survive in outer space, making it possible that life has traveled from planet to planet on meteors.

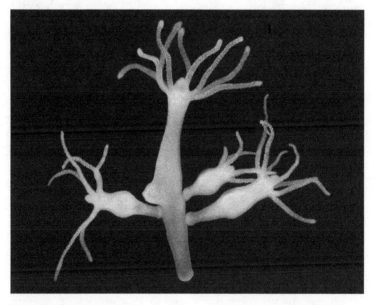

Figure 13. Freshwater Hydra.
This small animal, the freshwater hydra, grows to about 3/4 of an inch long and lives in lakes and streams. Hydras can reproduce sexually, asexually, or by being cut into pieces in which case each piece, if large enough, grows into a new hydra. It is believed that under suitable conditions hydras are immortal and show no increase in senescence with age.

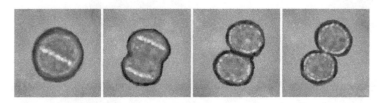

Figure 14. Single-celled organism splitting into two individuals.
The parent (left image) doesn't die or cease to exist when it splits into two
daughter cells.

Perhaps the best example of non-aging is closer to home in the human germline. A woman's egg cells are created before she is born. Decades later, a woman's egg cells can become her children. But babies born to twenty-year-old mothers and babies born to forty-year-old mothers are both babies, not little twenty-year-olds. Although human egg cells change in several ways between age twenty and forty, aging is not one of those ways. Development doesn't begin until fertilization.

While aging is a problem if you want to live forever, it's not the only problem. In addition to aging, we can die from trauma, toxins, bad conditions, or wear and tear. We will address each of these in turn, but first I'd like to dispel some possible misperceptions.

First: immortality doesn't mean patching together an increasingly frail body. The idea is to continue living in the body of a healthy young adult for hundreds of years.

Second: immortality doesn't mean death-proof. If you are living in the body of a healthy young adult, even for hundreds of years and you get run over by the future version of a bus, you'll still probably die. Immortality is always tentative, a work in progress, one day at a time.

Third: immortality will not lead to runaway population growth. This year, on Earth, about 140 million babies will be born and about 60 million people will die. The earth's human population will increase by about 80 million people. If no one ever died and we cut today's birth rate by slightly more than half, the world population would continue on its current trajectory. This is not unprecedented. We have cut the birth rate in half already. The birth rate in 1966 was double today's birth rate. Another comparable reduction would offset the population effect of eliminating all human deaths.

Fourth: immortality doesn't have to come in a single breakthrough and probably won't. Both average and maximum lifespans increase as we improve technology. If we can improve life-extending technology about 2.5 times as fast as we do currently, we will add one year to life expectancy every year. If we keep up this pace, we will achieve escape velocity. We won't stop increasing longevity at escape velocity; our advances will accelerate until we add a year or more to life expectancy every six months.

Fifth: we will not genetically deteriorate without death to cull the herd. We no longer evolve more fit bodies through natural selection and survival of the fittest. Human genetics hasn't been shaped by natural selection for the last several thousand years. Today, most people born survive to adulthood, and family size is based on personal choice, not survival of the fittest.

With those possible misperceptions out of the way, let's talk about why immortality is important. Based on population numbers, humans have been a remarkably successful species accounting for about 36 percent of all mammals by mass. Our domesticated livestock and pets account for another 60 percent. Wild mammals account for the remaining 4 percent.[9] We didn't fill 96 percent of Earth's mammal-niche because of natural selection in the usual sense. We became the earth's most successful mammal by our ability to collaborate and build things. We are now at the undisputed pinnacle of evolutionary success for a single mammalian species, as measured by conventional metrics.

Now we are ready to move on from becoming a successful species. Our unit of evolution has ceased to be the human species and has now become the individual. We improve ourselves individually at our own direction. Our species no longer improves because we have children who (hopefully) turn out better than the parents; we improve because we take responsibility for our own evolution. This idea of evolution applies both in terms of our bodily fitness and in a more metaphorical sense about what it means to evolve. We started this cycle when humans began to modify the earth to enlarge our niche. Now we complete the cycle. With immortality as a possibility, we're now in charge of our own evolution, like it or not. The evolution of life on Earth is now up to us.

I've mentioned that aging is not the only cause of death. Every year, some people of every age die. But the death rate varies greatly with age. At the current rates of death, about one ten-year-old in 12,000 dies each year worldwide. Does this mean that, if we perpetually had the bodies of ten-year-olds, we would live 12,000 years on average? No. Wear and tear still happens. If you eat candy every day and never brush your teeth starting on your tenth birthday, you might make it to age eleven with healthy teeth. But being perpetually ten years old won't prevent the cumulative effects of tooth decay. Brush your teeth!

LIFE EXPECTANCY IF YOU STAY AT THIS AGE

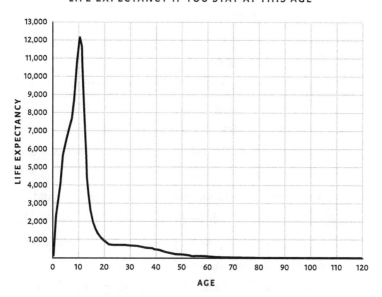

Figure 15. Life expectancy if not for aging.
This chart shows your life expectancy if not for the effects of aging. The vertical scale shows how long you could expect to live if you lived in a body that perpetually remained at the same biological age. That biological age is shown across the bottom. The peak is at age ten where you could expect to live over 12,000 years. But more interesting is the fact that you could expect to live 500 years or longer if your aging was arrested at any age between one and thirty-nine. *Data source: US Social Security Period of Life Table, 2010*

It is unlikely we will be reverting to the bodies of ten-year-olds anytime soon or even living perpetually in bodies of any age. We have over 200 cell types, most of them subject to biologically programmed development. Some cell types play a more important role in aging than others. We will likely develop different ways of retarding or reversing developmental inertia for many of these cell types so that you could have organs that appear to be different ages. It would be important to have a youthful heart, while olfactory receptor cells might be harder. So, you live in an otherwise youthful body with an old person's sense of smell.

How does technology work to keep us from aging and dying? There are two approaches getting most of the attention. One is called Strategies for Engineered Negligible Senescence, or SENS. SENS is associated with Dr. Aubrey de Grey, a brilliant and original thinker. In his 2007 book *Ending Aging*,[10] he described how although there are thousands of causes of aging and thousands of effects of aging, there are only seven mechanisms that connect the two. Then he proposed engineering solutions (not medical treatments) to address each of the seven deadly things.

There is another approach to ending aging, in addition to SENS. The second approach is focused on modifying our DNA. We are getting better at understanding DNA and developing safe strategies for editing the DNA inside our living bodies. Some of this requires a deep understanding of DNA and some involves taking traits from one species and giving them to another, like copy and paste. For example, if a salamander or an octopus loses an arm, a new arm grows in its place. Work is in process to add that trait to human heart muscle, so if heart muscle dies, it can be regrown.

Figure 16. Salamander.
An adult salamander is shown at two stages in regenerating a forelimb. In the top image, about ten days after amputation, the wound has healed and the end of the stump is beginning to enlarge. In the bottom image, about four or five weeks later, the new limb is well advanced and appears much like a normal forelimb except for its color and size.

Both of these approaches to extending lifespan have merit, and they can work together. Both are progressing rapidly. Both can be accelerated with attention, emphasis, and good policy. For example, aging is not yet considered a disease and doesn't qualify for certain funding or human trials under the regulatory structures of most countries.

Public policy tends to lag public demand by a few years, and the public demand for research into immortality has not been particularly strong. Why is this? Partially, the lag is because many people are not yet aware of the practical possibility of near-term breakthroughs. Partially, it is because not all those who think immortality is possible realize it is a good thing. It is easy to assume that the benefits of research now will only benefit future generations, and that is true for some, especially today's elderly. Some assume that life-extending treatments will only be available to the wealthy, and there is some truth to that.

But there is a significant portion of today's population that stands to benefit from current and near-term research. How big a portion of today's population? That depends on luck, timing, and crucially, how rapidly the research unfolds. Costs are an issue both for the research itself and for the application of treatments when they become available. But costs will decline rapidly, well within one generation. Research funding will increase rapidly when the wealthy have the option of paying for their own realistic chance at immortality. Some will opt to pay whatever they can; some already do.

Is it better to be rich or young? Currently, the poor die younger than the wealthy by a significant amount in countries around the world. The differences are stark between countries and within some countries. But longevity has been increasing among people at all wealth levels in most countries. By a lot![11] It is hard to see research proceeding at a pace so slow that generations of wealthy people will benefit while the poor die young.

Today, in most countries, you can expect to live slightly longer if you're wealthy. Most wealthy countries offer socialized medicine, yet some resist the call for sharing access to healthcare equitably. When the difference becomes dying soon versus living forever, the political pressure will increase, and public funds will be spent as necessary. In the long run, the research toward longevity will lead to cost reduction in the delivery of healthcare in wealthy countries.[12] Most healthcare spending is currently done in the last years of life, because old age leads to conditions requiring expensive care. If we don't deteriorate into a state of infirmity that requires expensive care, we can avoid many of those costs. Some diseases are associated with old age and can be largely avoided. But most diseases not specific to old age have an onset that is triggered, at least partially, by age.

Just as we can avoid infectious disease by eliminating exposure to certain bacteria or virus particles, we can avoid the onset of some otherwise chronic diseases by effectively remaining at an age before onset. In the short term, it may be this ability to avoid or defer disease that propels longevity research. Mechanisms, including funding and access to human trials, are available for treatments of diseases such as cancer. One way to reduce cases of cancer is to stop the aging process before people reach the age of onset. This may turn out to be more practical than other cancer treatment options.

Living forever is not for everyone. Many unfortunately are already too old or too infirm. Some are simply unlucky. Some will die of causes not related to aging. Some will refuse to intervene with aging for reasons related to their belief systems.

However, within a historically short period, those who will die will have mostly died out. That leaves those who choose to live forever and those young enough that they don't need to choose one way or the other just yet.

But despite the difficulty required to develop effective technology to address aging, there is a far greater reason that immortality is not more popular today. That reason is death psychology. Death psychology is the adaptive trait of avoiding inevitable negative consequences by denial. We avoid suffering by not thinking consciously about things to avoid unnecessary stress. Prisoners on death row experience the effects of death psychology. From the vantage point of death row, quitting smoking and maintaining a healthy weight are not urgent priorities. Today, it is fair to say that most of the world's population suffers from death psychology. We avoid thinking about death and how to prevent it because it is too unpleasant to spend any time on. Death psychology makes it harder to quit our nature-damaging habits and institute wide-ranging equity.

Immortality is key to our future, because death psychology underpins our destructive habits and our limited commitment to the future. Immortality is key because the world needs people who expect to live to see the results of society's current actions. This means you. You wouldn't be reading this book right now if you were content to die on a doomed planet. Understanding what possibilities are realistic is both a sobering wake-up call and a joyous invitation to transition from death psychology to something better. What is that something better? It remains a work in progress for all of us.

Immortality is coming. Will it come in time for you? Will you choose to live forever if that choice becomes available to you? Living forever is more desirable if you live in a healthy, fit body. Can most of us live in healthier bodies than we live in today?

OPPOSITE: *Figure 17.* Chart showing death thinking and immortality thinking.

	Death Thinking	Immortality Thinking
Plans	There is no long-term plan.	It is worthwhile to make long-term plans for coming centuries.
Life's phases	There is one cycle through: birth, childhood, education, work, retire, and die.	There are many cycles of education, work, downtime (temporary retirement), and the unknown.
Education	Learn about what is known now.	Education continues as new stuff is discovered; learn more.
Work	Employment or self-employment is traded for income.	It becomes worthwhile to find work that is a true joy.
Politics	Politics are limited based on voters' self-interest for the next few years or decades.	Much greater can-do attitude; voters are motivated for long-term societal benefit.
Evolution	Future generations will hopefully improve society.	Improving society becomes part and parcel of personal development.
Personal economics	Work → retire.	Contribution is a privilege and the main reward of working.
Feelings	Inevitable death is tragic and scary.	The unknown is scary too but in a different way.
Relationships	Annoying people will eventually go away; no real need to deal with them.	We need to eventually deal with everyone.
Wealth and poverty	The rich can maybe hold on to stuff by building walls to keep the poor out.	We need to eliminate poverty.
Death equalizes all	The rich and poor are equalized in death.	People born into average circumstances more recently may live richer lives than today's wealthy.
Economic implications	Some are rich, some are poor; we are destined to stay that way.	Now is time to reinvent the money system (like going from food → land → gold → money).
Personal motivation	It is not worth the effort to quit smoking on death row.	Anything worth doing eventually is worth doing now.
Perspective on right now	Procrastination may pay off.	Procrastination just delays the problem.
Catchphrase	Life sucks, then you die.	It gets better.

CHAPTER 8

HEALTH

L IVING FOREVER IS HARDLY WORTHWHILE IN A frail, sickly body. Until now, most of the world has defined health as avoiding a long list of known diseases. As we age, avoiding disease becomes less likely because our bodies become less able to sustain the conditions required for health. It is time to think about ways we can do better than today's definition of perfect health. Fortunately, vibrant health goes hand in hand with living a fun and satisfying life. Good health leads to greater satisfaction. Living successfully with purpose and the subsequent satisfaction improves health. It doesn't matter which causes which. We want to promote both health and vibrant living.

A life expectancy of eighty or ninety years masks problems that only show up later—specifically, problems caused by the accumulation of undesirable substances in our bodies. Toxins that accumulate to harmful levels over the course of 150 years don't cause acute problems in today's population. With a longer life expectancy, we will want to eat cleaner foods and drink cleaner liquids—cleaner in terms of both avoiding undesired substances, including organisms such as bacteria and the genetics of the organisms we consume.

The buzzwords of modern medicine are the four Ps: predictive, personalized, preventative, and participatory. We will want to follow each of these to its logical conclusion. The predictive nature of healthcare will change when the goal is to predict the course of our lives for centuries. Some predictions will have to do with what interventions we plan to make and when, such as modifying our DNA. Some of those predictions will be based on our expectations about which technologies will become available and when. There is no point in intervening now in something that won't bother you for decades if a better technology will become available in just a few years.

But the spirit of the predictive part of medicine has to do with knowing our individual bodies well enough to tailor interventions to suit. The personalized aspect has to do with medical interventions but will also encompass food, beverages, exercise, sunlight, sleep habits, and stress levels. Of the many thousands of edible plant species on Earth, we eat only a few. Mostly, we eat what we eat because of tradition and familiarity. In preagricultural times, there were survival advantages in not being too adventurous with food choices. Our ancestors only had to make one unsuccessful food choice to eliminate themselves from the human gene pool. We are the progeny of those who never made that mistake.

Today we see vestiges of this food-conservatism in immigrant communities who tend toward the food of their ancestors several generations after changing culture and language.

When we experiment with food today, our choices are limited and our measurement means are crude, consisting mostly of how food tastes and how we feel between meals. At some point, we will have biosensors that measure our body's reactions in various ways and participatory courses in food exploration, plus an expanded list of foods. The expanded list of foods makes more sense when you consider how much we do with some plants such as wheat. Or consider foods that are toxic unless we treat the plant material. Tapioca is an example of a food that requires processing. It requires the removal of a toxin (cyanide) from the cassava plant.

In our future, not only will you be more attuned to the foods that are delicious and healthy for your individual body but those plants and animals will be grown custom just for you. Plant genomes can be tailored to supply you with vitamins and nutrients in optimized doses. Seed-to-plate tracking and isolation from other organisms will ensure cleanliness. Likewise, animal products (to the degree we choose to ingest animal products) will be grown in ways that prevent cross-contamination from one animal to another.

Domestic animals will lead healthier lives, using many of the same technologies as people. Sensors for each animal's well-being will help select the healthiest plants and the right quantity for each animal. The animals might serve double duty by also growing cells and organs for later use in our human bodies, either in a routine fashion or for emergencies. We might raise pigs with immune profiles that match certain humans in case one of the humans needs a kidney transplant. Then before slaughtering the pig for food, we would ensure that a younger pig with the same immune profile is mature enough to offer a replacement kidney so that vulnerable people have a spare kidney available at all times.

I've referred to the things we do to extend our lifespans as "interventions" instead of "treatments" because it makes sense to think of these as the products of engineering rather than the products of medicine. Living in vibrant good health requires some of the same strategies we discussed in the chapter on immortality. Nature has made our bodies to last only a certain duration before we, as individuals, are replaced in the service of our species.

Now we are changing the plan. Earlier, I mentioned Dr. Aubrey de Gray's excellent book *Ending Aging*, in which he describes SENS, Strategies for Engineered Negligible Senescence. Dr. de Gray identified the seven mechanisms that lead to aging and discusses engineering interventions to address each of the seven. *Ending Aging* is well worth reading in its entirety, but I'll very briefly summarize the seven mechanisms and the seven engineering solutions here. Refer to Figure 18.

Some have compared SENS to keeping a house in perfect condition by replacing individual pieces as they age. To a certain extent, that is how our bodies maintain health—by replacing cells. For each cell type, there are several possible strategies for health improvement. We can replace old cells with new cells. We can find ways to prolong the health span and lifespan of existing cells. We can improve the way that cells are replaced so that we continuously grow the cells of a young person—or some combination. These strategies are not mutually exclusive.

Aging Mechanism	Engineering Solution
Stem-cell loss	A cell therapy using growth factors and stem-cell addition.
Cell senescence (zombie cells)	The removal of senescent cells via targeting, mostly by boosting "suicide" genes.
Waste accumulation outside of cells	Training the immune system to engulf the junk outside cells and transport it inside.
Waste accumulation inside cells	Putting genes from soil microbes with a taste for liposomal garbage into our cells.
Intercellular protein crosslinks	Adding enzymes that can break these protein links between the cells.
Mitochondrial DNA mutations	Transferring mitochondrial DNA into the cell nucleus.
DNA mutation (cancer)	Extracting cells. Modifying cells to not produce telomerase so they can't divide and to tolerate chemotherapy. Returning the cells. Using chemo to kill off any growing cancer cells.

Figure 18. Chart of Dr. Aubrey de Grey's seven deadly things.
Despite the thousands of causes that contribute to aging in the human body and the thousands of effects of aging, there are only seven mechanisms that connect the two. This chart lists the seven known mechanisms of aging with potential therapies for each. The potential therapies are different from what are traditionally thought of as medical treatments and more like engineering interventions to change the ways biology operates within our bodies.

Old people grow gray hair consisting of new hair cells. Why? We don't yet fully understand the cascade of events and internal body communications that make our bodies grow fresh old-person cells. At what point up the chain of causality do we need to intervene?

This question about the chain of causality is further complicated because, in addition to being a chain (with links in a specific order), the causality of aging and that of health in general is a system of synergy with multiple interwoven feedback paths. Unless we intervene, development routines in our cells continue to operate after we have developed into healthy adults, eventually modifying our bodies in ways that make us less able to sustain life. At first, the effect proceeds slowly. Then aging and disease progress more rapidly when one system falters, adding stress to other systems. For example, hypertension (high blood pressure) increases the risk of developing heart failure.

In emergency medicine, the first thing to do is to simultaneously stabilize the patient's vitals, such as breathing, pulse rate, blood pressure, and temperature. If any one of these vitals falls out of range, systemic problems occur and rapidly cascade.

In optimizing health for longevity, it similarly makes sense to stabilize many of the key parameters of aging before the effects begin to add stress to other biological systems. While not a perfect fit, Figure 18's list of seven deadly things offers valuable clues about how to organize a plan for stabilizing the slower-moving vitals of aging.

Only one item on the list of SENS interventions involves modification of the DNA in our existing cells by adding repair mechanisms from another species. There may be other opportunities to use genetics that evolved in other species. For example, an elephant has about one hundred times as many cells as a human and can live seventy years or more. Yet despite having many times the potential for a cell to go rogue in a way that leads to cancer, elephants seldom get cancer, and elephants die of cancer at less than one-third the rate of humans. One possible explanation has to do with gene p53. Gene p53 makes a protein that plays a key role in controlling cell division and cell death. The human genome has one copy of gene p53 while the elephant genome has twenty copies. Maybe we could advantageously add more p53 genes to our genomes. We are simultaneously learning how to modify DNA for longer lifespans (at least in mice) and learning how to engineer targeted viruses to safely install those modifications into the cells of living adult bodies. DNA modification is not just for future generations.

Our technology's range of possibilities is wide, but our knowledge here is limited. Prudent safety precautions and the long time required to evaluate safety in humans limit the pace of direct DNA modification in humans. But even with this limitation, the approach of adding traits from other species to our genome may happen soon enough to make one or more of the seven SENS interventions unnecessary for you.

DNA can be understood at two different levels. The more difficult level is that of computation or individual molecular reactions. Interventions based on understanding DNA at the level of computation are unlikely to be a significant factor in how we modify our cells any time soon.

Much simpler is a practical understanding of which chunks of DNA lead to which traits. Nature has a large library of possibilities. I mentioned salamanders, which can grow new limbs if one is severed. The DNA behind that trait is being explored for its applicability to regenerate human heart muscle. Of course, it is better to prevent heart muscle death in the first place, but the point here is to recognize that heart muscle regeneration may be possible.

As we understand the interrelated chains of causation that lead to aging, we will modify DNA using whatever tricks work best to engineer each intervention. The result is likely to be a new path away from old age but not exactly what we would expect from reversing the passage of time. In other words, the path from today's ninety-year-old body to that of a thirty-year-old will likely include stages unlike those experienced while aging from thirty years old to ninety years old.

Different organs and organ systems will become "younger" at different rates. The technology will be improved year-by-year, further complicating the picture. Someone who starts interventions to reverse aging on one date will have a different path than someone who starts the process a decade later.

Eventually, choosing your path through reverse aging will become a part of your health planning. Do you want mental focus now and the muscles to climb mountains later, or the other way round? What effective age is each of your 200-plus cell types? How will the combinations work together at each stage? If you want to climb mountains, strong bones are good too. How strong? No need to limit yourself to the normal human range. Tired of all that attention on healthy food grown just for you? Rats can be equally healthy with a diet of caviar or cardboard. Perhaps you'd like that ability too. These sound like frivolous or outrageous things, but someday we may discover that rat digestion is the safest way to avoid unpleasant and dangerous diseases. Our different cell types will have different researchers looking at ways to reverse the aging of that cell type and determining how each cell type affects the aging or reverse-aging of other cell types.

Not all aging is disease, and not all disease is aging—specifically infectious disease. Until now, our bodies have dealt with infectious disease with our immune systems, and we have trained our immune systems through happenstance exposure to certain organisms in air, water, food, and dirt. We also deal with infectious disease through vaccines and by generally trying to avoid pathogens. We will want to improve on all three: training our immune systems through exposure, vaccines, and avoiding pathogens. Instead of happenstance exposure to dirt and airborne particles, we will engineer a sequence of immune training exposures from a catalog or database and select our exposures based on our individual bodies.

Vaccine research is ongoing and can't be stressed enough. Along with general safety and efficacy, we can improve the technology to test in advance for adverse vaccine reactions on an individual basis. This way, even vaccines that might be dangerous for a segment of the population can be delivered to the rest of the population after testing the vaccine on each individual's cells in a lab.

But as important as vaccines are, avoiding exposure is probably the path with the most potential for dealing with infectious disease. Exposure comes from human-to-human contact, human-to-animal contact, and occasionally from contact with individual bacteria or virus particles that have been sitting on surfaces for a while. Some contagion is carried by spores that can survive for years; then, they can become infectious when they contact water.

For each virus capable of human-to-human transmission, there was an initial event that started a cascade of human infections. COVID-19, SARS, MERS, AIDS, Ebola, smallpox, polio, herpes—these are some familiar viruses, but there are probably many more that fortunately have not made the initial jump to humans. But we also have the common cold, the flu, and others that are not as deadly but still cause unnecessary human suffering. What would it take to eliminate all of these from our experience?

Transmission occurs through the foods and liquids we ingest, by touch, and through the air we breathe. I've discussed food and how we can keep the path of food separate for each person from seed to plate. Plants will be grown in glass containers that are specific to each person. Much of the handling and preparation that today's food entails will probably be done by machines in a continuation of the trend that has been happening for centuries. Kitchen robots are coming regardless of other trends I've discussed, and it makes sense to have our robots implement a higher level of cleanliness and disinfection than today's human-based standards.

We mostly solved the problem of contaminated drinking water many decades ago with plumbing, at least in the industrialized West. We have not improved water cleanliness much in the last few decades, and some places have fallen behind—for example, with poisoning from lead pipes. Anything we build now can take advantage of better techniques and materials. This becomes more economical in our high-density structure where overall distances are short.

Contagious disease is spread through the air, in our food, on the surfaces we touch, and through water. As we expand our systems to deal with air, food, and surfaces, we have several advantages over the people who built the water systems in our cities many decades ago. We can model the effectiveness of our designs, and we can build mechanisms that depend on computer logic to function. We can design systems to prevent contagion at the outset as we build. And since our current built spaces do so little to limit contagion, we will derive considerable benefit from even simple systems that are inexpensive and easy to implement.

For example, as I mentioned previously, with reactive laminar airflow, we can direct the airflow in our enclosed spaces. There are two major ways. The first way has to do with the design of buildings and furnishings. We can ventilate each occupied space with air that has been cleaned and disinfected since the last time it circulated through an occupied space. But occasionally, multiple people will be in the same space, for which there is a second way to prevent airborne contagion. For rooms with multiple people, we can build reactive systems with sensors, logic, and valves that operate in real time to regulate instantaneous airflow as people and objects move around.

We can engineer these reactive airflow systems with sensors that detect a sneeze and direct bursts of air to deflect the air from your sneeze away from other nearby people. We can make high-touch surfaces self-cleaning and build monitoring systems for lower-touch surfaces. The monitors can inform people or robots to come and clean those touch surfaces. Does this sound extreme? It's a trade-off between space and engineering. Enough space can effectively dilute the effects of person-to-person disease transmission, but so can engineering. The engineering may sound too complex or difficult until we do it. What's more, there is no limit to effective engineering. There is, however, a limit to the habitable area on our planet. If the goal is to reduce direct person-to-person air exchange, we can do that most effectively with imaginative engineering. We can choose a level of effectiveness such as 99 percent for everyday interactions and higher for more dangerous interactions. Higher effectiveness adds a slight inconvenience, such as more distance required between people.

Think about our current system for safe drinking water. As a thought experiment, a very small human population could achieve the same level of contagion-control with more space. But we would not think it wise to spread out so much that we each have our own personal aquifer and body of water. Compared to installing pipes for our water and sewage, spreading out seems absurd. But spreading out is exactly the way we deal with airborne contagion today, if we deal with it at all.

We can design our structures and the items inside our structures to reduce contagion from the outset. We can improve our methods over time. It will have helped that we designed from the start with an eye toward future improvements. But it will help even more that we can trace individual instances of disease transmission and learn from our results. With relatively few total infections, and most of those involving organisms that mutate quickly, we can make reasonable inferences about who infected whom by DNA-sequencing the infectious agents. We can build infrastructure with crypto that tracks the movements and touch of individual people in a way that doesn't violate anyone's privacy. Then, we can reconstruct the likely sequence of events that resulted in each case of human-to-human disease transmission. We can learn from each failure and improve our systems to prevent similar occurrences.

What about the health of nonhuman animals, such as domestic animals and pets? Animals are likely to receive many health and longevity benefits before humans. Why? Partially because animals, farm animals in particular, currently live under far worse conditions, and partially because, in the case of pets, it will be easier to test new interventions on animals. It is acceptable to take certain risks with the health and longevity of pets that we wouldn't take with people. Hypothetically, if we had a low-cost intervention that doubled the healthy lifespan of 99 percent of all dogs but killed the other 1 percent immediately, we would probably administer it to most pet dogs shortly after birth. We would accept the 1 percent dog fatality rate. We would have observable proof of effectiveness sooner with dogs, because dogs currently don't live as long as humans.

Farm animals are raised in conditions where health is not prioritized beyond a low level. Today, farm animals are often kept just healthy enough to reach the age of slaughter. Disease transmission in these unhealthy conditions is further increased because of crowding. We compensate for the high likelihood of disease transmission with antibiotics and growth hormone. Growth hormone speeds up the animals' development, allowing them to spend less time in situations where diseases are communicated. The shorter time allows for even more unhealthy conditions for the farm animals' short lives.

Animal disease, antibiotics, and growth hormone can all impact the health of the people who eat animal products. Human health can be bettered by improving the health of farm animals, for those who eat meat. The same methods of reducing physical vectors of disease transmission through air and surfaces that we use for humans can work for animals to a certain degree.

Another method of reducing disease involves animal-free meat, not simply vegetable-based meat substitutes. We are close to having practical methods of growing meat as cells in culture as opposed to meat grown as part of the body of an animal. With cells in culture, we can address health and taste with more flexibility than with animals. We can engineer meat that addresses infectious disease, improves the nutritional benefits, probably tastes more delicious, and is ultimately less costly. We can engineer our food supply with a simultaneous focus on healthy eating, animal welfare, and the natural world.

But food is only one aspect of health. For the foreseeable future, we will make discoveries about the mysteries of our physical bodies by the usual path of exploration. In other words, we will make increasing sense of our observations, especially regarding the workings of DNA. Simultaneously, we will refine ways to implement our increasing knowledge with useful interventions in the bodies we have. But later, we will unravel the workings of DNA by understanding the way DNA mimics computation at the molecular level.

Eventually, we will gain a mastery of life's DNA substrate that enables us to rewrite the DNA in our bodies using the full range of what DNA can do in any life form. At that point, we will be limited by the rules of chemistry and physics, but not so limited by the existing rules of biology. In addition to living as long as we desire, we will be able to incorporate features and characteristics from other species, plus new features we dream up. For example, eagles see in five colors compared to our three, octopuses and salamanders can regrow severed limbs, elephants can fight off cancer better than humans, bees can see the polarization of light and well into the ultraviolet spectrum. We could someday add those features to our bodies. But probably not soon.

I discussed outbound bandwidth in connection with brain machines in Chapter 6. As an example of something not inspired by other species, except maybe whales, we could genetically grow faculties for outbound bandwidth, for communicating our inner experiences to each other with the richness we experience inside— no brain surgery required. Machines would still be required, but nothing would be implanted inside our bodies.

I mention understanding DNA at the level of computation not because it is imminent. I'm pretty sure it is not. But the choices we make now can smooth the path to having this research (which will happen anyway) lead to better futures for all human beings.

I mention better lives for animals not only because the methods apply to human health but also because animal suffering is undesirable in its own right. I mention life extension for pets not because it is fundamental to our future, but because the discussion about life extension changes when the implications are curled up at our feet.

The prospect of immortality has immediate implications for our ongoing health. On one hand, the picture is more complicated because emerging health challenges that don't affect us in our first hundred years have not been a concern until now. In the future, they will be, especially the accumulation of environmental toxins in our bodies. On the other hand, it begins to make sense to calculate a health future for ourselves over the next several centuries. This justifies measures that would seem extreme by today's standards. But there's more of a risk, and more downside, in not cleaning up our food, air, and water. There's more of a risk in not constructing buildings with airflow that protects us from respiratory disease transmission. There's more downside if we don't improve living conditions for animals.

While good health makes living better, true well-being also requires fixing the world, and fixing the world requires lots of money. Building a new version of almost everything requires even more money.

CHAPTER 9

MONEY

REPLACING ALMOST EVERYTHING HUMANITY HAS ever built and curing death will be expensive, prohibitively expensive, with our current money system. I've been describing what is physically possible if humanity works together, not necessarily what we can currently afford. Without improvements to our money system, this better world is simply not going to happen. Today, money directs what most people do with their time and labor. We need a better way to organize our collective efforts.

Fortunately, improving the money system is unlike other big projects. With the money system, big changes can happen quickly. Of all the topics in this book, the money system is probably the easiest to fix. Why is this so? The money system has tremendous inertia. That inertia includes habits, institutions, knowledge,

familiarity, laws, regulation, and policy. Yet despite all this inertia, the money system can and does change rapidly. Because of
the ability to divide money into portions and the easy transfer of
money from one owner to another, new systems spread quickly
when they work. Sometimes new systems spread quickly even
when they don't work.

Money has not always been synonymous with wealth. At various times throughout our history, land or gold or cattle was considered real and money was more ephemeral. Even the definition
of money has changed. Cash, bank balance, checks, certificates
of deposit, near-term receivables—all these count as money by
some definitions. The proverbial Western cowboy would have
been a poor credit card customer. But eventually, his ability to
ride off into the sunset disappeared, replaced by Social Security
numbers and credit reports. The point is that our definition of
money morphs with the circumstances. What hasn't changed is
the money system's central role in organizing the behavior of billions of people. The money system adapts with whatever level of
detail it takes to organize this collective action. What I'm about to
describe will one day seem as normal as a debit card.

What is money? For our purposes, money can be considered
three things:

- A means of exchange
- A store of value for later
- An entry into the price system (because money is based
  on numbers)

More fundamentally, though, money functions as the means to an end. For the most part, money doesn't function as the end in itself. Having food to eat is an end; money is the means. Elevating your status is an end; money is the means.

Money is an effective means to get food but not as effective a means to elevate status. Unfortunately, many people treat money as if money is an end in itself. People acquire money in lieu of things that money cannot buy. The power of money is limited because it cannot buy many of the things that others would eagerly provide. I'm referring to personal interactions that would be satisfying for all involved, both buyers and sellers. I'm referring to personal interactions geared toward the four nonphysical levels of Maslow's hierarchy of needs: safety, belonging, esteem, and self-actualization. I will address the deeper question of how we align our actions with the essence of our deepest human desires in the next chapter. In this chapter, I will address the money system's more obvious flaws and how we can fix them. I'm going to propose ways we can use information technology, including well-being bots and crypto, in lieu of some of our existing institutions, especially those institutions that rely on centralized authority.

What are the flaws in our money system? Before I discuss what's wrong with our money system, let's review what our money system gets right. Our money system underpins the market-based capitalist economy that has lifted billions out of poverty. Adam Smith describes this in his book, *Wealth of Nations*.[13] Smith describes an invisible hand based on price signals that coordinate people to fulfill the needs and desires of others while in pursuit of their own interests.

Our money system is brilliant at efficiently allocating scarce resources. That efficient allocation of scarce resources underpins division of labor and specialization. The price system helps us prioritize between competing interests. Money measures success in a way that promotes what works and eliminates what doesn't. Our money system operates like Darwin's natural selection based on survival of the fittest, except it is the fittest businesses that survive.

Most of our ancestors perished from conditions we no longer face, things such as starvation, predation, exposure, easily treatable diseases, and injuries. The cooperation fostered by our money system has very successfully helped us address these conditions. Our money system helped people self-organize into an increasingly efficient system for supplying ample food to billions. Our money system helped us incorporate science into our understanding of how the world works. It helped people develop mechanization and build industry. Science and industry brought us technological capabilities that changed our lives for the better. We owe our money system a tremendous debt of gratitude. But there are some problems.

Partly because of its success, our money system has been given too central a place in our culture. Money guides both personal and public choices in areas where a different lens would lead to better outcomes. The finance industry, developed to operate the machinery of the money system, has become too large and powerful. Now the finance industry directs actions for the benefit of the finance industry itself instead of simply facilitating the smooth operation of signals to coordinate people's actions. Adam Smith's invisible hand has developed a mind of its own, a mind with its own rules, some of which don't operate in our best interests.

For example, some businesses are focused on moving money from one owner to another while producing nothing that fulfills real human needs or desires. And money tends to concentrate, leading to gross and unfair wealth inequity because, beyond a certain level, wealth itself earns more than a person's labor. Whole categories of valuable things are not measured by the money system. Because things not measured by the money system (externalities) don't count, we have organizations designed to fulfill the needs and desires of a few people, while causing a greater loss to everyone else and to nature. Our money system fails to measure this greater loss. Meanwhile, surveillance capitalism invades our privacy. And when surveillance capitalism is successful, it undermines personal agency.

But the biggest problem with our money system is that it prioritizes acquiring and consuming over creating. Consuming is key if you lack the basic necessities of life, but people whose physical needs are securely met want to be creators of value. Wanting to create and contribute is a natural human desire.

Can we improve our money system to fix these problems? Definitely! Adam Smith and his contemporaries didn't have information technology, ubiquitous connectivity, or crypto. We now deal in financial details that are spelled out and well defined. Today's public has an expectation of progress and a willingness to accept innovation. People today have experienced the effects of disruptive technology and inherently understand that successful innovation works alongside existing norms and institutions. We have working examples of distributed systems not subject to single-point failure or coercion. These things provide a platform for our new money system.

The amount of detail in this next section is a compromise designed to make the mechanics of this proposed new money system comprehensible. I expect some readers will find these details woefully vague, while others will find this section too dry and technical. But think about describing today's money system to someone unfamiliar with it. How would you teach an intelligent human visitor from prehistoric times about prices, interest rates, taxes, checking accounts, and choosing a retirement plan?

The new money system I am about to describe substitutes information for institutions, especially institutions of centralized authority. Currently, we rely on centralized authority with the means and mandate to discourage bad behavior, such as crime and fraud. But if we have reliable information alerting us to crime and fraud before we fall victim to it, we will have a better system than the threat of punishment after the fact. I'm going to describe a distributed information system that provides information about each player in the marketplace. Players can be individuals, businesses, or any organizations that deal with money. But organizations are always tied to individual people in this system. The goal is to provide trustworthy information upon which we can safely make decisions without revealing more personal information than is necessary and without a centralized authority keeping track of individual behavior.

The legitimate purpose for getting personal information is to reduce risk, usually the risk of not getting paid. We have institutions to mitigate this risk, such as credit reporting and escrow services, yet there are costs associated with these services, and there continues to be a trade-off between trustworthiness and intrusiveness. Ideally, we would be able to accurately access the risk in any potential transaction without needing to calculate the risk from the details. Conversely, it would be advantageous to benefit from being honest without having to prove yourself over and over.

Suppose you are a plumber. You receive two requests for assistance at the same time. You can only take one. One is a sweet, easygoing customer with a history of generally being satisfied with satisfactory work. The other is angry, litigious, and never satisfied. It would be helpful to know which is which. We're beginning to see this sort of information in online platforms that match buyers with sellers, but they do not have much privacy and are limited to a specific type of transaction. We will expand this sort of transparency so we can enter into each transaction with visibility about how well the other party has behaved in the past. A money system with embedded crypto can help simultaneously deliver useful predictions and good privacy.

How can a money system do all that? Here's how. In this system, you mint your own money. You create your own currency backed by your full faith and trust. But others don't need to evaluate your trustworthiness. Your history determines the strength or exchange rate of your individual currency. Your currency is stronger if you have a history of trading with many people over time and exchanging lots of money. But more important to your exchange rate is whether the people you dealt with had positive experiences with you. Yet the only person who sees your individual exchange rate is you. You are also shown how your exchange rate compares with others in aggregate and how your exchange rate can be raised. Others see only the price that you charge, denoted in their own currency. As a buyer, you see only the price you pay for each item you might buy. Your well-being bot calculates exchange rates and handles the details.

Today, we have credit scores that set the rates people pay for borrowing money and for certain services. A credit score is like a report card for good behavior. A perfect credit score means you usually pay in full before your bills become overdue. That's a low bar. There are better ways to interact than simply not being a deadbeat. In this proposed system, you can earn a better-than-perfect credit score by consistently being a positive influence on those with whom you interact. If you offer unexpected positive value beyond good customer service, there is a market for that extra value. The best kind of gift is when you surprise the recipient with something delightful because they didn't realize that such a thing could exist. That sort of opportunity will exist whenever you buy or sell. There's a limit though. No one wants annoying and superfluous gifts. Whether physical items or wastes of time, unwanted gifts become clutter. Yet the market would be different if each participant was focused on how to better serve and delight each person with each exchange.

In our current system, discrimination is a bad thing. Credit is measured by institutions according to fair standards based on rules that are designed to be consistent from person to person. In this proposed system, individual experience becomes a valuable signal; others' discernment becomes valuable feedback. Knowing others' perception of you is valuable for what it teaches you and also valuable in a direct way. Others' perception of you adjusts the exchange rate of your individual currency and the prices you pay for everything.

The exchange rate between any two currencies is set by both parties' parameters. A buyer can set a curve to value others' exchange rates. Sellers can choose whether to offer people with histories of good behavior a discount and, if so, how much of a discount for the level of good behavior. Perhaps for certain transactions, you just want the goods. You don't care if the other party is annoying, so you offer no premium for good behavior. In this case, you set your price curve to be a flat line with no such premium. Or the opposite could be true. You simply don't want to deal with anyone who is likely to be an energy drain. As a buyer, you set your price curve so it offers to pay zero to anyone without a history of excellent behavior.

Each transaction is priced by the intersection of the buyer's and seller's price curves. But each transaction (and the other party's evaluation of satisfaction) subtly affects both parties' ongoing exchange rates. As a seller, consistent good behavior potentially increases the prices you receive. As a buyer, consistent good behavior can earn you a discount. You are shown how much your good behavior is worth. You can decide how much effort to put into serving others with good behavior (beyond the terms of your agreements). The idea is to create a marketplace for good behavior—a race to the top, not simply a minimum acceptable service level. You are shown your own exchange rate, how your exchange rate compares to others' exchange rates in aggregate, and why. But no one else can see that information. You are also shown any trend in others' perceptions of you soon enough to catch yourself if your exchange rate begins to fall.

Societal trust has real value, but only if that trust is well placed. How much is good behavior really worth? Our proposed money system has a mechanism for answering that question. Investors can buy and sell positions along the behavior curve, the general curve that applies to everyone. If you think that today's behavior curve overvalues good behavior by more than people are really willing to pay for good behavior, you can sell some (overvalued) currency that represents good behavior and buy some mediocre-behavior currency at a bargain. This market for investors keeps the price of good behavior honest.

I have described a money system that rewards people who interact in mutually beneficial ways above and beyond simply paying on time. But there's a catch. Personal discrimination based on perceived value opens up our system to bias based on limitations in our psychology. These psychological limitations include racism, sexism, ageism, and all the other isms, as well as cognitive biases that come into play whenever people interact. Examples of cognitive biases include confirmation bias, priming, anchoring, fundamental attribution error, and dozens of others. It is not crucial that you know the meaning of each of these biases. The point is that psychological biases can be detected and measured by your well-being bot, which also quantifies the effect of each bias on your exchange rate and the prices you pay.

Would there be less racism if the cost of racism was made visible with each transaction? A goal of this money system is to provide an invisible hand that signals the most honest and beneficial ways for us to interact with each other. With well-being bots, the hand can be made visible to those who choose to look under the hood. But even without that understanding, people are automatically guided to behave in mutually beneficial ways.

Bottom line: satisfaction varies greatly. People are willing to pay extra when it reliably leads to greater satisfaction. Satisfaction is largely predictable and measurable. We will use information to measure and promote behavior that delivers greater satisfaction.

Our money system is used by more than just individuals. We also have to consider how companies and organizations use the money system. Like individuals, businesses have the opportunity to profit from behavior that goes above and beyond what is expected. Businesses have the opportunity to buy from suppliers with low exchange rates for a discount and sell to customers at a higher exchange rate, earning an extra premium. This is not unlike what brands do today. Brands add value by attaching their reputations to the goods they select or have produced.

In business-to-business transactions, some companies do a better job than others. Today, the actual cost of doing business with different companies is hidden, to the detriment of all. Buying from a flaky company costs more than the amount on the invoice.

Maybe the flaky company delivers late, bills incorrectly, or just takes more effort to deal with. Businesses learn the true cost of dealing with other businesses through experience, but few businesses have information systems that accurately measure this. At best, this information is costly to gather, slow, and based on a partial picture. Our proposed money system provides businesses an accurate way to compare the real costs of dealing with each other. These real costs are reflected in each business's exchange rate.

Minting your own money in this money system is not that different from trade credit in today's economy. Most businesses today initiate transactions not with cash but with credit, credit that businesses issue to each other. Retailer A places a purchase order with Supplier B. Supplier B delivers the goods and trusts Retailer A to pay. Money (in the form of credit) is created by trust each time an order is placed. Usually that trust is warranted, but not always. Today's financial tools measure returns with great precision but measure risk poorly, mostly because risk is hard to calculate. Risk comes in large, uncertain chunks, and the nature of risk events is hard to predict. Even the definition of risk varies. Sometimes business failures cascade when one business fails and leaves suppliers unpaid.

Credit rating agencies exist to mitigate some risk, but credit reporting is imperfect and delayed. Part of the problem is that a company being shrewd and a company in trouble look almost identical from the outside. Both accelerate receivables and delay payables. Both demand discounts. People in positions to sound the alarm increase their own risk of not getting paid unless they remain silent until they do get paid. Further complicating things is the fact that there is no internal signal inside a business to indicate exactly when the business becomes nonviable. At first, all that's needed is a pretty good sales month, then a string of really, really good sales months. But that's not impossible. There is no warning alarm that sounds at the moment when it becomes too late.

Sometimes business failures cascade. Supplier B fails because Retailer A failed and didn't pay Supplier B's invoices. The system would be more robust and fairer if Retailer A could see the moment of failure coming in an objective and certain way. Once past a predictable point, Retailer A fails immediately, and failures don't cascade. The key is information—information that is hidden in today's world, although the facts were known by some people, just not communicated.

Today's investment capital prefers to invest in things already proven instead of more innovative and interesting things. Part of the reason for this investment conservatism is the uncertain nature of risk. If risk was measured better and failure was detected more quickly, overall risk would be reduced. With better information, investors stand to gain more from success and lose less in cases of failure.

In this proposed money system, each party's solvency is measured in a uniform way. That measure of solvency is visible internally but not to others. High risk of insolvency is reflected in a lowered exchange rate with an abrupt falloff curve. The point where your exchange rate plummets is likely a point of no return. Failure turns your business into a liquidation sale predictably and seamlessly, unless you can pull your business back from the brink. The brink is easier to avoid because you see it coming with certainty and precision. That certainty and precision are based on your account balances plus the totality of others' experiences interacting with you.

Today's dollar-based money system will continue to operate and underpin money minted by individuals. Each individually minted currency can be exchanged for currencies such as dollars or euros at the individual's personal exchange rate. But as a seller, you'd probably prefer dealing with someone who mints their own money, someone known to be a positive influence. There have been many alternative currencies, but these usually trade at a discount compared to the national currency. In this proposed money system, your personal currency, minted by you, trades at a premium compared to the national currency.

As a seller, you offer those with their own individual currencies discounts equal to what their positive influence is worth to you. As a buyer, you get a discount proportional to your positive influence. But dollar- and euro-based transactions without additional information will continue. Individual currencies add a layer of information on top of the underlying national currency. That layer of information is optional, not required. Accounts in new currencies can be settled in dollars or euros. At one time, dollars could be redeemed for gold although few people demanded gold for their dollars. Over time, society came to trust the value of dollars without the promise of gold. Similarly, we will come to trust the value of currency based on information and backed by individuals.

Democratizing currency creation based upon accurate information has the added advantage of reducing the risks related to national currencies. Your exchange rate can be denoted in a basket of national currencies or based on a formula such as purchasing-power parity. Multiple currencies backed by multiple originators are not subject to the weakness of a monetary monoculture or misbehavior by any one entity.

So far, what I've described is a view from the level of individuals and businesses. No government or central bank policy is required to make this money system work. But there is the opportunity for governments to enact policies that would make it work better. Conversely, individual currencies can make government policy work better. Mechanical things, such as tax collection and automated bookkeeping, can be built into the money system. Statistics based on the economy can be measured and reported in real time. In addition to GDP, we can calculate another measure, a measure of overall good behavior or the total benefit generated by well-earned trust.

Under our current money system, policy decisions lead to monetary actions to promote aims such as maintaining a desired rate of inflation. Or the goal could be to maximize employment, maintain wages, or regulate the balance of trade. Usually, the aim of monetary policy is some combination of these. Monetary policy acts by regulating the supply or cost of money, directly or indirectly. But monetary policy makes coarse adjustments after the fact and is based on human judgment. Human judgment can be unpredictable and subject to political pressure.

In this new money system, monetary policy is built into the algorithms ahead of time. Algorithms act predictably, transparently, immediately, and in a graduated manner. The policy objectives are programmed into the algorithms, and the algorithms are public for all to see. The value of today's cryptocurrency is not regulated by monetary policy or controlled to maintain a stable value over time. Earlier we discussed money as three things: a means of exchange, a store of value for later, and an entry into the price system. Current cryptocurrencies work well as a means of exchange but not so well as a store of value for later. You would regret having agreed to a ten-year lease, payable monthly for a fixed amount of Bitcoin.

Can a new money system fix inflation, deflation, fluctuating foreign exchange rates, bubbles, and gyrations of the business cycle? Can we reverse the tendency of money to intrude into areas where it doesn't truly serve human needs? Can we develop better behavior than what we currently think of as good customer service or paying on time? I think we can. Here's why: what gets measured gets emphasized; what gets emphasized gets maximized. Our money system operates on signals that only report some of what we care about. We need signals about each other's needs and desires that are personal and measure deeper human qualities than what we think of as successful transactions today.

Measuring success only in terms of money accumulation misses signals about personal desires—signals that don't exist yet anyway. After we create signals to measure well-being, we will have new ways to measure success. There's a market for well-being beyond the stuff of our physical needs. Ironically, addressing genuine well-being will also expand our conventional dollar-based economy. In Chapter 1, I showed a grid of self-interest and altruism. Our current money system values self-interest but not altruism. This new money system values both.

But there is a more glaring and immediate example of how our current money system is not up to the task at hand. I've mentioned how our current money system is great at allocating scarce resources. But much of today's economy involves neither scarcity nor resources. Technology has made formerly scarce things abundant and made new things that never previously existed. Many of our creations have zero or almost zero marginal cost. All the cost is up front. A movie can cost hundreds of millions of dollars to make and almost nothing to stream. The cost is the same whether the movie is watched by one person or viewed by billions.

Like movies, many technological products have most of their costs up front. Those up-front costs include scientific discovery, research, design, testing, building factories, educating people, and our industrial infrastructure. Making experiences for others will become a big part of our future economy. As we get good at making experiences for others (with brain machines) more of our economy will take on this zero-marginal-cost attribute.

One effect of zero marginal cost is that competition switches from a balance between supply and demand to winner-take-all. The dominant player (the winner) incurs no additional cost by supplying more customers. The winner can then underprice others who have not yet incurred expensive up-front costs.

The network effect is the tendency for some products to become more valuable the more people use the products. If you have the only telephone in the world, it is not valuable because there is no one you can call. The more people with telephones, the more valuable each telephone becomes. Combine network effects with winner-take-all and competition suffers. Competition suffers further if there are effective ways that the winner can erect barriers to competition. One way to outcompete others is by offering good service or low prices. But there are other, more detrimental ways to erect barriers—barriers to competition that make it harder for those with competing products or services, even better ones, to succeed.

Today, even with zero marginal cost, the winner is motivated to price services not at the price where the most people benefit but at the price that generates the most income. There's a curve of what people will pay; some people are able or willing to pay more than others. As the winner, your income is higher if you limit how many people you serve to only those who will pay high prices, while excluding others. As the winner, you do even better when your product can be priced in tiers so that those willing to pay more can be charged more.

Think about software, electronics, online services, lifesaving drugs, and medical devices. The price system is poor at maximizing the overall societal benefit from this type of product and poor at directing investment in a way that does the most good. The money system emphasizes concentrating more wealth with the current holders of wealth. We would be better served by a system that rewarded investment based on doing the maximum societal good.

Today's measurement of some values to the exclusion of everything else is especially detrimental to the poor but also detrimental to the wealthy. There are significant benefits not available to the wealthy, either as consumers or as investors. This is good news. Improvements to the money system have a better chance of success when today's wealthy are incentivized.

Unrestrained, the tendency for wealth to concentrate makes the rich get richer and the poor poorer, until the poor are mostly left out of the economy. Eventually, society splits into haves and have-nots. Programs exist to mitigate this split and promote a middle class. Some of those programs are very effective, but the tendency of our money system is to concentrate wealth among those who are already wealthy. Investments are made to maximize return on shareholder value, not to serve humanity at large. But the wealthy are not served by great wealth that cannot buy what they really want. In the following chapter, I will describe a whole new economy for things that money cannot buy today.

The rest of this chapter addresses the need to eliminate poverty, which denies some people the physical goods they need to thrive. By today's logic, eliminating poverty requires sacrifice from the non-poor. All of this makes perfect sense if wealth is about accumulating scarce resources. The poor are poor because they lack resources. Each of us has a need for resources, such as food, clothing, and shelter, that have real marginal costs. No amount of safety, belonging, esteem, or self-actualization can feed the hungry. But there are both psychological and practical costs to maintaining an economic system that inherently concentrates wealth. We are affected by the unfairness and suffering of others at an emotional level, while money is spent erecting barriers to prevent the redistribution of wealth.

We need a system that shifts eliminating poverty from sacrifice to the investment opportunity it could be. People are creators of value when given the opportunity. Wanting to create and contribute is a natural human desire. It helps to have a stable, healthy environment, education, healthcare, and a marketplace for the fruits of your labor. Another factor that helps is a solid foundation of ownership. Having an ownership stake in the future helps each of us contribute to making the future better. Homeowners often add value to their homes while renters, at best, do no harm. Buying a fixer house and fixing it up can be a good deal if you know to find and fix homes, including the removal of hidden rot.

Similarly, there may be psychological rot that needs to be removed from society. Like the deferred maintenance in our hypothetical fixer house, there is a backlog of needed health, education, and recovery from stress or trauma. Some people may need a period of rest before shifting from survival mode to creative-industrious mode. Many people who are not poor but are stressed from years of unrewarding work may drift through a period of restful laziness before becoming inspired creators.

How do we measure the opportunity lost to poverty? How do we benefit from investing in people? Can we afford to pay people to not be poor? Or would we run out of steam before seeing any return? I don't know the answer with certainty, but I have reasons to be hopeful. In Chapter 11, I will describe a series of multipliers that can quickly multiply the size of the world's economy.

Our money system has helped us deal with scarcity in amazing ways. Can it do as well with the fruits of abundance? Many people are still poor, and even more people work in ways where they don't benefit from their imaginations or creativity. The key to fixing this is a better money system. But a better money system is only half of the solution. Money can't buy love! Or can it?

CHAPTER 10

INNER PEACE
FOR SALE

I N THE TWENTIETH CENTURY, THE WORLD'S POPU-
lation quadrupled while the world's economy increased by
more than thirty times. Economics is a perfect lens to view
this past success in conjunction with science and the industrial
revolution. But economics may seem overly dry when describing
a similarly significant leap in our psychological well-being, which
includes what it's like on the inside to be alive as a human being.

Think of economics not only in reference to markets and prices
but as the study of what people do in the real world, or the not-so-
real world. Prestigious economics journals have published papers
from Princeton and Harvard professors on why people brush their
teeth and why Cinderella wasn't invited to the ball.[14] This is economics too. I'm using the lens of economics to stand back and

take a detached look at what people choose to do, even the very personal and mostly private ways we each experience reality inside ourselves. Businesses, prices, credit, division of labor, currency: these are all familiar concepts. I will use them in ways they don't exactly fit, but by using these familiar concepts, we can understand an economy for healthy interpersonal relations and improved individual psychology.

I am going to describe a system to measure and emphasize emotional well-being that has as much nuance and specificity as today's financial system. Like Adam Smith's invisible hand, we will be guided to develop ways to cooperatively improve our own and each other's emotional well-being.

What does emotional well-being have to do with the hard-and-fast world of economic reality? By emotional well-being, I mean more than ways to feel good. I'm oversimplifying a bit by using Maslow's hierarchy of needs, but Maslow's four terms for well-being beyond the physical will suffice for now. Collaboration at a high degree and across millions of individuals sets humanity apart from other species. It is that same wide-scale collaboration that allowed us to build most of what underpins our technological civilization from spoken and written words to space travel, artificial intelligence, and our increasing understanding of the foundations of life.

Except for a few enlightened individuals, most of us contain internalized limitations based on fear, compromised autonomy, and other psychological limitations. We have these limitations for a reason. This psychology predates language and helped us survive under much different conditions. Today, almost no one perishes from the conditions this psychology developed to protect us against. We would be better off if we could truly see ourselves as others—guided by their kindness, wisdom, and courage—see us.

Today, even our best relationships seldom lead us to be our best selves, and those who might help us be our best selves have limitations of their own. Why do I think we will become the better people needed to operate effectively in a society of emotional well-being? My answer is a bit of an over-simplification: it's because it will pay you to do so. You will not be paid in any kind of cash you are familiar with. Instead, you will be paid in something better, a whole new type of currency unlike anything I have described so far. People will find ways to do well in this new economy because it pays in ways that are valuable, real, and measurable.

Previously, I discussed simulations and the way influence can flow asymmetrically. I also talked about brain machines that allow us to experience another person's reality almost firsthand. Now I will describe an economy that provides signals to harness the forces of collaboration and competition to promote emotional well-being. Like our existing economy, this economy filters results to promote success and eliminate failure. Except this economy's products are not resources for survival but experiences that promote internal well-being.

In addition to increasing personal satisfaction, emotional well-being promotes better collaboration in the ways that we traditionally collaborate. Our traditional collaboration helps us build things and furthers our understanding. In other words, emotional well-being helps us make wealth of the traditional kind—the kind we are familiar with, only better.

In the next chapter, I will describe how we multiply the world's output of goods and services in order to replace poverty with abundance and simultaneously repair the natural world. In this chapter, I want to focus on benefits to our inner selves and our interpersonal relations. What will we do with additional clarity, better interpersonal alignment, increased creativity, and all the other good things that come with emotional well-being? The long-term answer to that question is we become better people and form a more advanced society. Shorter term, we fix the natural world and improve the ways we treat each other.

Even though today's money is poorly suited to the purpose, people attempt to use it to seek emotional well-being. Discretionary spending is largely spent in pursuit of emotional well-being. Or discretionary funds are spent in pursuit of plain old fun. Fun is emotional well-being too. Yet there are many possible win-win deals that never materialize.

What if you could reliably receive genuine safety in proportion to the degree you help others, in terms of both safety from harm and safety on a personal level? What if esteem flowed in an honest and measurable way from the good you do in the world? That's different from esteem that flows (or not) from today's purchase and display of status items.

Today's currency is designed for those whose goal is to acquire or receive money. Money is received by offering things that others are willing to pay for. The focus is on receiving and maximizing income. Much creativity has flowed from this. Generations of people have developed valuable goods and services based on the desire to receive money for their efforts.

But our exclusive emphasis on receiving leaves out half of what we can do with our creativity. People are also good at giving. Part of the emphasis of well-being currency is to tap the potential we have for improving the lives of others by our own initiative. There are many ways we can improve the lives of others in terms of supporting their safety, belonging, esteem, and self-actualization. In addition to the ways obvious to all, we can use our creativity to improve others' lives in ways they might not anticipate. How do we make a system that harnesses and maximizes our best creative juices to find ways to make each other's lives better? We make it pay! We make it pay to maximize other's well-being as much as it pays to maximize our own. The payment comes not in dollars or the mint-your-own money of Chapter 9 but in currency that best supports our own desire for emotional well-being.

Today's currency and those I have described previously emphasize receiving from a limited supply of resources using orders and transactions. In the future, multiple emotional well-being currencies will be designed for giving others the fruits of our creativity and acknowledging gratitude. Today's currency works equally well whether the item you sell is valuable or not, so long as the buyer pays you. Today's currency is equally valuable if you earn it by providing genuine value or if you acquire it in a way that simply shifts money from its previous owner to you. Emotional well-being currencies help measure what is truly valuable and help us better understand our own healthy desires. Knowing ourselves better, with help from information technology, will predict what we are likely to value (or not) before we enter into an exchange. Much of the value in emotional well-being comes not from increased output but from increased alignment between our desires and what is created.

How does this relate to the economy we know, the economy of today? Remember economist Angus Deaton and Nobel prize–winning psychologist Daniel Kahneman, both from Princeton University? They analyzed 450,000 surveys from 2008 to 2009 and determined that after some threshold, additional income doesn't make much (or any) difference in satisfaction. The measured threshold was about $75,000 a year.

According to the World Bank, in 2019 (the latest year for which they have figures), the world's economic output was about $133 trillion a year in current US dollars based on purchasing power parity around the world. With today's world population, that works out to about $17,000 each. To make enough stuff so that each person gets $75,000 worth each year (assuming equal distribution) we would need about five times today's total world economic output. At current annual growth rates of 3.5 percent to 4 percent a year, and with expected increases in population, fivefold economic growth will take approximately another fifty years.[15]

Fifty years from now is a good vantage point to imagine looking back from. If we continue economic growth with business as usual, looking back to now, about 22 percent of all our stuff would date from before the time this book was published. The remaining 78 percent would have been made in the intervening fifty years. I'm suggesting that we largely replace the 22 percent we already have and do it quickly. I'm suggesting we start over and build almost 100 percent new. By starting over, we can build a much better version of our physical stuff.

Under business as usual, fifty years of economic growth would likely trigger effects that threaten our survival. Under business as usual, nothing leads to a more equitable pattern of distribution. What will it take to get fifty years' worth of economic growth quickly? What will it take to distribute the world's economic output in fairer and more equal ways? In the next chapter, I will describe a series of multipliers that can multiply economic output quickly; then, I introduce an alternative to redistribution that is inherently fairer and more fun. But first, let's look at our current economic system versus a system that maximizes alignment.

It doesn't require an understanding of new currencies to understand a fundamental problem with today's money-based economy. Economists talk about capacity utilization in terms of idle factories, unused agricultural output, and unemployed workers. According to economic theory, when there is a mismatch between what people want and what is available, enterprising entrepreneurs find a way to fill the gap. Where there is inefficiency, there is opportunity. Or so the theory goes.

But even at the most basic level, our current economic system fails this test. Think about what actually happens every day in the economy of products, jobs, investments, and services. Then think about what people (including you) most deeply want. There's a gap. The alignment between what people most deeply want and what the economy emphasizes is poor. Much of what happens is simply what has been happening previously, whether it serves anyone or not. In other words, most of the economy is built upon inertia, not personal fulfillment. Some businesses simply shift wealth from one party to another, creating no new societal value. Only a portion of economic activity genuinely makes human lives better. In reality, all the rest is waste. Any business or investment focused on something other than making lives better is generating waste. By this measure, many products and services in today's marketplace are 100 percent waste.

Where are the entrepreneurs to turn the inefficiency of this waste into opportunity? How can we make an economy that uses the majority of human talent to serve healthy human desires? With better alignment, we'd spend our days at meaningful jobs and come home to an environment of increasingly thoughtful and surprising delights. We will address how to fix this shortly. For now, let's examine how today's economy distorts the relationship between what we each want and what we collectively do. Making stuff no one really wants can be profitable if people buy it.

Marketing furthers the goal of concentrating wealth by creating desire and demand for products that people can be influenced to buy. People can be influenced to buy things that are not ultimately in the interest of their well-being, especially since there is no way to reliably buy emotional well-being. Consumerism's cultural dominance has become a mindset that organizes society. Why? Because we don't have a more compelling narrative than consumerism. Even if we did, we don't have a mechanism in place to organize that more compelling narrative into an effective market structure. Meanwhile, marketers' influence only increases as personal data is used to effectively predict and shape the behavior of consumers on an individual basis.

Marketing and consumerism sell the dynamics of poverty to people with higher and higher incomes. The dynamics of poverty displace freedom and flexibility with the need for regular paychecks. The dynamics of poverty leave little or no cushion for unexpected events or to make far-reaching life changes. Another dynamic of poverty means accepting things that are not exactly what you want while lusting after things that seem just out of reach. Making consumer items of dubious value contributes to traffic, noise, and pollution, while careers are spent pursuing the meaningless goals of others.

But the biggest dynamic of poverty that has been successfully sold is the elevation of consuming over creating. Consuming is important if you don't have enough sustenance, but additional consumption becomes less satisfying than creating. Especially if what you create is significant and others recognize that significance. There's a reason many prominent people continue to do challenging work long after they could have chosen a life of leisure.

In a life not mired in the dynamics of poverty, once you reach a suitable income, it makes sense to switch your focus from consuming to creating. The satisfaction of creating should be available to all of us. According to economic theory, spending time creatively after your material needs are met is maximizing utility. If you have existing wealth beyond a certain plateau, it makes sense to find ways to efficiently convert some of your wealth into currencies that enhance emotional well-being. What would give you the most satisfaction: increased safety, more belonging, greater esteem, or achieving self-actualization? Why not choose the whole set? Or create your own categories!

In the spirit of Adam Smith and his "invisible hand," I'm going to describe the underlying pattern of signals that coordinate actions for the betterment of all as each person pursues self-interest. I will not be describing the specific products and services that individuals and businesses will deliver in the well-being economy. I'm leaving that up to the same kind of invisible hand that Adam Smith described. Except I'll predict that brain machines and simulations will be involved. Many of the products will be in the form of realistic experiences communicated between people for the benefit of the recipient.

With people focused on maximizing their own and others' well-being, we will collaborate and use structures not unlike the things we are familiar with: competition, prices, currency, and multi-person organizations. Except, instead of producing traditional goods and services to sell each other, the aim will be to enhance each other's emotional well-being. Making this system work requires an accurate way to measure results. Those results are measured in multiple currencies that each behave differently. And each currency behaves differently than dollars or euros, or the mint-your-own currency from Chapter 9.

An organized way of improving each other's well-being is key, but a large part of emotional well-being is the inner work of personal development. New currencies can help, but they won't substitute for the hard work of making inner shifts. People will find innovative ways to earn what's valuable. New currencies will help by delivering feedback showing each of us how we're doing. New currencies measure success while maintaining individual privacy. Individual privacy means that it will not be possible to compare one person's wealth to that of another. This reduces competition based on who is wealthier. The way to be wealthy is to be aligned with your inner desires. Wealth is measured by your level of deep satisfaction. One way to gain satisfaction is through the esteem that comes from delivering genuine well-being to others and being rightfully acknowledged. Besides, who's to say who is wealthier in satisfaction when we each find satisfaction from different things?

Inner development is key to satisfaction and success. Successful inner development requires both motivation and means, in addition to help from other people and technology. Motivation comes from inside, but this is equally true in the current world of work. People adapt to the current world of work by fitting themselves into jobs that only poorly fulfill their inner needs. As in getting a job today, preparation may include education, help from others, trial and error, plus years of experience.

Specialization allows the well-being economy to develop into multiple niches for different people with different needs. Competition fosters innovation and hard work. Accurate measurement of the results allows for pricing that values more effective means more highly. Effectiveness is measured in the successful well-being of those we touch or influence (customers). I'm using concepts such as prices and customers from today's economics, even though the fit is imperfect. The key economic principle that does fit is the role of accurate measurement. What is measured can be emphasized, optimized, and maximized.

How will a well-being economy affect employment? Labor and jobs were once mostly focused on agriculture, or manufacturing, or depending on the historical period, information and services. As we become more efficient at transforming thoughts into things and things into experiences, the experiences sector of the economy will grow, and with it, employment in the experiences sector.

Brain machines will help us bypass the intermediate step of making physical things and go more directly from our imaginations to experiences for others. Jobs will be about creating experiences that others can receive in an almost first-person way. Sometimes simulations will have multiple people focusing simultaneously on the experience of a single recipient. In other cases, experiences will be conveyed one-to-one or one-to-many, as in a classroom. In some cases, the relationship will be zero-to-many with stored experiences from a library.

Some jobs will entail going into unusual human realms and bringing experiences back for the rest of humanity. Do you go to places internally that would be of value to others? Some jobs will be about creating experiences simply for entertainment. Experiences communicate both the intentions and the inner states of others in ways that words alone cannot. Full-bodied experiences become the medium for new products. These new products support the recipient's persistent experience of some combination of safety, belonging, esteem, and self-actualization. Or products get created to deliver whatever form of well-being sells best in the marketplace.

What will sell in the experiences market? Any experience that has ever been experienced by a human being is fair game. Love? Connection? Discovery? Accomplishment? Enlightenment? These are just words, but today, if you experience these things, you alone are the beneficiary of your experience. That will change in a well-being economy empowered by brain machines and mediated through currencies that measure what you and others most value.

Brain machines won't deliver an exact replica of accomplishment, for example. For that, you need to actually accomplish something. But communicating a realistic representation of your experience of accomplishment will grease the skids for others to follow in your footsteps—potentially many others. Conversely, each time someone exceeds the current outer bound of a certain type of human experience, you can go there too, after a fashion.

Plus, there will be many opportunities for those good at translating peak human experiences into forms more accessible to those of us on the journey but not so close to the peak.

Jobs of the future will be different, but so will the nature of work. Employment was once a lifelong relationship between employer and employee, including retirement. Then employment became more of a step along a career path. Responsibility for the career path switched to the individual employee. Jobs in the future can be thought of in a way that more corresponds to ownership: you own your job. You continue to own your job independently of any specific employer. Even the notion of ownership is probably not strong enough. Think super-ownership.

How does ownership work? Today, people only partially own many of their possessions. There's planned obsolesce. Houses come with mortgages. Appliances come with warranties or service contracts. Electronic devices require firmware updates. License terms dictate what you can and cannot legally do with things you own. True ownership is stronger. True ownership has value. Most people are served by the things they own, yet for some people, the reverse is true. The person is owned by their stuff, even stuff without ongoing manufacturer relationships.

True ownership is where the relationship is completely one way. You own your stuff. Your stuff doesn't own you. With true ownership, there is an incentive to master your possessions. You maintain your possessions and possibly make improvements because they serve you in a satisfying way. If your job truly creates value for others, it makes sense to own your job this way, too. You own your job both in the sense of owning a possession and in the sense of owning your job as part of your identity.

The social trend has moved away from identifying with a job, even a good job. That trend reverses with portable job ownership. It is healthy and desirable to identify deeply with a job that is meaningful, creates genuine value, and engages more of your whole person, especially if you can take your job with you independent of any employer relationship. Eventually your job will be a valuable possession: valuable in currencies of emotional well-being and valuable to your sense of self. That's what happens to jobs in the future.

Meanwhile, there will be many good jobs of the more conventional type while we build a better world. Building a better world is a good job by any measure, and there's much work to be done in building everything a better world requires. A better world requires a new city for 11 billion people and almost everything in that city. A better world requires brain machines that are today only partially developed. A better world requires the development of well-being bots to leverage crypto for societal good.

Plus, there's the job of restoring nature in the 99 percent of the world not occupied by our city. We can't just leave our destruction behind and expect natural forces to repair our damage. We will not be able to recreate the natural world that existed before us, and there will not be universal agreement on what is worth doing. There will even be disagreement about what is ideal. But many potential disagreements have an easily reached consensus. The level of atmospheric carbon dioxide is too high. Forests are good; toxic waste is bad. We can agree to prioritize wild elephants over additional mosquitoes. I oversimplify here, but the point is that it is good to have a discussion now about what nature is to become when we restore nature as best we can.

These tasks of building almost everything new and restoring nature will require lots of money. Mostly, that's money of the conventional kind and the mint-your-own money of Chapter 9. These tasks will support many good jobs. The amount of work needed fits well with the decade or more it may take to shift internally and recalibrate our inner expectations.

A plan that is robust enough to inspire people also calls forth an expanded capacity in our thinking and commitment. One boost will come from the realization that many of us will be here to experience the consequences of our actions or inactions centuries into the future. There's a different mindset when long-term problems fall to future generations and those future generations don't include us. When we didn't expect to be here in the future, it was easier to look the other way because no one would notice until after we're gone. Not anymore! Those of us who take long-term responsibility will gravitate toward the meaningful kind of work that will later become the kind of job that is a privilege to own, the kind of job you proudly identify with.

With empathy enhancement fostered by brain machines, we can collaborate in more powerful ways, especially if we share a sense of alignment as we work together toward a positive outcome. And meaningful collaboration toward a positive outcome is fun! That positive outcome can be further refined, both individually and collectively, by honest self-reflection. Self-reflection can be aided by feedback based on others' perceptions and made friendly through well-being bots.

Specifically, we will be guided by a system not unlike an improved version of today's individualized predictive evaluations, which anticipate what is likely to lead to satisfaction. We are familiar with individualized predictive evaluation systems based on one through five stars for choosing music and movies. We will develop an improved system of predictive evaluations to choose our human sources of influence. This system of predictive evaluations for influence will work the opposite way from today's world of marketing and advertising. Today, influence is pushed from the would-be influencer to the recipient of that influence. Our new system will allow each potential recipient to choose what to be influenced by and indirectly how to evolve. We will choose to be influenced by those we are most drawn to, those who have most earned our admiration and respect.

I'm using terms such as buyers, sellers, and one through five stars because those are familiar, but this system for trading emotional well-being is more than a system of transactions. Influence includes all the aspects that we have control over regarding who we are, what we do, with whom we do stuff, what for, and in a sense, our purpose in life. In today's marketplace, influence occurs first, then transactions happen, then the buyer becomes satisfied to a certain degree (or not). Maybe you evaluate a product or experience to help a recommendation engine predict your tastes next time. The future will look similar, except in the future what you will buy is well-being.

Now put yourself in the role of a future buyer. You, the buyer, will continuously and retroactively adjust your evaluations (the prices) of past experiences. How have past experiences affected your ongoing well-being? Each time you evaluate something you bought, the recommendation engine will change predictions for other possible transactions or experiences. Your well-being bot will show you predictions, and some of the predicted evaluations shown to you will be for things you already happen to be familiar with. Do you agree with your well-being bot's prediction? If not, you can inform your well-being bot. The result is that your well-being bot will move some sources of influence closer to you and others farther away.

But there's a further twist. There will not necessarily be a transaction corresponding to each evaluation. Where I've been describing things in terms of transactions, buyers, and sellers, you can substitute any relationship where any person, place, or thing influences you. You can evaluate experiences, people, places, and things with which you have only a passing association. Your evaluation will help your well-being bot decide what to expose you to, but your privacy is maintained. Others will not see your individual evaluations or that you are choosing their influence. Others will only see a total showing how many others have chosen their influence. Conversely, you will only see how your behavior and your choices affect others' perceptions of you in aggregate. You won't be shown who likes and who hates your influence, choices, or taste.

Compare that to today. From today's vantage point of limited emotional well-being, there's a temptation to select what we think fits us, what we deserve, and not what we most desire. This is especially true in terms of relationships (platonic, romantic, and professional). Today, individuals can only influence those whose influence is reflected in return. Today, it makes sense to aim only for the best we think we can realistically get. But if influence—especially brain machine almost-first-person experience—can be shared asymmetrically (one-to-many), there's no need to rein in our desires. If a person who is highly sought shares their first-person experience widely, that influence will be recognized for delivering value. The highly sought person's wide influence will increase the exchange rate of their well-being currency.

You may think to yourself, "I'm intrigued by something I heard this person say. I'll move closer and find out what else they are all about." Through your well-being bot, this can be as simple as moving closer to what you choose and away from what you don't choose. If you choose to move closer to another person, that person will not necessarily know you moved closer. That person will only later see that the value of their well-being currency has increased when multiple people move closer.

Moving toward what we choose is similar to the way we interact with people in our daily lives now. But with our well-being bots, we can choose sources of influence with more honesty because we are in a safer, more private, more trusting environment. We can choose what we really desire, not merely what we think we can get or what we deserve, because interactions are no longer limited by the formerly reciprocal nature of person-to-person influence.

The nonreciprocal nature of person-to-person influence becomes especially important when experiences become shareable, and the shareable experiences are created almost as a byproduct of having that experience. One of the most valuable things a person can do is have unique experiences that are shareable, and then make those experiences available to others. Like movies, experiences can be created once and shared an unlimited number of times at little or no additional cost.

In this chapter, I've tried to bridge the world of economics with what it will take for us to become better people living in a better society. To reach that better society, we need to collaborate better, compete better, and communicate better. I'm convinced we can do all three. It's hard to imagine looking back from this advanced society and thinking it wasn't worth the bother.

We have the technology, or we will soon. Do we have the imagination and the will to use this technology wisely? That's a trick question. The key to making wise choices is to accurately measure well-being. We will do just that by using currency that makes it pay to be a better person—currency that aligns our actions with our deepest desires. If you take away one thing from this chapter, take away the notion that we can create a functioning economy not built around more stuff but made to function on the inner planes where we actually live.

CHAPTER 11

AN ECONOMY FOR A WORLD THAT WORKS

I N THE FUTURE, MANY OF THE WORLD'S RICHES WILL be in the form of shareable experiences. It makes sense to share experiences, or any zero-marginal-cost items, as widely as possible. New currencies will help distribute the world's riches in ways that are much more equitable by measuring and emphasizing overall well-being.

But not everything is zero marginal cost. People still need food and many other things where resources are required. We need enough stuff for 11 billion people. In Chapter 9, I mentioned multipliers that can deliver prosperity rapidly to the world's population, sooner than the fifty years it would take at the current rate of economic growth.

I will now describe what those multipliers are. Each multiplier can work individually, or the multipliers can work in any combination to multiply each other's effects. I have mentioned these previously, but I have not described them as economic multipliers.

Multiplier #1: Redefine Value

First, we redefine what is valuable. If we redefine what is valuable to include only what truly makes lives better, we can free up a sizable portion of today's economy. We free up the economic capacity that today is producing waste. We need to produce enough physical goods for each person to reach the threshold where satisfaction plateaus sooner than the fifty years it would take at current growth rates. Through efficiency gains, we can probably reduce the threshold for satisfaction from $75,000 a year to a significantly lower dollar value. Eliminating waste gets us a higher growth rate immediately. Growth rate is a focus of today's policymakers, so policymakers won't need to embrace completely new thinking to support this multiplier.

Multiplier #2: Prioritize Creating Over Consuming

Some work will always be required to satisfy our ongoing physical needs. If the other portion of work, beyond what's required to support a comfortable lifestyle, is focused on creating instead of additional consumption, that work will create more interesting and more innovative products and services.

Multiplier #3: Longer Life Expectancy

Those who expect to live long enough to experience the consequences of their actions will take more consequential actions and produce more of what matters. Careers will span more decades. Most of us will find work we love and never want to retire because work gives us energy and satisfaction. Do you like academia? Teaching? What will we gain from those with one hundred years of higher education? We could know the answer several decades from now. Maybe this is you.

Multiplier #4: Support the Poor

Today, a significant portion of the world's population is functionally left out of the productive economy due to underinvestment in health, education, and the capital required to make each person maximally productive. We will eliminate poverty not only because it is the right thing to do, not only because we all bear the psychological costs of leaving some of our fellow humans behind, but because it makes urgent economic sense. We will benefit from the efforts and goodwill of formerly poor people to help us build our new city and repair our damage of the natural world.

Multiplier #5: Leverage Brain Machines

Communicating experiences more directly using brain machines increases the power of collaboration and education. Much work today consists of explicit collaboration. The purpose of meetings is to share what is going on in our minds and stimulate thought, which can then be expressed in communications to others or in products and services. Both thinking and expressing are improved if the other meeting participants can effectively be with you in your head in an empathetic, cooperative way. Collaboration can also be a lot more fun.

Multiplier #6: Shift to Virtual Goods

Much of what we produce can be made virtually when the product is an experience to be communicated to someone else. As often as practical, we will replace physical stuff with virtual stuff. The making of stuff is easier when so much of what is valuable can be made virtually.

Multiplier #7: Reduce Friction

Life in one big city will create a new level of convenience and logistical ease. The friction of business and daily living will be reduced, including shipping, time zones, space utilization, and commute time.

Multiplier #8: Better Health

Healthy people don't only reduce healthcare costs and life interruptions that accompany illness—healthy people function better. Health, in this case, is not just physical, but also emotional and relational.

Multiplier #9: Reduced Destructive Behavior

Destructive behavior, such as crime, will be deterred by the almost certainty that bad actors will be identified and caught quickly. Honest people will interact more easily and need to worry less about security. Deterrence will be more certain, more immediate, and more proportional. As in more honest countries today, we will not need to devote the same level of resources to suspicion and protection from each other.

Multiplier #10: Reprioritize Investment

More than simply avoiding fraud and crime, we can make investment decisions based on better knowledge about who and what is trustworthy. This will reduce the losses from failed business attempts and the contagion of business failure. But more importantly, it will encourage healthier risk-taking, leading to more innovative inventions and businesses.

Those are ten multipliers that will help the world economy provide for our physical needs. But there is one more multiplier, which is in a different category. In this eleventh multiplier, we apply ourselves to the nonphysical aspects of well-being not only in personal ways but in a coordinated, societal way. What happens when we combine an emotional well-being economy with abundance of the conventional kind—abundance of the goods and services that can be made of materials, labor, and ideas?

Think of how we so successfully collaborated to satisfy our physical needs. We organized around a system of economics based on money and invented an industrial economy. As information technology emerged, we learned to use information to get more out of both labor and materials. We learned to listen to nature and advanced science in a way that is ongoing and builds on itself.

Now, we do the same for safety, belonging, esteem, and self-actualization, or for any definition of emotional well-being you choose. We organize around a system of economics based on new forms of currency and invent industries to generate a new form of measurable wealth for our inner landscapes. We use information to make an industry of mutual and reciprocal well-being increase. Through experience over time, we make that industry more efficient.

I'm going to stick with the language of economics and transactions, despite the limitations of that language. The words are familiar, and it helps make this understandable. But please hear this next part in a more general way that applies to lasting value as well as momentary transactions. Today, we use GDP as a measure of a nation's economy, and I previously mentioned a metric for overall good behavior. Now we will need another new measure and another new set of initials for the measure of total human well-being. The key concept here is that we measure emotional well-being with specificity and precision.

I've mentioned the notion of abundance. Abundance denotes having enough, as opposed to scarcity. Enough is not just a plateau where it makes sense to focus on something else, like Deaton and Kahneman's $75,000 a year. Enough is the situation where no additional amount makes life any better. Now let's look at what it means to have enough safety, belonging, esteem, and self-actualization.

Safety is avoiding harm. Safety also exists in more subtle and personal ways. Feeling personally safe inside allows you to act with more vulnerability externally. This leads to better ideas, more creativity, better collaboration, and more deeply being in touch with the essence of your authentic self. Being in touch with your authentic self helps you discern what you most care about, your unique values, and your purpose. Safety also allows you to be closer to others in ways both gentle and bold. How much safety is enough? Enough is where more safety no longer makes your life better. Can we make this level of inner and outer safety a normal part of living for most people?

Belonging is a reward in itself. What does it take to have an experience of enough belonging? Think of this as belonging, maxed-out. Belonging is an all-or-nothing proposition to a certain part of our brains: you either belong or you don't. So belonging maxed-out is really the only satisfactory level of belonging. Nothing less will do. Maxed-out belonging allows you to choose with whom to identify, not because you get increased status by association but because you use your sense of belonging (or not) to discern. You can afford to move freely toward those you are drawn to and away from those whose influence you are not drawn to. Belonging helps you to be your best self. You naturally align with those who can appreciate who you are. This is what it is to receive belonging. But belonging is a gift to be given as well as received. Through your kindness (and because it is rewarded in well-being currency), you also extend yourself to those who stand to gain belonging from their connection with you.

Esteem is trickier. There are two keys to having enough esteem. The first key is to recognize value in yourself and others. The second key to having esteem is to truly deserve it. This requires healthy ego alignment between your inner creative and your inner critic. Esteem is amplified and made more robust when you collaborate with others who have healthy egos. Truly collaborating with others who have healthy egos allows you to see yourself through different eyes. You gain, seeing yourself from the perspective of others with diverse points of view—from varied experiences compared to your own.

Self-actualization means acting in alignment with your unique or unusual personal gifts, then applying those gifts in a way that is meaningful and real. Enough self-actualization means living a life where no amount of better alignment or more meaning would make your life any better. Self-actualization includes balance, so in addition to living a life of meaning, self-actualized living is fun. Until self-actualization is the norm (and possibly then too), many of us will find meaning through service to others. This is the point of building an economy based on emotional well-being.

Does this sound unrealistic for all but the most enlightened among us? Can we each really get enough safety, belonging, esteem, and self-actualization, so no additional amount would improve our lives? Remember that, to our ancestors, reliable year-round food availability was only for a privileged few, and current news from across the sea was physically impossible. I think we will look back upon these times with a similar perspective.

Currently, we don't have an infrastructure for addressing our healthy human desires beyond the stuff of our physical needs. We don't even have a very good description of what our nonphysical desires and needs are, although Maslow gives us a clue. We certainly don't have a system to measure what we have versus what we are missing on all the planes of emotional well-being. When we try to use our current economy to satisfy emotional well-being needs, various distortions occur. Even calling them needs is a distortion, one that I'm using simply because I have no better words to describe this.

In the following section, I use the words "prices," "buyers," and the like to fill in for concepts that have to do with ways we influence each other. Here, we are measuring positive influence or satisfaction, not the value of goods or services. I could call what we are measuring love, and that would be just as accurate as calling it value. But the word "value" fits more with our understanding of measurement, and this is all about measurement.

Despite these limitations in our language, and despite the incomplete details in this description, now is the time to start building our well-being economy. We often develop technology first and over time come to understand exactly what it is for. Since the beginning of the industrial age, the world economy has increased by orders of magnitude even on a per-capita basis. We didn't start industrialization with the same level of understanding we have today. When we apply economic methods to emotional well-being, we can expect similarly significant results. This is especially true considering how impoverished many of our inner lives are in terms of safety, belonging, esteem, and self-actualization.

So far, I've described the implications of an economy that values, measures, and emphasizes emotional well-being, but I have not specified how it works. How exactly does this economy work? What are the technical underpinnings? The rest of this chapter describes that technology. The key takeaway is that we can measure, emphasize, and maximize emotional well-being on the inner planes where we actually live. We will use a form of collaboration to maximize total well-being, a form of collaboration not unlike what we think of as an economy. The hardware to run the needed well-being bots and leverage crypto requires nothing beyond today's computers, internet, and phones.

How does the emotional well-being economy work? As in the previous chapters, the level of detail here is a compromise designed to make the mechanics of a system based on well-being currencies comprehensible.

Chapter 9 discussed individual currencies minted by each person. I explained that each person's currency could be converted to anyone else's currency at some exchange rate. And each person's currency could be converted to conventional currency, such as dollars or euros. In this chapter, we will discuss new forms of currency for measuring emotional well-being. I use the term "currency" loosely because these currencies behave unlike currencies we are familiar with.

Emotional well-being currency attaches to people, locations, experiences, or anything else you choose in addition to transactions. Well-being currency also attaches to things you don't choose if you have an idea, prediction, or hunch about how satisfied or unsatisfied you would be with something or a place you don't choose or someone you wish to avoid. When currency is attached, it means that you've generated and communicated information to your well-being bot or received information from an exchange between your well-being bot and the well-being bots of others. Your well-being bot communicates with others' well-being bots using crypto to maintain privacy.

The choice to avoid certain people and things (but especially certain people) can be either a wise decision or indicative of an inner trait we avoid when we see that trait reflected by others. We stand to gain depth and maturity by observing our reactions and confronting the aspects of ourselves that we currently reject. Some call the embodiment of these traits our shadow selves. If we develop a negative sense of someone, how do we tell if this negative sense is a healthy preference versus an opportunity to expand self-acceptance by embracing our shadow self? Ultimately that call is up to each one of us to decide, but emotional well-being currency and your well-being bot can help. Well-being currency illuminates the considered perceptions of others as we consider making an internal shift. Then after we shift, accurate self-reporting reflects the satisfaction gained (or not) as we grow in self-acceptance. To benefit fully, we need awareness, introspection, honesty, imagination, and courage. Each of these traits occupies a different emotional plane.

Well-being currencies will similarly occupy multiple planes. There are multiple ways to get to self-acceptance in this example of embracing your shadow self. You can get there via various combinations of awareness, introspection, honesty, imagination, and courage. Strength in one trait can partially compensate for less strength in another. There will not be an exact correspondence between the planes of well-being currencies and emotional traits, but the comparison is apt. Both well-being currencies and emotional traits operate on multiple planes that interrelate, but not in parallel. Both emotional traits and well-being currencies can be used in various combinations to reach a desired destination: in this example, self-acceptance.

What does it mean, technically, that currencies operate on different dimensional planes? The conventional currencies we are familiar with, and those I discussed in previous chapters, have just one dimension, and all these currencies operate on the same dimensional plane. When I pay you in any of these currencies, I have less, and you have more in equal amounts. You can have more or less, but that is the only thing that these currencies measure. You can freely give or throw away any of these currencies, but receiving currency usually requires doing something in return. When you accumulate any of these currencies, you have the sum of all the separate amounts you have collected.

Compared to conventional currencies, interactions between the dimensional planes of well-being currencies consist of reinforcing relationships and counter-forcing relationships. For example, Currency A might add 50 percent to Currency B and subtract 30 percent from Currency C, but only up to a point. The relationships can be linear or based on any monotonic mathematical function.

Transactions don't have to be equally additive. On some planes, currency is generated whenever an exchange occurs. On some planes, if I give you currency, the amount you have goes up, but so does the amount I have. Or maybe mine goes down but only half as much as yours goes up. In these cases, multiple back-and-forth exchanges generate additional well-being currency with each round, mirroring the way that caring and affection operate between people. On some planes, recipients can freely receive currency, but giving currency away is impossible without earning the right to give it away. In another scenario, no exchange takes place unless both parties independently and anonymously choose each other, and even then, neither party necessarily knows with whom they are interacting.

Instead of adding separate amounts together, some currencies act as multipliers. These currencies accumulate super-linearly. Say you receive currency worth 10 percent. What does it mean if you receive a currency worth 10 percent? Ten percent means that whatever amount of currency you currently have on that plane gets increased 10 percent. Then, if you get another 10 percent, your original amount is increased 21 percent. (110 percent × 110 percent = 121 percent.) Super-linear (multiplying) currency favors and supports capital concentration. Other dimensions add sub-linearly, which favors spread-out (not concentrated) wealth.

Other currencies add super-linearly up to a certain amount, then linearly, then sub-linearly.

Many of the currencies for emotional well-being share common features, and all require well-being bots. These common features include privacy enabled by crypto and "price" that is established after the fact by the recipient, once the recipient has had time to reflect. As a recipient, you can change the price you paid repeatedly and forever to reflect your considered experience. Each time you change a price, the relative price of everything else changes for you according to the best information your well-being bot has for predicting how much you will likely value each other person, place, or thing.

Another common pattern is purchases that are initiated (or not) as an acknowledgment of gratitude after the fact instead of purchases that originate when a buyer initiates a transaction. Your choices and evaluations influence the predicted prices of people, places, and things, but your individual choices and evaluations remain private behind a wall of crypto. Even the fact that you made a purchase is kept private from everyone else, including the seller, for items of zero or very low marginal cost.

In addition to setting prices to indicate satisfaction or gratitude, information is fed forward by your well-being bot and becomes the basis for predicting what others of similar taste will find valuable. What I've been referring to as a "price" is actually a measure of how satisfied you are. Or price can be a prediction of how satisfied you are likely to be. You can attach prices to people, places, experiences, and transactions. You can attach prices to both transactions that occur and potential transactions, to indicate and keep track of your preferences. Your well-being bot will show you others' prices but not the details that form the basis for that price. Prices here are indicators of your satisfaction, either satisfaction that you indicate or your well-being bot's prediction of your satisfaction.

Predicted satisfaction will be based both on the character of the parties involved and the nature of the interaction. For example, if you are choosing a brain surgeon, your satisfaction will be more strongly predicted by surgery skill than the surgeon's poor golf game. If you are an excellent golfer seeking a golf buddy, the same surgeon will not be as strongly predicted to deliver satisfaction.

As a user of this prediction information, your well-being bot adjusts your parameters to tailor predictions for you by empha-sizing the aspects of well-being that you most value. You set your parameters by accurately evaluating the effects of people you encounter, places you go, and experiences you have. Each time you assign a price, it refines not only other predicted prices but also the dimensions of your personal currency. The dimensions of your personal currency predict the satisfaction you would receive from the influence of other specific people.

In addition to the quantity of currency you have, the dimen-sions of that currency also determine your "overall measured inter-nal satisfaction level". Your overall measured internal satisfaction level indicates how well you are doing at successfully navigating the landscape of your own and others' cooperative attempts to maximize your own and others' well-being.

Your overall measured internal satisfaction level is your metric of success. In today's economy, the analog for that would be your net worth. You get to see your overall measured internal satisfaction level, but others do not. You get to see how you compare to others in the aggregate and the ways that others have improved from circumstances similar to yours. Your measure of success depends on both your inner work and feedback from others. The global sum of overall measured internal satisfaction level indicates how well we as a society are helping each other to improve and maximize global well-being.

Your well-being bot gives you feedback on how positive a force you are in others' lives. The basis for this evaluation is not simply successful transactions but every type of influence that one person, product, service, or institution can have on another. The degree of personalization in the way this information is fed forward varies with the nature of what is being evaluated. The prediction for a satisfying book-reading experience is personalized to your reading preferences. The prediction for a replacement appliance part is less personalized. The appliance part has a prediction based on factors such as quality and reliability that don't vary much based on personal taste.

What I'm calling "prices" are predictions of satisfaction to a potential recipient. But to someone who is already a recipient, prices are measures of satisfaction or gratitude. Assigning a higher price indicates more satisfaction. Prices for the same thing can vary greatly between individuals. In the book-reading example, you would give your favorite book a high price reflecting its worth to you. This doesn't predict that everyone will like your favorite book. But it does help predict who will like your favorite book and what other books you might like. If you change your mind later, you can retroactively adjust the price to reflect your changed perspective.

The prices others set help predict what you are likely to value. The prices others set on you and your creations also set your level of influence. The more good you do, as measured by others' experience of your influence, the more "wealth" you earn. Except this wealth accumulates both additively and as a multiplier. Each person's definition of what matters and how much each thing matters can be different.

One requirement to make this work is a solid mechanism of identity authentication with privacy. One reason for that is because pools of sublinear currency won't accumulate sublinearly if you can keep them in multiple independent accounts. Each person can have only one identity in the system. Privacy protections in your well-being bot hide that identity unless you choose otherwise. And even then, your identity is revealed only incrementally and only under certain circumstances. Another key requirement to make this work is an accounting system to keep track of which unit of currency goes with which person and what dimension each unit of currency occupies. Well-being bots collaborate through a behind-the-scenes infrastructure (and use crypto) to make this happen.

Knowing yourself and what you desire helps you maximize your real well-being. This is true today, but without a good way to measure and compare results, the effect is weak. Today, people strive to get emotional well-being by accumulating more money.

This makes sense because we don't currently have a better way to prosper. In our future system, the accuracy of knowing yourself is based on the same information that sets prices throughout the system. Self-development leads to more accurate self-knowing which leads to more measured wealth. So, one benefit of this measure is to help focus self-knowing. Your overall measured internal satisfaction level reflects, among other things, how well you are doing at knowing yourself.

Your personal development also increases your influence. If people are drawn to you, that further increases your influence on others. The measure of your wealth in this system aims to reflect your genuine satisfaction as accurately as possible. Reporting your self-evaluation accurately is worthwhile because it leads to an increase in both measured wealth and real satisfaction.

This organizes society around a form of wealth that is based on doing good. The societal good you do is calculated as perceived by others. Instead of concentrating at the top, wealth will flow to the places where the smallest amount of wealth can do the most good. This includes conventional dollar-based wealth. Today's poor are the best investment opportunity for dollars because relatively few dollars can significantly increase the real well-being of a poor person. Wealth can be converted from one form to another through actions, but not in a direct exchange like between dollars and euros. It takes both ingenuity and work to convert conventional wealth to well-being wealth. It takes some work to go the other way, converting well-being wealth into conventional wealth, but probably not as much.

To get the most well-being currency in exchange for your conventional dollar-based wealth, you'll need to figure out an effective way to best put your dollars to work for the good of others. Conversely, you can convert the beneficial effects of your influence on others into conventional wealth at some exchange rate, at least up to a point. Your well-being bot helps figure out the most efficient way to convert between currencies and indicates your prices or income from various potential courses of action.

In terms of personal motivation, there is a race to deliver the most positive influence in the lives of others. Except unlike a conventional race where the goal is to beat others, the winners of this race will be those who help others as much as possible. The idea is to combine the most intense competition with the most thorough cooperation. We are all on one team: humanity versus meaninglessness. The way to win is to give away what you can afford to give, including your positive influence, as quickly and efficiently as you can.

Compare this to today's situation in terms of a business's intellectual property. Intellectual property includes patents and copyrights as well as useful knowledge or expertise in the minds of employees. In today's business world, the winning strategy is to keep secrets in order to confer an advantage to your organization.

The winning strategy in a well-being economy is to find where each piece of information or knowledge can do the most good. With a currency that measures overall societal benefit, it makes sense to collaborate at a more granular level. But it also makes sense to compete at a more granular level because your best ideas are applicable at every decision point, and so are everyone else's.

Is positive influence a resource with ongoing marginal cost (like agriculture) or only up-front cost (like a movie)? It can be either or both. You can serve others by offering to wash all your neighbors' dishes. This has marginal cost and becomes more costly to you the more dishes you wash, the more tired you get, and the farther you have to travel. But there are ways to serve others where you do the work once and everyone benefits. Your own inner work is one example. Creating valuable experiences for others with brain machines is another. Business competition is different when success is measured by how well you further the goals of team humanity, including people currently seen as competitors. The nature and flavor of businesses (and other multi-person organizations) will be different when the "customer" is the overall well-being of anyone and everyone, not just the people who have agreed to pay you.

In our current world, success in a zero marginal cost endeavor leads to a winner-take-all situation and hurts all the non-winners. That's everyone else. In a well-being economy, zero marginal cost endeavors serve everyone who can benefit. In our current world, you benefit by acquiring and holding. In a well-being economy, your incentive is to give what you can afford to give to everyone who can benefit. You receive currency from each recipient in proportion to the recipients' honest evaluation of the benefit received. The safest and most productive way to store your wealth is in the immediate service of others. Your well-being bot will predict what course of action is likely to benefit you the most and screen out much of the rest, so that the number of choices is not overwhelming.

The details of the last few pages may make an emotional well-being economy seem more complicated than it is. Optimizing your and others' well-being in this system will become as second nature as choosing groceries at the supermarket. The multiple dimensions of currency and the automated transactions will be visible if you choose to examine and understand the details. But just as you can eat well without reading every food label, you will be able to live well while ignoring most of the details.

As with many of today's technological products, you would only need to operate the user interface of your well-being bot. The user interface is as simple as moving toward what you like and away from what you don't. As a user, your role is to be honest with yourself and aware of what you like and want. Your role is also to decide how you prioritize your time. Your well-being bot helps you choose what to do with your time by indicating a price you'd pay or receive for different possible courses of action. Price, in this case, is a measure of your own and others' predicted satisfaction or gratitude for your choice of action. Your well-being bot will handle the details, maintain your privacy, establish dimensions for your currencies, and set how those dimensions interact with each other. Your well-being bot will interoperate with other well-being bots according to the settings you choose. Your well-being bot will be supported by an infrastructure that you will probably ignore, just as you don't think of towers, antennae, radios, cables, switches, servers, and software when you use your phone.

With use, your well-being bot will adjust your settings to reflect your values and desires. But before that optimization happens, your well-being bot will come preloaded with pretty good initial settings. As soon as you start working with your well-being bot, you can experience many of the benefits of a society where people are motivated to make their own and each other's inner lives better. Over time, you can tune your settings to better fit your unique flavor of emotional well-being. Accurate tuning improves your overall measured internal satisfaction level. Your overall measured internal satisfaction level is the emotional well-being equivalent of your net worth. Except this net worth is not directly comparable to another person's net worth because each person's definition of satisfaction is different. And whatever esteem or bragging rights might come from having a high net worth will pale in comparison to the real esteem that an emotional well-being economy will deliver.

I started this chapter describing economic multipliers that can work together to multiply our production of goods that have real marginal cost, such as food. I described ten such multipliers. Then I claimed that building an emotional well-being economy will work as an eleventh multiplier. Is this really true? When we become rich in emotional well-being, will we also become more productive at growing and building things? Or will we choose to meditate contemplatively, avoiding getting our hands dirty? If we find that emotional well-being makes us less concerned with conventional wealth, is this a bad thing?

To create safe and comfortable living standards for the world's population, we will need industry for several decades at a scale several times greater than what's in place today. In several decades, we may have robots doing most of the labor. Meanwhile, we have work to do.

Emotional well-being can work as a multiplier of labor through several mechanisms. One is simply helping to establish better priorities. Another is more efficient teamwork because our priorities are better aligned.

But the primary mechanism that leads to higher productivity is the power of expectations. Expectations help groups work together to quickly create the conditions we expect. For example, after a war or weather event, society sometimes comes together to rebuild after vast destruction. The rebuilding happens more rapidly than the original building or new building in undeveloped places. Why is it faster to rebuild than to build in the first place? One reason is expectations. People are already familiar with the rebuilt conditions and expect them to exist.

In a well-being economy, one type of product is new expectations—expectations powerful enough to help pull reality into their wake. Remember the author Yuval Noah Harari's intersubjective reality and his example of car companies (versus cars) from Chapter 3? Things that exist in intersubjective reality are especially powerful when many people simultaneously believe, expect, and are familiar with them. Until now, those expectations and the corresponding intersubjective reality only happen after the fact. In a well-being economy, new human institutions on the scale of nations and the rule of law can be prototyped, tested, refined, and experienced by millions before we start building anything. Then, only after a new institution gathers widespread acceptance do we make it real. But when we make it real, the work can proceed at the rapid pace we associate with successfully rebuilding after a disaster. It is this rapid leap from societal expectation to reality that makes emotional well-being the most powerful economic multiplier.

For more detail, Appendix 3 compares conventional and emotional well-being currencies.

CHAPTER 12

RIGHT NOW

W E KNOW AT SOME LEVEL THAT WE NEED TO take bold action to avoid continuing down the destructive path we are on—a path leading to our annihilation as a species and the end of the human experiment. Building a new version of almost everything humanity has ever built at first seems like an overwhelming task. In retrospect, it will seem like a good choice and an obviously wise step for us to have taken. This moment in history is probably the best chance for a restart that we will ever have. But from here, it looks hard. How do we gear up for such an undertaking?

The first step is to embrace the prospect of living forever. The direction of the world today and in our recent past is largely determined by the relationship between the haves and the have-nots. The rules are designed to favor the haves. Today, the haves own wealth, and the have-nots mostly don't. But the purpose of wealth is to live better, and the ability to live better is lost if you die. Wealth confers some advantage when it comes to living forever, but not nearly as much advantage as youth. A healthy child in dire poverty today has a better chance of living forever than a middle-aged billionaire. So, who is the have and who is the have-not?

Figure 19. Haves and have-nots.
Traditionally the "haves" were those with money and the "have-nots" were the poor. But with life extension technology advancing decade by decade, it is not clear who is more likely to experience the riches of the ongoing future and whose riches will be defined by having existed for only a moment in history.

Mostly due to year of birth, some people are probably destined to die while others have the chance to live forever. This realization is likely to create an unprecedented fissure in society. It remains to be seen how this fissure will play out. We may have a graceful but profound parting of the generations, or we may have something much darker. The realization of this fissure will likely lead to a push for life-extending technologies, but not right away. Today, the age threshold for immortality is vague. Today's children have different prospects than today's elderly. You are more likely to live forever if you are poor and young than if you are wealthy and old, but the transition point is unclear. In time, the cutoff date will become more specific. Is it better to be a wealthy forty-something versus a healthy-but-poor thirty-year-old? When the question gets this specific, expect to see a big, urgent push for life-extension technology. The timing of this big, urgent push will determine the fate of billions of us alive today.

Those who expect to live forever will find the resolve to take actions that are beyond what is politically feasible today. So, the first step toward making the world we want is to embrace living forever. This means you! Immortality is more realistic for you if you are below a certain age, but the age depends on how soon we take the necessary steps as a society. Results depend on how hard the problems turn out to be, the resources we devote to research, how quickly we mobilize, and luck. But luck favors the prepared. The best preparation is to push for and begin to expect life-extension technology now. If you are a biomedical researcher or intend to go into that field, your path is clear.

The psychological effect of embracing immortality cannot be overstated. Embracing immortality is like being released from death row. Formerly, you were sentenced to die after a possibly long, slow, torturous decline—an inevitable decline in your physical and cognitive abilities. Now, the future is open-ended. I've written about immortality as if ongoing life will always be similar to that of a healthy thirty-year-old adult. That's a useful image as far as it goes, which is perhaps a century or less. The longer-term future is equally interesting but beyond what I address in this book. Unless we annihilate ourselves, we will go on living for the foreseeable future. We will go on living in some recognizably human form, or maybe in a form not recognizably human. It is possible that, longer term, it makes sense to think about what we become post-human.

What is a post-human self? What will you become after your human phase? I think it makes sense to answer this in two ways. First is the simplistic answer that you will become whatever you choose to become. The second is the more detailed answer, and this has two parts.

Eventually we will probably master our biological substrate at the most basic level. We will master DNA at the level of molecules and computation. In other words, we will understand and be able to choose our biological characteristics at the level of molecules. We will learn to avail ourselves of the full library of living organisms. We will learn to incorporate features from any living thing into our bodies. We could choose to see like eagles, breathe underwater, receive our energy from sunlight, or have eight legs like an octopus. But it is not this sort of trait that will define us in our post-human phase.

A more substantial aspect of defining the post-human self may have to do with the question, "What is a self?" Today, it is clear what a self is. One human body with one brain contains one self. Later, this relationship may become more fluid. We could have more flexible associations between bodies and selves, or non-bodies and selves. In other words, we may have much more vivid connections between our bodies and the inner experiences of others through our technology.

Meanwhile, we will learn to modify our bodies enough to make us question whether we remain the same self after switching from, say, a land-mammal to an aquatic life form. If you can roam the thoughts, memories, feelings, and experiences of others with as much realism as your own life, who is to say where one self ends and another begins? Add in an archive of historical first-person experiences, and the relationship between selves becomes even more ambiguous.

These thoughts about humanity's long-term future are only wild speculation and certainly not my predictions. I bring this up only because immortality sounds like something that lasts a very long time. I think it is unrealistic to presume that we won't evolve into something quite different in the centuries to come, regardless of individual lifespans. I mention this long-term outlook only to set it apart from the more urgent matter at hand.

My discussion of immortality in this book is about the near-term future in the next few decades. In the near term, we are at risk of destroying or seriously damaging the natural world upon which we depend. The solution to that problem requires a deeper level of commitment. That level of commitment seems overwhelming to someone expecting to die. Don't be that person expecting to die! Find the courage to rise above the tunnel vision and inertia of death-row mentality. Excuses become harder to justify when you expect to live with the consequences of your actions.

One practical step is to make a plan for your next one hundred years (or more). How old will you be in the year 2100? In 2150? What do you see yourself doing? What steps will you have wished you had taken? Some trends are reliable enough to make plans around. Machines will get smarter. Jobs will be automated. Humans will continue to work together in powerful ways, usually, but not always, for positive results. Pick your place in the world at each age. Calculate backward to today and outline the steps you'll need to get there. Invest your wealth and your time in ways that position you for genuine well-being and reap the kind of rewards you will want in future centuries.

Some of the tasks at hand require major investments and significant changes in public policy. This book is light on the role of public institutions such as governments. What form of government works best for a highly interconnected city of 11 billion people in a single time zone? What are the roles of that government compared to today?

Embrace crypto! Given your sense about how seemingly logical contradictions can be accommodated with crypto, what public rules make sense? If you are involved with the formulation of public policy, make understanding crypto part of your agenda. As a citizen, support politicians and candidates who understand the opportunities that crypto offers.

Today, most countries treat death-from-aging differently from other things that kill people, such as identified diseases. Funding for research and regulatory approval is available for curing these diseases but not for addressing the more general and more deadly course of aging. This needs to be reversed. Dementia is a good example. Regardless of the likelihood of experiencing dementia in old age, you can likely avoid dementia by avoiding the deterioration of old age. Previously, your alternative to age-onset dementia was to be lucky or die young. We are on the cusp of a better alternative, an alternative that is probably less costly than dementia care and definitely leads to higher quality of life.

Don't be misled by others' fears—for example, fears of overpopulation, or a world of feeble old people, or the inability to dislodge entrenched ideas. Be suspicious of any would-be reasons that living forever is undesirable. Rationalizing that death is good is a symptom of death-row thinking. Recognize the symptoms of death-row thinking in others and offer them compassion. Having assumed and planned around the notion of inevitable death, possibly soon, the stress involved in releasing that burden of doom can be significant. One common reaction is an attempt to make the conflict go away by clinging to the idea that death is inevitable. Today, there are enough people in various stages of letting go of death psychology that you can possibly find others of like mind. Ally with your immortality-friendly peers.

When enough people release death-row psychology, bigger things become possible. As life-extension technologies become available, attitudes will change, although some of that change will at first be weak and begrudging. People will agree to just a minor lifespan increase but make no commitment for the long term. Eventually, these people will look silly or die out.

In addition to embracing immortality and policy changes, the world needs technology entrepreneurs and developers. If you develop software, there are opportunities that become much more valuable as the world takes on some of the shapes I've outlined. Specifically, products that leverage crypto to deliver services that counter surveillance capitalism. The precursor to a well-being bot is simply a layer on top of today's social media. Social media platforms have lots of personal information and may continue to store and deliver that data. But the platforms are not the best parties to make decisions about what influences to prioritize. That role is best performed by services with only the best interests of users in mind, not the financial interests of platform owners and their advertisers.

Other opportunities abound in the intersection between technology and the public sector. There are opportunities for technologies to counter common forms of crime and corruption. Opportunities abound to counter everyday nastiness that doesn't rise to the level of crime. Demonstration projects can be solicited with a straightforward request for proposals. This book has examples, but they're not completely thought out. For example, I discussed a camera that records what it sees in a way that can only be decrypted if almost everyone recorded in the video agrees. There are limitations to this approach. Horrific crimes are committed with only two witnesses: the victim and the perpetrator. How does the requirement for a supermajority work in that case? Others will invent things with the same general focus as my examples and come up with better ideas. Maybe it will be you.

Despite my focus on empathy and seeing the world from the perspective of others, I have not adequately addressed racial, economic, gender, and other specific forms of injustice. Those injustices have perpetrated specific damage in ways that call for specific solutions, such as antiracism to address the damage caused by racism, not just the discontinuation of ongoing racism. Remedies for specific past mistakes are also needed to get humanity from where we are to a future with enough safety, belonging, esteem, and self-actualization for everyone. What are the specific remedies and how do we implement those? Deeper solutions become possible in the context of making a world that works.

Our current economy has worked as well as it has in part by borrowing from the future for gains now. The gains we realize now help make that future possible. Examples include home mortgages, publicly traded company valuations, and burning fossil fuels. The wisdom of borrowing from the future can be questioned, but the effectiveness of this technique is proven. We can do the same on a limited scale as we build new technology to improve relationships. Organizations of mature and trusting individuals can create teams to alter members' expectations. Humans can do some of the roles that later will be assumed by virtual reality and well-being bots, with a reduction in anonymity, while people take on the roles of AI.

We will make products and services that cannot be effectively monetized today but provide real benefits that will become apparent and measurable under a system that values and rewards emotional well-being. Some of today's most successful companies started by offering clear benefits but without obvious ways to get paid. There are more options if the ways to get paid in the future include currencies that trade in the stuff of Maslow's higher levels. If you direct investment capital, consider how your potential investments will perform in an economy that values emotional well-being. Think of ways today's investors can reap earnings in monetized safety, belonging, esteem, and self-actualization.

The biggest challenge and opportunity of the coming decades will probably have to do with the burgeoning realization that some of us will die and some will not. Those at the ends of the age spectrum can predict their futures based on date of birth. Those in the middle have a more interesting challenge. The challenge is to hold those who will die with true compassion, dealing with the loss and grief while processing the unprecedented opportunity provided by this change in what it means to be a human being.

The unprecedented change in what it means to be human includes the ability of wealthy individuals to affect the cutoff age of who gets to escape death. There is probably no better example of a place where altruism and self-interest align. If your goal is to improve your own well-being, there can be no better philanthropy than to hasten the arrival of life-extending technology. Your early investment helps drive down the costs for others. Those others may be the ones who will solve problems such as repairing nature and reducing inequity. Sooner is better.

Continuing with business as usual likely leads to the end of the human experiment or at least a world that is worse than it otherwise could be. Immortals will replace business as usual with the creativity and commitment it takes to fix the world. Hastening the transition to the day when humanity escapes death psychology is a worthy and achievable goal. Empowering those who expect immortality by promoting their education, opportunity, and power will accelerate the pace.

The plan in this book is nowhere near complete, and no doubt contains errors. My personal pattern is that I ponder a problem for some time, not deliberately seeking a solution. Then, suddenly, a far-reaching vision pops into my mind. My vision often addresses both the problem I started with and the bigger problem that my original problem was hiding inside.

But my initial vision is riddled with flaws. I work as an engineer. This is how I design electronic devices. In the world of electronic devices, nature reveals hidden flaws. When my designs refuse to work, each flaw is a teacher showing me where my understanding is wrong and patiently allowing me infinite retries until I get it right. Writing a book has no such guardrails against error. Nature doesn't point out my mistakes—you do. This book illustrates my vision of a world that works based on what I think is possible. This book is limited because I am one individual with one perspective and one plan. That's where you, the reader, come in. Please take my plan as your starting point. Please let me know of any errors I have made and any places where my ideas can be improved.

As a child, I loved to take things apart. Later, I learned to put them back together, and sometimes they worked. Then, I learned to take apart things that didn't work, fix the internals, and put them back together working. Eventually, I started a business making electronic interface products so that otherwise incompatible devices could work together. Does this qualify me to fix the world? Can anything? I say yes, not because I have enough knowledge or wisdom, but simply because there's a need. If we endeavor to implement any part of my vision (or yours), the flaws will be revealed.

You too are qualified to fix the world, because...why not? Who better than you? Someone who cares, someone who has skin in the game. What is your plan? There's almost nothing I'd like more than a robust discussion around many people's ideas for a better world. Almost nothing. But one thing, better than any discussion, would be the reality of a future forged from the synergy of my plans and yours.

Compare that with today's inertia, inertia that is heading us toward annihilation. Is it hyperbolic to equate inertia with annihilation? I don't think so. Hopefully we will never know.

CONCLUSION

I started out by saying that the future can go one of three ways:

1. We annihilate ourselves and go extinct.
2. We continue to muddle along.
3. We learn to live forever and fix everything.

I lied. Number two is not an option. Number two is a perspective. Up close, everything looks like number two. We're always just muddling along.

Pocket-sized devices that connect us with the world's knowledge and each other? The latest smartphones are just a predictable improvement over last year's models. Worldwide pandemic kills millions? Stuff happens! Telepathy becomes real? That's predictable technological progress. Tipping point climate collapse kills us all? We saw this coming! No matter what happens, you can see it from the perspective of just muddling along.

So really, our choice is between extinction and fixing everything. We won't be choosing extinction in the normal sense of making choices but as a side effect of inertia that depends on ignorance and a defeatist mentality. For every problem with a good solution, there is a dystopian alternative.

Problem	Positive Solution	Dystopian Alternative
Damage to the natural world	The city	Earth becomes uninhabitable for humans. Humans go extinct.
Injustice, inequity	New measures of wealth that advantage all	Super-rich own everything and hire private armies to defend against everyone else.
Surveillance capitalism, loss of privacy, online trolls	Own and manage your own data	Omni-surveillance capitalism. Single market winner takes all.
Weak personal connections, loneliness	Satisfying relationships, empathy	Increasing pressure on mental health often leads to suicide.
Relations between humans and other species	We cooperate with nature according to our best ideas and wisdom	Mass extinctions; pathogens and pests multiply.
Death	Immortality	Those above a certain age embrace destructive envy and sabotage younger generations' escape from death.
Disease	Health	More illness and death with a deteriorating natural world. Multiple ongoing pandemics most of the time.
Limited outlook, despair, withdrawal	Immortality thinking	Death-row thinking intensifies as we witness impending doom from the likely oncoming death of all humanity.

Figure 20. Dystopian alternatives.
Positive outcomes are not guaranteed. For each problem with a positive solution, there is also a range of very real dystopian alternatives. This list shows one possible dystopian alternative for each of the problems discussed in this book.

We are used to the notion that global problems are interconnected. Poverty leads to political unrest and poor stewardship of the earth, which leads to crop failures and more poverty. Population growth is highest in the poorest countries. With too many people and not enough wealth, some people become refugees. The institutions that otherwise maintain peace and order are strained. I could go on, but you get the idea.

The good news is that the converse is also true. Wealth, security, and education work together to strengthen society. Educated people in a stable society produce more, leading to more wealth, health, education, and the like.

But it's different now. Where previously multiple cultures existed side-by-side, now the world is one culture, mostly a culture based on consumerism. Where previously we could only see a path leading into the future, we can now see a destination. A destination where we live safely in our relationship to nature while supplying all of humanity's basic needs and wants. Then what? Then the nature of living changes. Our cultural focus becomes not only the external world of material objects and interactions but our inner landscapes where we actually live. The challenge is to get to this destination before our unwise actions cause irreparable harm. Can we fix the world before we seal our doom? From the perspective of what's physically possible, the answer is yes.

But maybe not if our future is limited by old attitudes and expectations. For all of recorded history, some people have been impoverished and everyone was destined to die. We can be forgiven if we assume that this is an immutable reality. It is not. Now, the opposite is true. Everyone can have enough, and some need never die. For many of us, the threat that we perish together is greater than the individual threat of dying from old age. Consider that for a moment. Many of us, especially the young, are more likely to die from human extinction than from old age. Humanity has never been bound together like this before. What does it mean to have humanity bound together in a common fate like never before? It is up to us to determine the answer. This is new territory. We know of no other intelligent life in the universe. The human experiment is precious.

How precious? Let's explore by the numbers. Numbers may seem a cold and calculating way to ask ourselves how precious all of humanity is, but bear with me.

As far as we know, there are no other planets with intelligent life. Until recently, we could only speculate about life on other planets, but we are discovering planets at an increasing clip and the universe is a big place. But still surprisingly limited. There are 133 visible stars within fifty light-years of Earth and maybe 1,300 star systems, comprising about 2,000 stars in total. Most of those 2,000 stars are red dwarfs. I'm not going to say how many planets have been discovered, because by the time you read this, today's number will be out of date. NASA has a fascinating website that is continuously updated with the latest information at exoplanets.nasa.gov.

I mention fifty light-years because the speed of light seems to be a hard limit and anyone farther away than fifty light-years would take over one hundred years to exchange one message. If we continue to fund and develop space telescopes, we will soon know if there's anyone out there with whom we could exchange a message within a century. There is a very real possibility that for practical purposes, we are alone. Soon we will know.

But there are many humans already here on Earth and possibly other intelligent species such as whales. How many? As I write this, we're just a few short of 8 billion humans. It took 200,000 years to reach the first billion, and we can expect a billion more in the next thirty to thirty-five years. Running the progression backward, it looks like about 108 billion humans have lived so far on Earth, of which 93 percent have died and 7 percent are alive today. You are among that 7 percent. Most of the humans who have died lived relatively short lives, so the 7 percent alive today represent more than 7 percent of all the years of human living that have occurred. The effect of life extension will further increase the proportion of total human experience among the living. Meanwhile, we will learn more about those who came before us through archaeology, radiocarbon dating, and sequencing genomes from ancient bones.

By total mass, humans account for about 36 percent of all mammals. Domestic animals, mostly cows and pigs, account for another 60 percent. Wild mammals comprise the remaining 4 percent. That's by mass. By individuals, humans account for only about 6 percent of mammals, because we are relatively large compared to more populous mammals such as rats. But the large number of rats is due mostly to human activity, so by any account, Earth is the planet of the humans.

Speaking of Earth, we have a very special planet in what astronomers call the "Goldilocks Zone." That's the area around a star that is neither too hot nor too cold for water to exist in liquid form. But Mars and Venus are also in the Goldilocks Zone, yet only Earth has suitable conditions for life to flourish. Why is that? One reason is the greenhouse effect.

Venus is about 800 degrees hotter than Earth, of which about 90 degrees is because Venus is closer to the sun. The other 710 degrees is because the thick carbon dioxide atmosphere of Venus has a larger greenhouse effect. Mars is about 140 degrees colder than Earth, of which 90 degrees is because Mars is farther from the sun. The other 50 degrees is because the thin atmosphere of Mars has almost no greenhouse effect. To be habitable, in addition to being in the Goldilocks Zone, a planet needs to orbit a suitable star in a stable orbit, have enough mass to keep an atmosphere, and be composed of suitable chemical elements. Refer to Figure 21.

We first saw photographs of the whole Earth in 1972, after the astronauts on Apollo 17 took a picture on their return from the moon. For the first time, we could see our planet as a whole, a place teeming with life and vibrant in a way unlike other planets that we can see through telescopes. The iconic Blue Marble photo of Earth against the black background of space was taken on December 7, 1972, on the last human visit to Earth's moon. It was shot during a time when the sun was almost directly behind the spacecraft relative to Earth and from a distance of about 18,000 miles above Earth's surface. No human has been as far from Earth since then.

	Venus	Earth	Mars
Distance from Sun	0.7 AU	1 AU	1.5 AU
Diameter relative to Earth	0.95	1	0.54
Mass relative to Earth	0.815	1	0.107
Atmospheric composition	Carbon dioxide 96.5% Nitrogen 3.5%	Nitrogen 78% Oxygen 21% Argon 0.9%	Carbon Dioxide 95% Nitrogen 2.7% Argon 1.6%
Atmospheric pressure	1335 psi	14.5 psi	0.087 psi
Surface temperature	850°F	60°F	−80°F

Figure 21. Venus, Earth, and Mars.
Our sun has three planets in the Goldilocks Zone, but only one has vibrant life.

But to my mind, the Pale Blue Dot photo does a better job of showing just how precious we are. This was the last picture taken by the Voyager 1 space probe after it had traveled 3.7 billion miles over a thirteen-year period. As I write this, forty-three years after its launch, Voyager 1 is the most distant device ever launched from Earth and is still functioning, sending data from outside our solar system back to Earth. Just after the Pale Blue Dot photo was taken in 1990, the camera was turned off. Earth is shown as a single blue pixel.

The idea of turning the Voyager 1 spacecraft around just before shutting down the camera and taking a final picture of the earth was the idea of the late astronomer Carl Sagan. I think his intention was to highlight just how extraordinary it is that our universe contains intelligent life. That intelligent life is us. The human experiment is precious. Let's not blow it!

Both the Blue Marble and the Pale Blue Dot photos are available on NASA's website.

Sometimes, the easiest way to finish a complicated project is to start over. I propose building a new place to live and new...almost everything else. I think the city would be grand, and I'd love to live there. I hope you would too. What better than a new home to communicate to ourselves that things are different now? People innately understand that doing too little to repair nature is disempowering and sad.

New behaviors paired with technology can definitely improve human relationships, especially relationships that are already fairly good. The current economic model doesn't emphasize this, but I'm surprised a market for emotional well-being hasn't arisen already. There are enough good-hearted people with skill and means that we should at least have a layer on top of social media looking out for the interests of users over the interests of platform owners and their advertisers.

Likewise, in the civic sphere, why don't we have technological means to root out petty corruption and deter most violent crime? Why don't we have reliable systems to predict our satisfaction with each discretionary expenditure? There are genuine efforts to protect personal data underway in capitals around the world, but regulatory power is weak compared to the abuses of surveillance capitalism—surveillance capitalism (or just plain surveillance) that too often allies with the worst features of statecraft. Hopefully, as the understanding of crypto becomes more widespread, citizens will expect and demand more benign uses and fewer abuses of the public trust, including online services.

I described a budding technology that turns brain activity into actions. Then I extrapolated to machine-mediated telepathy. Maybe I'm over-optimistic, but I don't think so. There is a general principle that more outbound bandwidth leads to a simpler form of communication. Ironically, simplicity communicates more. This principle is robust and based on solid information theory. Information theory has been developed and refined over the last seventy-five to one hundred years.

Think it and make it so! That is the basis of all deliberate action. We will soon have the option to bypass many of the intermediate steps between thinking and creating experiences for other people. Can we learn to deliberately operate attachments to our brains that haven't previously existed? Time will tell. We may need to simulate early developmental stages like when we first learned to wiggle our fingers.

Sometimes, the truth is hiding in plain sight. This describes our current fixation on an economic system that addresses only a very limited understanding of our healthy human desires and who we are. There is an opportunity here proportionate to how poorly the current system serves the totality of our humanity. Can we make an economic system that promotes genuine well-being and deemphasizes our intermediate desires? Can we make a system that helps us see the essence of what we most deeply care about? Any cynical calculus that says no will simply fall away when this opportunity becomes real. Spend time with those who are rich in emotional well-being, and you will see how consumer lust loses its grip.

Today's money system is owned by everyone and no one simultaneously. That causes it to be deeply entrenched in our habits and sense of understanding; further so because it has worked so well for the limited purposes to which it is well suited. But the disequilibrium between the weight of current reality and what is possible cannot stand forever. When the disequilibrium can no longer hold, the shift will be abrupt. Now is the time to prepare. When the disequilibrium corrects, pent-up energy will release a burst of creativity—the creative energy of people who yearn to make a better world but currently need to earn an income.

I hope and believe that this burst of creativity will be sufficient to propel us to address inequity and build everything we need. We need enough industry to supply the world's people with enough stuff to meet everyone's physical needs. We need about five times the amount of worldwide material wealth we have now. If labor and investment are not focused on improving lives, then what are they for? Today, they are focused on making more money. When money as we know it operates alongside well-being currency, this will shift. Our unmet desire for emotional well-being will mostly be addressed through experiences created by others. Creating experiences for each other will be streamlined and expanded by technology created for that purpose.

We need to rapidly reach a suitable level of material wealth and simultaneously reduce our negative impacts on nature and each other. The needed ingredients are creativity and labor, neither of which is in short supply. And we also need money, today's money, the kind of money we are all familiar with: dollars, euros, rupees, yuan, and yen. We need paths for the wealthy and those in power to employ money advantageously so that the future can turn out well. But we also need better safeguards to minimize risk when things go wrong.

Probably the biggest opportunity hiding in plain sight is the way the money system doesn't address most of what we care about. I have only superficially explored organizations and products that we will create to foster emotional well-being at scale. It will take time to hone the mechanics of a currency for emotional well-being, and it will take time to develop the products and services that make up the well-being economy. Expect trial and error, with some notable errors along the way. But it is glaring how thoroughly we have remade our physical surroundings and how little we have done to address the inner landscapes where we actually live. This is the legacy of a money system so well adapted to scarcity and so ill suited to abundance.

Immortality changes everything. Progress is happening. Will it happen in time for you? I'm reluctant to put specific numbers here, but if you were born before 1950, your chances are slim, and if you were born in the twenty-first century, your chances are good. For those born during the fifty years between those dates, it depends. It depends on how fast the ongoing research bears fruit, and it depends on the pace of research. And it depends on luck. There is a big, unknown luck factor here.

The best thing we can do for the planet right now is accelerate the push for human life extension. Even more urgent is spreading the understanding that this is true. Some people hold the misconception that immortality is either bad for the planet or personally indulgent. Both beliefs disintegrate under scrutiny. Immortality is a state of mind as well as a set of conditions. Immortal does not mean death-proof. Death is optional for everyone every day. Hopefully, you will have many, many more days, but there is no point at which you or anyone else achieves immortality, just one day at a time. The difference is that those days hold a different view of the future. A view of the future that makes actions practical that are otherwise too difficult to undertake.

Immortality also releases us from a debilitating psychological burden. Without the specter of inevitable death, possibly after a long and torturous decline, people become more creative, ambitious, calm, energized, and thoughtful. These are exactly the traits we need. We also need compassion for those unable to escape death. When people die today, we feel sadness and loss. That won't change. What will change is that it will seem so much more unfair. Prepare yourself!

Humans have a finely tuned sense of fairness that is part of our evolutionary heritage. In the best-case scenario, this strong psychological motivation will propel us to focus on advances not only toward life extension but also toward the other actions we need for a world that works. In a worst-case scenario, this psychological trait will lead to conflict that prolongs the period before we escape the inevitability of human death and furthers the destruction of our niche in the natural world.

Currently, our bodies follow similar progressions as we age from fertilized egg to centenarian. A thirty-five-year-old looks like a thirty-five-year-old. Reverse-aging will not look like running the clock backward, especially when the reverse-aging technology is new. Our efforts to reverse aging will affect different body systems differently and may include some unusual intermediate states.

New versions of reverse-aging technology will be developed faster than the aging process unfolds. So someone who starts interventions to reverse aging at a later date may go through a different series of steps. There will be enough variation that it will not be easy to look at someone and guess their actual age, level of anti-aging (if any), or version of anti-aging technology.

I've spoken of life extension and immortality somewhat interchangeably. This makes sense in light of the never-ending and tentative nature of continued living. But also, I've purposely not delved into what happens longer term. What happens longer term is one of two things. One possibility is we annihilate ourselves, go extinct, and end the human experiment. The other option is, in the near term, we fix the world. Fixing the world has been the focus of this book. But if we survive, in the longer term, we evolve into something else. Both annihilation and evolving into something else have the similar feel of staring into an unimaginable void. Some liken this to the event horizon surrounding a black hole in space or a singularity.

Don't fall into the trap of believing that the future is an unimaginable void. The future is only unimaginable if you lack imagination! Lack of imagination is the greatest impediment to a positive future. To an unprecedented degree, the future is what we collectively imagine and choose. Individually, we know this, especially in terms of not destroying our place in the natural world, but as a society, we act like we don't have a clue.

Everything in this book is based on today's technology and predictable progress. But I would be remiss to assume that there are no wildcards in our future, especially unpredicted scientific breakthroughs. That doesn't mean that the longer-term future is unimaginable. Unpredicted scientific breakthroughs make the future more interesting.

Lack of imagination is mostly from simple psychological inertia. For millennia, psychological inertia was mostly a good thing; it kept us safe from taking unwise risks. Now the opposite is true, but psychological inertia lives on. So coordinated collective action takes time. Now, we are short on time. Fortunately, we now have the tools to act. We can make our situation glorious, both in terms of creature comforts and something deeper. What's the ultimate purpose of living forever in healthy bodies telepathically connected to each other and maxed out with enough safety, belonging, esteem, and self-actualization?

I don't know.

I purposely have not discussed the spiritual dimension to life. Immortality for some falls in the domain of spirituality or religion. Bringing immortality to Earth may seem like interfering with divine will. Having an inner landscape with enough safety, belonging, esteem and self-actualization may seem to be the exclusive role of heaven. Are these things out of place in earthly life?

Previously, it was believed that the earth was flat, the sun revolved around the earth, pi was three, and humans were not animals connected to other species by evolution. We didn't trigger divine wrath by understanding these things differently. Changing death from mandatory to optional neither invalidates nor confirms what may happen afterward. Death and afterward is always a possibility. Additional time can help us grow in kindness, caring, and understanding—all good things according to most belief systems.

The picture I've painted is one of a world that works for me. I would choose everything in this book if it was up to me. But I wrote this book, not you. You may have a different vision. Or something I propose may rub you the wrong way. You know that business as usual won't lead to a good outcome, but is it realistic to expect so much? Yes! It is if we make it so.

The future is what we choose or what we choose instead by failing to act. The goal is to shift humanity's internal conversation, our expectations, and the course of our collective actions. Looking back from the future, it will appear unrealistic (and suicidal) to have chosen a less optimistic path. Let's shift the conversation from "Can we muster the will to overcome inertia?" to "Which vision of a better future shall we create?"

I hope you'll join me in refining this vision, and I invite you to develop your own vision of a future that works. Then, let's build it!

Keep the conversation alive.
To contact the author, visit:
www.liveforeverfixeverything.com

ASSUMPTIONS FOR THE CITY OF CHAPTER 4

Part 1: Space Utilization

SPACE PER PERSON

The central core where people live, work, and play is a cylinder, sixty to sixty-two miles in diameter and 150 stories high.

The area of a circle is πr^2. For each floor, that works out to (30 miles)^2 × 3.14 = 2,827 square miles. I round that down to 2,800 square miles.

Floor area includes usable space, the structure itself, and mechanical items such as equipment, elevator shafts, and plumbing, but not squished rooms. Squished rooms are part of each resident's usable space. Each city resident gets about 2,000 square feet of usable space. I calculated the area for each floor starting with the bottom floor (floor 1). The bottom floor has only 25 percent usable space because the other 75 percent is the structure holding up all the higher floors. Then 20 percent (that's 80 percent of the remaining 25 percent) is dedicated to mechanical items, leaving only 5 percent for occupancy. Each higher floor has proportionally less area dedicated to the structure itself and mechanical equipment. This continues until the top floor is only 5 percent structure and 0.134 percent mechanical equipment. Refer to Figure 22.

So, of the total floor space, 76 percent is usable space.

- Floors 78–150 (those above the transportation floors) have 55.9 floors' worth of usable space.
- Floors 1–73 (those below ground and below the transportation floors) have 20.3 floors' worth of usable space.
- If we have 11 billion people living on the 55.9 floors' worth above ground, that's 42,200,000 people per floor's worth.
- Arranged in a square pattern, that's 6,500 × 6,500 people per floor.
- Each floor's worth is 2,800 square miles.
- In square feet, 2,800 square miles is 2,800 × 5,280 × 5,280 = 78,000,000,000 square feet (78 billion).
- That works out to 1,850 square feet per person (based on a central core that's sixty miles in diameter).

I rounded 1,850 up to 2,000 square feet per person in the text to use round numbers. To get a full 2,000 square feet per person, we could increase the diameter of the central core to sixty-two miles, or

Floor #	Usable % (not structure)	Portion usable	Usable space less the four transportation floors	Mechanical Equipment %	Usable % after mechanical
1	25.0	0.250	0.250	20.000	5.000
2	25.5	0.255	0.255	19.867	5.633
3	26.0	0.260	0.260	19.733	6.267
4	26.5	0.265	0.265	19.600	6.900

The four transportation floors in the middle (floors 74 to 77) have all their open space dedicated to transportation, so none of the space on these four floors is usable.

Floor #	Usable % (not structure)	Portion usable	Usable space less the four transportation floors	Mechanical Equipment %	Usable % after mechanical
72	60.5	0.605	0.605	10.354	49.966
73	61.0	0.610	0.610	10.400	50.600
74	61.5	0.615	0.000	0.000	0.000
75	62.0	0.620	0.000	0.000	0.000
76	62.5	0.625	0.000	0.000	0.000
77	63.0	0.630	0.000	0.000	0.000

...*from previous*

		Total % usable	% usable less the four transportation floors	Mechanical %	Usable % after mechanical
78	63.5	0.635	0.635	9.734	53.766
79	64.0	0.640	0.640	9.600	54.400

The top floors are mostly usable space.

		Total % usable	% usable less the four transportation floors	Mechanical %	Usable % after mechanical
147	98.0	0.980	0.980	0.534	94.466
148	98.5	0.985	0.985	0.400	98.100
149	99.0	0.990	0.990	0.267	98.733
150	99.5	0.995	0.995	0.134	99.370

The total space is shown in units of a "floor's worth." One floor's worth is the total space of a floor as if no area was needed for structure or mechanical items. One floor's worth is about 2,800 square miles.

	Total % usable	% usable less the four transportation floors	Mechanical %	Usable % after mechanical
This many floors' worth → 93.375	90.885	14.698	76.19

Figure 22. Chart showing floor-by-floor space utilization

assume the total peak world population is 10.18 billion people, or reduce the portion of floor space dedicated to the structure itself, or use some of the space below the transportation floors for living space.

The space below the transportation floors has 20.3 floors' worth of space that can be used for storage and industrial functions, which benefit from being close to where people live. The total belowground floor space works out to 670 square feet per person.

Part 2: Energy Requirements

How much energy will be required to give each person the experience of enough energy if we start over based on new technology? I'm using 2,000 watts per person as my benchmark. That means an average of 2,000 watts per person, 24/7, or 48 kilowatt hours per day. This includes direct energy use by each individual and each individual's portion of the energy used in industry, agriculture, transportation, temperature control, plumbing, and everything else that society uses energy for.

By comparison, a gallon of gasoline releases about 33 kilowatt hours of energy when burnt, so our 2,000-watt figure (48 kWh/day) is equivalent to about 1.5 gallons of gasoline per person per day. Today's average US citizen uses about 12,000 watts, an average European uses about 6,000 watts, and an average citizen of India uses about 1,000 watts. Is it realistic to assume we will get three to six times more efficient at using energy compared to Europe or the US today? My guess is that a three- to sixfold increase in efficiency is about right.

But the assumptions are not straightforward.

Take heating and cooling, for example. Compared to today's world, heating and cooling will have lower losses to the elements through surfaces because the city will have much less surface area per person than today's buildings. But the heat dissipated in the middle of the core area needs to be pumped somewhere, probably into the earth below. Pumping heat takes energy, and pumping heat over a distance of miles takes additional energy to move a heat-carrying medium such as water.

Or consider transportation. Because distances are shorter, the energy to transport people and things will be able to get each person in potential contact with more people using less energy per trip. But will this lead to more trips and more use of transportation when now it is more convenient to travel and you can order lunch from the other side of town?

The Jevons paradox is the explanation for increased use of a resource in response to increases in efficiency because people increase their use of things that are more efficient or economical. Eventually, people no longer use more of a thing, because they have enough, and more wouldn't make life better. I don't know at what level increased energy use no longer makes life better. So, I chose 2,000 watts per person.

In 1998, the Swiss Federal Institute of Technology proposed a plan to deliver first-world living conditions to Swiss citizens on 2,000 watts by the year 2050. For more information, read about the 2,000-watt society. But really, the 2,000-watt assumption is arbitrary. I had to pick a per-person energy level to take into account the effects of economic growth, poverty elimination, new technology, the effect of replacing almost everything with new versions, the benefits of pumping heat around from where the heat is excessive to where heat is needed (instead of dissipating excess heat mostly into air or water), and the effects of shorter distances.

I make the assumption that about 25 percent of total energy use will be for pumping heat. As a rough approximation, I'm assuming that heat pumps pump about three times as much heat as they dissipate, including the energy needed to move the heat a distance to its heat-sink destination. This means that only 1,500 of the 2,000 watts-per-person is available after accounting for heat pumping. I think this is a fair way to look at things. A sizable portion of today's energy use is for heating and cooling. I'm assuming we will use pumped (otherwise waste) heat for domestic hot water, drying clothes, and most processes that require heat but not especially high temperatures.

For higher temperature needs, we can focus the sun's energy with heliostats. Heliostats are arrays of mirrors that track the sun and concentrate solar radiation. High-temperature needs include the manufacture of steel, concrete, and glass. The manufacture of concrete today releases approximately the weight of the concrete in carbon dioxide, in addition to the carbon dioxide released by the source of heat used to make the concrete. Hopefully, we will develop a concrete substitute that releases little or no carbon dioxide, but concrete substitutes are still likely to require heat at high temperatures.

I'm assuming that the manufacture of steel, concrete, and glass will take place in the same outer-circle area that contains solar panels. The energy that is concentrated for high-temperature processes is included in the 2,000-watt per-person energy budget. But how the energy collection area is used will change over time. As construction progresses, we will need increasing quantities of steel, concrete, and glass to build the city itself until near completion, when we will no longer need as much. After construction is complete, most of our ongoing needs for steel, concrete, and glass can be met by recycling, which uses less energy and costs less. Then, we can convert some heliostats to recycling and some heliostats can be decommissioned to make room for more solar panels.

As we build the city, it makes sense to overbuild the energy infrastructure first and focus on efficiency later. That's a low-risk method to benefit from more efficient technology, if we invent more efficient technology. But if we don't become as efficient as I predict, we will later need to cover more area with solar panels.

I'm also assuming that the city will be built in a desert near the equator where the length of each day remains more or less constant all year, where the sun is almost directly overhead at noon, and where cloud cover is rare. If the city is built somewhere other than a desert near the equator, the size of the energy collection and storage area will need to be scaled to account for the different latitude and weather.

Here are the numbers and calculations I used for energy. I've rounded numbers, and I jump back and forth between American and metric units, depending on which units are most often used in the literature. For example, in measuring solar irradiance, watts per square meter is more common than watts per square foot.

The total energy needed is 2,000 watts × 11 billion people = 2.2 × 10^{13} watts continuously.

Over one year, that's 2.2 × 10^{13} watts × 365 days/year × 24 hours/day = 2 ×10^{17} watt-hours.

Sunlight delivers about 1,000 peak watts per square meter when shining directly overhead on a clear day. Assume that over the course of a day, we get the equivalent of six hours of peak sunlight. Assume that solar panels cover 75 percent of the area. That's more closely spaced than solar farms today, but I think not unrealistic. Assume the panels are 25 percent efficient. That assumes an increase in efficiency over today's most economical solar panels.

So, each square meter in the outer ring produces the equivalent of a continuous 1,000 watts × 0.25 (for 6 hours per 24-hour day) × 0.75 (for coverage area) × 0.25 (for panel efficiency) = 47 watts.

But we need to store some of that energy for nighttime use. Let's say the storage mechanism is 80 percent efficient, a reasonable assumption for pumped hydro. Batteries or fuel cells are probably more efficient, but batteries have to be replaced or recycled from time to time, which takes energy. So, I'll stick with 80 percent efficiency for nighttime storage.

Only half of our energy needs to be stored for nighttime use, so our 80 percent efficient system leads to another 10 percent loss (based on a 20 percent loss in half of our energy). Assume that the electrical energy conversion and distribution system is 75 percent efficient. That's more efficient than today's electrical grid, but I'm assuming we will make better electronics to convert DC to AC and to convert between voltages, and that we will build more efficient transmission lines than we have today.

I think it makes sense to be optimistic about electrical conversion and distribution efficiency because we will be replacing old technology with new at unprecedented scale, and the distances are relatively short. Also, these levels of efficiency are in keeping with current trends.

- So, 47 watts − 4.7 watts (for nighttime storage losses) = 42 watts.
- Taking into account the conversion and distribution losses: 42 watts × 0.75 = 31.5 watts.
- At 31.5 watts per square meter of land, we need this much land: $(2.2 \times 10^{13}) \div 31.5 = 6.98 \times 10^{11}$ square meters.

The square root of 6.98×10^{11} is 836,000, so we would need a square area 836 kilometers in each direction. That's approximately a 518-mile square. How large does that make the outer ring? The core area plus the farm area is a circle 120 miles or about 200 kilometers in diameter.

- The area of a circle is 0.25π of the square area.
- 200 km × 200 km × 0.25π = 31,500 km² or 3.15×10^{10} square meters.

Add that to the 6.98×10^{11} square meters we need for solar collectors for a total area of 7.3×10^{11} square meters for everything inside our outermost circle.

How big a circle is that?

- Area of a circle = πr^2
- $\pi r^2 = 7.3 \times 10^{11}$ m^2
- $r = 482{,}000$ m
- The radius is 482 kilometers.
- The diameter is twice the radius or 964 kilometers (about 600 miles).

That gives us a diameter of the outside of the energy collection area of about 600 miles. The square area equivalent is $0.25\pi \times 600$ miles square or a 470-mile square or 2.2×10^5 square miles.

How much of the earth's land is that?

- Earth has about 57 million square miles of land, of which about 33 percent is desert.
- 57 million $\times$ 0.33 = 19 million square miles of desert.
- If the city is built in a desert, our 2.2×10^5 square miles will take up about 1.2 percent of the world's desert area.

Earth also has about 25 million square miles of habitable land. If we built the city on habitable land, our 2.2×10^5 square miles would take up about 0.9 percent of the world's habitable land.

Or compared to the whole of Earth's land, the city will occupy about 0.4 percent.

Part 3: Travel Times

Travel will usually consist of your room moving in a vertical segment, like an elevator ride, followed by a horizontal segment like a train ride (on one of the middle four floors). Then your room will take a short vertical ride and move to a different floor of tracks oriented in a different direction. Then another horizontal segment followed by another vertical segment up to your destination.

Let's look at that in more detail. Say you're sitting in your living room or your Zone Pod on the 100th floor, near but not quite at the southernmost edge of the city. You decide to meet in person with a friend who is on the 125th floor and northeast of the city center, at the far edge of the city. This is almost a worst-case scenario in terms of travel time. Most people will be closer to you, but I want to show that even the farthest-away person is conveniently close.

You tell your well-being bot your intention. You and your well-being bot decide whether you will go to your friend's location, your friend will come to your location, or you will meet up somewhere in the middle. In this case, you and your friend decide to meet up somewhere in the middle. You're planning to simply hang out and chat, so you decide to take your comfortable living room to the central meeting location.

Here's the sequence of events. First your living room (with you inside) descends from floor 100 to floor 76. Floor 76 has rail lines that run north to south. Imperceptibly to the occupants, the rooms directly below your living room part, opening a vertical shaft, so that your living room can descend to floor 76. You may or may not notice your weight change slightly due to vertical acceleration and deceleration (as with a conventional elevator today). Your well-being bot knows your haste versus g-force preference and calculates acceleration for all your travels. In this example, you prioritize haste.

On floor 76, your living room is placed on and attached to powered rail carts that ride on tracks. The vertical shaft above you may close up or not, depending on the needs of others for space. Powered rail carts move your room north and simultaneously tip your room slightly to the north as the rail carts (and your room) accelerate. You might notice a slight heaviness (or not) as your weight increases due to acceleration. You and your room are heading north. When your room reaches full speed, acceleration stops and your room un-tips, returning to vertical. As you near the next stop, your room tips toward the south and decelerates to a stop on the north–south track. The tipping from vertical makes gravity always appear to pull straight down, as experienced by you and the stuff inside your room. No need to worry about objects sliding around or drinks spilling.

Next, the section of north–south track below you and a section of east–west tracks below that open up, and your room descends to floor 74. Floor 74 has tracks that face northeast–southwest. The rail carts move and rotate you and your living room onto floor 74's northeast–southwest tracks. You make another horizontal journey, this time to the northeast. The sequence of events mirrors the previous segment: acceleration with tipping, maximum-speed travel with no tipping, deceleration with reverse tipping, stopping, and un-tipping back to vertical.

Now you and your living room are directly below your meeting destination. As in your previous vertical journey, everything between you on floor 74 and your destination floor above opens up so your room can ascend into position at your meeting location. Your friend, who has simultaneously traveled to the meeting location, opens a door into your living room and enters.

How long did that take?

Assume you and your friend are at almost opposite edges of the sixty-two-mile-diameter central city. I say "almost opposite" because if you're exactly opposite and directly north–south, you could take a single set of tracks. But in most cases, you and your friend will each need to take two sets of tracks and transfer. Theoretically, you could each take a single set of tracks and meet at the point where the tracks cross, but I'm going to assume for this case that each of you transfers tracks.

Now, instead of describing track directions as north–south and east–west, I'll use headings in degrees. Tracks carry vehicles in both directions, so instead of calling north–south tracks "0°–180°", I'm just going to call it 0°. The four floors of tracks go 0°, 45°, 90°, and 135°. I'll explain below why I chose four floors for rail tracks and not some other number. If your destination is 22.5° from your starting point, you will need to go half the distance in the direction of 0°, then transfer to a track that goes 45° for the other half of your trip. This adds about 8.24 percent to the length of your trip, compared to traveling on a single set of tracks that head exactly in the 22.5° direction you are going.

I'll assume that your trip length will be no longer than 32 miles because you are going to meet up near the halfway point between your and your friend's locations, but not exactly at the halfway point. The exact halfway point would be a maximum of 31 miles from your starting locations if you both start at the outside perimeter of the 62-mile-wide area. You should be able to find a suitable space to position your two rooms within a mile of the mathematically optimal spot. So, I'm assuming 32 miles for the longer of both trips. Add 8.24 percent for the indirect route. So we will calculate a 34.64-mile trip.

For longer trips (including this one) maximum rail speed is 300 mph. That's below the top speed of the French TGV line, which goes up to 357 mph. I'll discuss air-friction losses (which are considerable) below. I'm going to limit g-forces from acceleration and deceleration to 0.2 Gs. This means you would weigh up to 20 percent more during parts of your trip. Typical elevators in the US are limited to about 1.15 Gs; passengers on commercial planes typically experience up to 1.3 Gs during flight and more as the plane decelerates on landing.

Acceleration from a stop to 300 mph at a constant 0.2 Gs takes one minute, eight seconds. The four acceleration-deceleration events cover 20.67 miles and take one minute, eight seconds each (four minutes, thirty-two seconds total). The remaining 13.97 miles at 300 mph takes two minutes, forty-eight seconds. Add in one minute for the vertical transfer between tracks and one minute each for two elevator rides. That's in keeping with today's elevators. Elevators in the world's tallest building (the Burj Khalifa in Dubai) take one minute to reach the observation deck on the

124th floor. Total trip time is 4:32 + 2:48 + 1:00 + 2:00 = 10:20 (ten minutes, twenty seconds).

Most trips would be much quicker, because most of the people you want to see and places you want to go are not at the opposite side of the city. But in this case, you will have scheduled ahead and remained in your living room while the room traveled to your destination. So, while your trip took just over ten minutes, your perceived travel time was zero.

I will now explain my choice of four floors for rail lines. It would be possible to get from any point to any other point with only two floors of rail lines, one going north–south and one going east–west. To go northeast, you'd first go north then east. Or first go east, then north. But the distance to go north and then east is 41 percent longer than going directly northeast. More floors of rail lines reduce travel times unless you're going directly north, south, east, or west.

How much are travel times reduced by having more floors? I've calculated the effects of having between two and eight rail floors versus a theoretical infinite number of floors with rails heading in every direction simultaneously. Refer to Figure 23.

I'm figuring that the additional distance for the average trip is only half the worst-case scenario. On average, the two additional floors save 16.6 percent of your travel time. An additional four floors would save only 3.1 percent more. Three rail floors are a possibility and would save 13 percent of travel time versus two floors, but for most of us, it is easier to visualize coordinates and directions with tracks oriented in four directions versus three. And there are two more reasons to choose four rail floors versus two.

Number of rail floors	% of additional travel time (worst case)	% of additional travel time (average)	% of travel time saved by one additional floor	% of travel time saved by two additional floors
2	41.4	20.7		
3	15.5	7.7	13	
4	8.2	4.1	3.6	16.6
5	5.2	2.6	1.5	5.2
6	3.5	1.8	0.8	2.4
7	2.6	1.3	0.5	1.3
8	1.9	1.0	0.3	0.8

Figure 23. Chart showing diminishing benefits of more than 4 rail floors.

One reason has to do with geometry, and one has to do with congestion, or the maximum number of people and things that can be in transit at any given time.

Regarding geometry, the whole of floors 74 through 77 are rail lines spaced apart every two feet. A single pair of rails accommodates a small vehicle for delivering packages. Wider vehicles can carry people, rooms, and whole buildings up to 120 feet wide. Two of the rail floors have high (120-foot ceilings) for carrying tall items. The occasional tall item will have to go up to 41 percent farther to get to its destination if it needs to go at an angle halfway between the directions of the two high-ceiling floors.

Some of the tracks extend beyond the perimeter of the sixty-mile-wide central core to serve the farms. Some tracks extend beyond the farms and serve the energy collection zone. Some can extend to other places such as Earth's existing cities and places of interest during the time when the city coexists with our present-day civilization. Parallel rails radiate out from the city's core like sixty-mile-wide spokes. The spokes are not solid sixty-mile-wide swaths of tracks but are a subset of the tracks. For example, every quarter mile might have a set of eleven tracks for carrying up to twenty-foot-wide loads. (Eleven tracks span ten two-foot spaces.)

Two sets of tracks (north–south and east–west) that radiate straight out from the full width of the sixty-mile core fully cover a sixty-mile square. The corners of a sixty-mile square are only twelve miles past the perimeter of the circular sixty-mile center. There are four triangular areas (triangular as seen from the central core) that parallel tracks don't serve, starting only twelve miles from the edge of the central core. That's with only two floors of tracks. Beyond twelve miles, the tracks would have to curve and diverge to cover parts of the farm area. Diverging tracks would be spaced more than one mile apart, significantly more at the outer perimeter of the farm zone and the energy collection zone. Refer to Figures 24 and 25.

With four floors of tracks, all the area out to the edge of the farms is served by parallel tracks. I'm not going to go into further detail about tracks and geometry because the concentric circle design I am using is unlikely to exactly fit with real-world geography. The actual shapes of the farm area and energy collection zones will be a compromise between theoretically ideal circles and whatever shape best fits the terrain.

In addition to geometry, there is another reason that four floors of rail lines make more sense than two. This reason has to do with capacity and congestion. Four floors can carry approximately twice

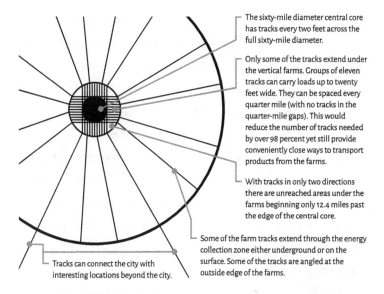

The sixty-mile diameter central core has tracks every two feet across the full sixty-mile diameter.

Only some of the tracks extend under the vertical farms. Groups of eleven tracks can carry loads up to twenty feet wide. They can be spaced every quarter mile (with no tracks in the quarter-mile gaps). This would reduce the number of tracks needed by over 98 percent yet still provide conveniently close ways to transport products from the farms.

With tracks in only two directions there are unreached areas under the farms beginning only 12.4 miles past the edge of the central core.

Some of the farm tracks extend through the energy collection zone either underground or on the surface. Some of the tracks are angled at the outside edge of the farms.

Tracks can connect the city with interesting locations beyond the city.

Figure 24. Two levels of tracks oriented north–south and east–west (density of tracks is not to scale)

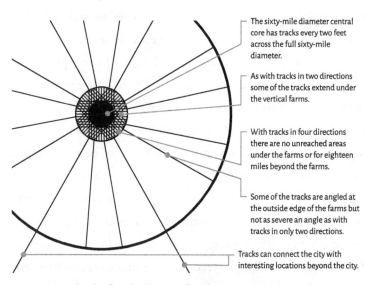

The sixty-mile diameter central core has tracks every two feet across the full sixty-mile diameter.

As with tracks in two directions some of the tracks extend under the vertical farms.

With tracks in four directions there are no unreached areas under the farms or for eighteen miles beyond the farms.

Some of the tracks are angled at the outside edge of the farms but not as severe an angle as with tracks in only two directions.

Tracks can connect the city with interesting locations beyond the city.

Figure 25. Four levels of tracks (density of tracks is not to scale)

as many people simultaneously as two floors. I say "approximately" because each floor needs to open up in spots to let cars travel vertically. This reduces capacity. But less distance needs to be traveled (because tracks are angled closer to your desired direction of travel), which increases capacity. I'm going to assume that, in terms of congestion, these two factors cancel each other out.

The big unknown is how many people and objects will be traveling simultaneously. Today's trends are not helpful because, today, people schedule their travel to avoid congestion and choose to not go to places inconveniently far away. Hopefully, in the city, there will be little or no perceived slowdown, even when many people want to be somewhere else at the same time.

Regarding friction losses, 300 mph trains (or anything moving through stationary air at 300 mph) have significant wind resistance regardless of aerodynamics, especially in an enclosed space. Two possible ways around this are to reduce the air density, or continuously pump the air through smooth tubes at 300 mph, propelling the vehicles, partially or fully, with moving air. Some subset of tracks in each direction can be flexibly partitioned off and turned into one-way corridors of moving air. The friction losses are still significant and will create heat, which needs to be pumped out. But much of the time during the day our solar panels will be collecting more energy than we can use, so it makes sense to build transportation systems to operate at high speed when energy is essentially free. When energy is free, it is okay to lose energy to friction in return for high speed. At other times, maximum speeds can be reduced to save energy.

Part 4: Costs

The numbers above for space utilization, energy, and travel times can be calculated based on assumptions with which you may agree or disagree. But if you want to try different assumptions, you can calculate the effects. Costs are different. Calculating the cost of the things I propose in this book is not straightforward, and I don't have numbers or calculations to price the pieces and make a shopping list. What will it really cost to rebuild almost everything we have ever made while restoring nature in the rest of the world? In many cases, restoring the world involves unbuilding what we previously built. Unbuilding and restoring nature have a cost which is hard to calculate too. By any metric, the plans in this book will be expensive.

How expensive? Part of the problem in understanding cost has to do with the limitations of economics. According to the website Visual Capitalist, the total wealth of the world in 2019 totaled about 360 trillion US dollars (not adjusted for purchasing power parity), while worldwide GDP totaled around 88 trillion dollars. This implies that all the world's wealth could be created from just over four years of total world GDP. Of course, people need to eat regularly, so not all the world's resources could be used to build new things, even if building new things became our total focus for four years. But economics fails us here because it fails to reflect our true priorities. Economics measures the value of the house where you live but not the air that you breathe. Economics measures the value of the food that you eat but not the ability of soil to grow plants. Yet even with these limitations, we can gain valuable insights by applying cost figures to our plans. If 2019's wealth and income were distributed evenly to each of the 7.7 billion people alive in 2019, each person would have about $47,000 of wealth and an annual income of about $11,500. These figures would be higher if adjusted for purchasing power parity.

How does this compare with the cost of building everything new? Let's look at today's costs for building skyscrapers. According to Statista, high-rise construction for Class A office space costs between $580 and $2,000 per square foot. Luxury residential construction costs about the same.

The wide variation between $580 and $2,000 depends on location. New York costs are around $2,000 per square foot; in Kuala Lumpur, the cost is closer to $580 per square foot. Even at Kuala Lumpur's lower cost, if each person has 2,000 square feet, at this rate, the cost per person for living/working space would be around $1.2 million. That's over twenty-five times the world's per-capita total wealth or over one hundred years' worth of income. If all this construction was done over the next twenty years, we would require about forty times as many finished square feet as all of today's worldwide construction (not just high-rise construction). This doesn't take into account construction of farms, energy collection zones, or transportation systems, so realistically, this plan might require a fifty- to hundredfold increase over today's new construction. So from this perspective, our new city is clearly unaffordable.

But we won't be using the same methods we use to build today's skyscrapers. There are many realms in which the world increases output by one hundred times or more over the course of just a few years. Our plan requires robots that ramp up to scale, and assumes that we get better as we gain experience.

Some of our technologies increase in capacity continuously and reliably enough that we regularly consider many multiples in advance. Moore's Law describes this exponential increase for computing power. When considering encryption algorithms or computers that will someday outperform brains, we regularly think in terms of millionfold increases. At the cost trajectory of computing power, our $1.2 million home of 2019 should cost about $1,000 in 2040. At the cost trajectory for DNA sequencing, our $1.2 million home of 2019 would cost just over $10 in 2040.

How relevant is this sort of cost trajectory to the plans in this book? Building large physical items includes costs that cannot be significantly reduced through innovation, but there is a world of variability between different technologies in terms of cost reduction over time. Which cost curve will rebuilding our world follow? How much of what we desire can be built with technology that is subject to Moore's Law–like behavior? Answering these questions is beyond the scope of this book but not beyond the scope of what human ingenuity can begin to estimate.

Yet past experience is not the only way to look at costs, especially in comparison to the cost of inaction. We need to construct living and working space at fifty to one hundred times today's rate. Likewise, we need to increase manufacturing capacity fifty to one hundred times, especially for construction materials and solar panels, but also for many other things. How realistic is a hundredfold increase in construction and manufacturing? What I hear when I ask this question is typically: "For the whole world, a hundred-fold increase is unrealistic, but my company would eagerly expand a hundredfold over several years if the market was there and our suppliers could keep up." Extractive industries don't answer this way, but manufacturers usually do.

I've tried to make the case in this book that the benefits of working simultaneously and synergistically on many facets of our situation outweigh the cost. I've tried to make the case that inaction would cost more and benefit us less than if we choose a future limited only by what is physically possible. I've tried to make the case that through the multiplier effects of improving both ourselves and our world, we can take the wisest path into the future. That path includes a lot of new construction and manufacturing.

Have I succeeded in making this case? In pure cost–benefit terms, according to the ways we currently measure cost, the answer is no. I can't adequately make the case purely in terms of measurable costs and benefits, at least not using only today's measurement tools. Yet even so, putting cost numbers to this plan hopefully offers the reader some useful insights and points in a direction that can lead to further fruitful exploration.

CRYPTO

Throughout this book, I use examples of possible inventions enabled by crypto. My intent is to give the reader a feel for what crypto makes possible and what crypto cannot do. I refer to this as "general cryptographic literacy" and compare it to the way most of us have a good intuitive idea of what electricity can and cannot do.

We know that electricity can:

- Provide motive power for small things like electric toothbrushes and big things like locomotives.
- Send pictures and sounds from place to place and make recordings to show accurate pictures and sounds from the past.

We also know that electricity cannot:

- Teleport people and things from place to place.
- Show us accurate pictures and sounds of events in the future.

My hope is that enough people develop a similar feel for the capabilities and limitations of crypto. In the book, I mentioned these examples of things that crypto and related techniques can do:

- Support asymmetric human influence and attention (Zone Pods, *Tool #5* in Chapter 3).
- Intermediate our interactions with others and the world through an AI agent (well-being bot, *Tool #9* in Chapter 3).
- Enable anonymous evaluations (choosing a movie, Chapter 5).
- Administer taxes privately (tiers of request for personal data, Chapter 5).
- Offer security plus privacy in public places (ubiquitous cameras, Chapter 5).
- Reduce bribery and extortion (switch feature added to money, Chapter 5).
- Offer tiered identity authentication (two-way anonymity, Chapter 5).
- Base money on trust and evaluations of satisfaction (mint-your-own money, Chapter 11).
- Organize social-network feeds based on the interests of users (including those of existing social networks, Chapter 12).

In addition to the inventions I mentioned, most readers use and expect to use crypto in online communications (for example, with any website address that begins with https) and with secure online portals.

Now I'd like to place these concepts in a wider context.

For our understanding, it probably makes sense to place crypto in the context of information theory. Information theory dates back to at least 1948, when Claude Shannon published "A Mathematical Theory of Communication,"[16] in which he laid out the notion that information can be described in mathematical terms and measured. When information is digitized, it becomes possible to trade off one parameter for another. For example, by reducing sounds or pictures to digital representations, copies and copies of copies can be made without loss of accuracy.

But even before that, in a strictly analog world, engineers were trading off one parameter for another. In 1927, Harold Black came up with the principle of negative feedback for an amplifier.[17] (In this context, negative feedback is a good thing.) Negative feedback makes amplifiers more accurate (more linear) by trading gain for accuracy. Specifically, a negative feedback amplifier inverts and amplifies the difference between its input signal and a small portion of its output signal, driving the amplifier's distortion toward zero.

More relevant to us are ways that digital information can be manipulated to trade one parameter for another. In most cases, the parameter traded away is some information overhead (additional bits). For example, by encoding a signal with additional bits, errors in transmission or storage can be detected and corrected, up to a certain limit. That limit can be pretty large. Radio signals are transmitted through deep space over channels with error rates over

99.9 percent. Most of the received bits are noise. Hard disks and flash memory are inherently more accurate than deep space radio, but still too error-prone to be useful without error correction.

A crude way to implement error correction is to send or store each chunk of information multiple times, hoping that at least one chunk will be error-free. This has the disadvantage of being inefficient, and also there is no obvious way to determine which, if any, of the chunks are accurate. Math to the rescue! There are various ways to make errors detectable, and correctable, even errors consisting of large missing chunks. Read up on parity errors, Reed–Solomon encoding, and fountain codes for more on this.

As an interesting aside, biological processes also use forward error correction to trade additional information for the ability to correct errors. For example, our cells have mechanisms to repair errors in our DNA. Longer-living species (at least among mammals) typically have more of these error-correction mechanisms and devote more energy to correcting errors. This provides an interesting window into possible areas for longevity research. As a long-lived mammal, we have many built-in repair mechanisms, but there are biological repair mechanisms in the animal kingdom that we don't have.

Crypto allows us to communicate privately over a public channel. People have attempted to send private communications through public channels since at least 400 BCE, when Greek military commanders sent encoded written messages by runner that could only be deciphered with a decoder key. But even before that, as far back as 1900 BCE, Egyptian tombs had carved inscriptions using nonstandard hieroglyphic symbols. In all these examples, both the sender and the receiver needed to have identical secret keys. Until the 1970s, this is how encrypted messages were sent.

Public-key crypto (also called asymmetric crypto) solves the problem of needing to share prearranged secret keys by using a system that involves pairs of keys. A message encrypted by one key of the pair can be decrypted by the other key but not by the encrypting key (and vice versa). One key of the pair is kept private, and the other key is published in a public directory. So, if I encode a message with your public key, only the holder of your private key (that's you) can read the message. Conversely, if you send a message encoded by your private key, if I can decrypt and read it with your public key, I can be sure it was really sent by you. Using both my private key and your public key on the same message allows me to send you a message that only you can read and that you can be certain came from me. Also, you can prove the message was sent by me (not an imposter), and I can't credibly deny it. This combination of encryption, authentication, and non-repudiation makes public-key crypto suitable for important agreements and business contracts.

But third parties who overhear our secret communications can tell that we have communicated, when we communicated, and approximately how much information we exchanged. Mathematical ways exist of obscuring who is communicating with whom and even the fact that someone is communicating. Investigate onion routing and steganography for more information on this.

The crypto technology that currently gets a lot of news is cryptocurrency, such as Bitcoin. The blockchain technology that underpins most cryptocurrencies does away with the need for a centralized bank or administrator to run the machines that store data and perform the calculations. Blockchain incentivizes multiple parties to collectively run the machines by making it pay to do so. Those who run the machines are mining cryptocurrency for their own benefit while serving others because the mining operation is what makes the system run. To keep it honest, a majority needs to independently arrive at the same answer with each round of computation.

But there are some limitations to today's cryptocurrency technology. First, there is no mechanism like monetary policy to keep the value of the cryptocurrency constant or predictable. Money is not a commodity that should be subject to the pressures of supply and demand. In the short run, that can make cryptocurrency seem like a good bet because the value increases, sometimes dramatically, for a while anyway. Then it behaves like a bubble. Another limitation is that each blockchain is subject to being forked, meaning that if even for a moment, one entity gets control of over 50 percent of the total computing infrastructure, that individual can take over the blockchain. This in itself is probably a manageable problem. The bigger risk is that the dishonest individual in control can hide that fact.

Theoretically, a dishonest individual's surreptitious control could take ownership of a cryptocurrency for themself. That would be immediately obvious to the next people who tried to spend or send funds, when they discover funds missing. It would be obvious unless the dishonest individual redeposited just enough to cover today's expenditures, but not much more. It would benefit the dishonest individual to do this daily, so long as more money is being added to the total cryptocurrency system each day than is currently being spent and withdrawn.

The likelihood of one entity building a secret crypto mining infrastructure sufficient to run more than half of the total transactions on a large blockchain is slim. After all, that entity would have to acquire computing capabilities larger than the sum of all the other users combined. But the possibility of introducing an exploit that secretly takes over the computing resources of others' mining machines is possible. Just as bugs in the code of popular programs and operating systems can be exploited, so can the code of popular blockchain-mining machines. You wouldn't necessarily know it when this happens. The dishonest party running the exploit would likely let the system appear to run normally while watching their ill-gotten wealth increase. This has happened, not with blockchain itself, but with services that supposedly store cryptocurrency for safekeeping. Read about Mt. Gox for further information.

A further problem with blockchain technology is the total electrical energy used. Every round of mining (and running the infrastructure) is a competition to find the next chunk of value buried in statistical noise. The more computation you perform, the higher your likelihood of successfully mining a nugget of value. This leads to a race to have more and faster machines. More and faster machines use more electrical energy. This has led to a noticeable fraction of the world's energy going to cryptocurrency mining, with a trend that increases over time.

These problems can be solved with better technology. Cryptocurrency can be developed with a mechanism to keep the value predictable or constant, detect attempts to hijack the ledger, and keep the total energy consumption reasonable. When blockchain was developed, it broke new ground in many areas and justifiably became a success. Now, we are more sophisticated.

The above examples describe what is currently being done with crypto. In the future, when general cryptographic literacy becomes widespread, it will make sense to focus on the qualities we want from any new system with confidence that it will be possible to implement the plan. More important than understanding the specifics is an accurate general sense of what is possible and a fertile imagination.

A key to understanding what is possible is being able to visualize possible trade-offs. So far, we have discussed trade-offs that trade:

- Additional bits of information for the ability to correct for errors or send accurate communications through a noisy channel (forward error correction).
- Additional bits for the ability to send information privately over a public channel (public key).
- The ability to verify the sender of information and prevent forgeries (public key).
- Additional bits for the ability to send information without revealing to whom we are sending information (onion routing).

- The ability to send information without revealing that we are sending information. This trades additional bits for metadata such as the fact that we are sending messages at all (steganography).
- The ability to exchange and verify information in a public record with no centralized authority. This trades additional computing power for the need to have a centralized node (blockchain).

What other trade-off possibilities can we envision? Can we develop new ways to detect bad behavior (and its perpetrators) without reducing privacy? What about tracking biological contagion from person to person (or animals) without privacy intrusions?

Crypto can be leveraged to help form more interesting and satisfying relationships. What if we could share our most private thoughts with a high likelihood of finding understanding and empathy, because the only people we share them with are those who have had similar thoughts?

Crypto can also help us collaborate in more powerful ways. Have you ever had an idea about how a product, service, or business could be improved? Currently, collaboration is restrained by the need to protect proprietary rights. The main way to protect proprietary rights is to not collaborate with people outside your organization because collaborating would share otherwise secret information. Crypto offers a way to establish honest broker software to accurately track each individual's contribution to a collective endeavor on a granular level. So instead of a marketplace of product-versus-product competition, each product can be a collaboration based on feature-by-feature competition.

If we think imaginatively about what we want, we can work backward to see if there is something we can trade for that. If we simply need to trade more bits for some quality we desire, we are rich in bits and can usually afford the trade.

For example:

- Is there a way to determine who is most attuned to your individual thoughts and feelings, perhaps because they have independently had similar thoughts or feelings?
- Is there a way to choose whose influence and what influence would best help you become more of who you want to become?
- Can we develop a way to find and choose colleagues and friends with whom you are most likely to have success and fun?
- How do you determine who would most benefit from your influence or most appreciate your company?

Could you significantly improve any product or service you use? Would your contribution be valuable? Perhaps we can engineer ways that most products and services benefit from the creative imagination of anyone with a good idea. Perhaps those with good ideas can be compensated fairly.

Technology can offer something in each of these cases and in thousands of others. But people are unlikely to use the technology unless it offers transparent and trustworthy privacy and security. That's where crypto comes into play. Crypto offers us the ability to promote simultaneous competing interests in new ways, limited less by technical constraints than by failure of imagination.

COMPARISON OF CURRENCIES

Comparison of Conventional Currency and Emotional Well-Being Currency

	All existing currencies from barter through dollars, data, and credit, plus the improved currency described in Chapter 9	Emotional well-being currencies operating on multiple dimensions as described in Chapters 10 and 11
	STRENGTHS AND WEAKNESSES	
How well does this currency function...		
as a means of exchange ?	Excellent	Good
as a storage of value for later?	Okay	Good
as entry into the price system?	Excellent	Okay
for prioritizing and distributing scarce physical resources (examples: agricultural products and raw materials)?	Excellent	Poor
for maximizing the fruits of abundance (examples: products of information (movies, music, computer programs) and products of emotional well-being (genuine safety, belonging, esteem, self-actualization))?	Poor	Good to excellent (depends on how well the individual currency's dimension fits with the nature of your desired emotional well-being)
for improving self-knowledge?	Poor to okay	Good
for receiving from others?	Excellent	Excellent

for giving to others?	Poor	Excellent
	IN PERSONAL TERMS	
What is the purpose of this currency?	Means of exchange. Get the money first, then you get what you want.	Measure of satisfaction after the fact.
How is winning determined?	Receiving the most: more is better.	Customized measure of your own well-being (including having the most).
What is the role of ownership?	Centralize and consolidate wealth for benefit of the owner.	Own your job, role, and identity to strengthen self-actualization and esteem.
How much is enough?	There is no such thing as enough.	Conventional money is a means to an achievable end or multiple ends. Then you have enough conventional money. After that you can prioritize more important achievable goals.
What is the role of your job?	Individuals sell their labor to employers.	Individuals' skills predict accurately how valuable their contributions will be to others.
What is the role of an entrepreneur?	Find ways to accumulate dollars by manipulating and fitting expectations.	Find ways to invent stuff that delights people who may not suspect that such a thing could exist.
What is the role of investment?	Accumulate more dollars.	Find the most efficient ways to benefit others.
What is the role of inner development?	It has little or no role.	Attunement to your inner desires leads to better alignment with your actions. Currencies in this column offer useful feedback along the way.

continued...

...from previous

How does the economy of this currency change our view of ourselves?	Manual labor was replaced by machines. Mental calculators were replaced by computers.	People benefit individually and collectively by association with certain others. The system promotes healthy and beneficial flow of influence at large scale.
IN SOCIETAL TERMS		
What is the purpose of having an economy?	Coordinate actions to produce stuff.	Focus actions and self-knowing. Prioritize actions that are most wanted.
What is the role of nature in the economy of this currency?	It acts as a resource.	It offers a relationship.
How is data used?	To influence others through means mostly hidden from them.	To understand self, to predict what others want, and to determine what is or will be truly valuable and to whom.
How is wealth and poverty viewed?	The poor are a drag on the economic system of this currency, yet marketing is both crucial to business and functions to sell the dynamics of poverty to consumers.	In terms of emotional well-being, everyone is poor today. As part of improving this situation, we will invest in those who are poor by the conventional definition of poverty because their lives can be improved the most for the fewest dollars.
How much economic activity do we need?	We need 4.5-5 times today's world economic output to provide enough material well-being for everyone to live in good-enough conditions so that further focus on material well-being no longer takes priority over emotional well-being.	Unknown, since we're starting from almost zero. Also, it is hard to answer this question because the same activity (most activity) in this sphere counts as both contribution and reward.

What is the role of specialization?	It improves productivity by having each job done by someone good at that job.	There is a wider range of possible emotional well-being than a single individual can encompass. Specialization allows the breadth of human experience on everyone's inner landscapes to accrue to more people.
What is the role of competition?	Chooses winners, kills losers. Winner-take-all situations disadvantage everyone but the single winner.	Mostly operates as winner-take-all. Each new invention, product, or service operates in its own category until something better comes along and displaces it.
What are the failures of the economy and sources of waste?	Most work and investments are not focused on improving lives. There is a gap between what is wanted and what the economy does.	We need currency of the kinds in both columns of this chart and successful interaction between the two. There is no guarantee that any attempt to make life better will succeed.
How do large organizations work in the economy of this currency?	Organizations can do bigger and more complicated things than individuals working independently.	Bigger organizations can develop independent ecosystems of well-being-improvement technology.
How will brain machines affect the economy of this currency?	Increased economic output is possible because groups can better coordinate, collaborate, and focus their actions.	We can learn better what we want, what others want, and how to connect the two.
How will the multipliers of Chapter 11 affect the economy of this currency?	They will create more wealth.	The first step is to fix the world's problems. In general, multipliers work together to help us live better.

continued...

...from previous

What is the trajectory for the future?	Most lives are unfulfilled. Collective failure and inaction are likely to lead to humanity's self-destruction.	Fixing the world is the first step toward being guided by healthy inner yearnings.
CHARACTERISTICS AND ACCOUNTING		
How many dimensions exist?	Only one. You can have more wealth or less wealth.	Multiple dimensions behave differently and interact according to vector math on many planes.
What are the mechanics of exchanges and accumulation?	Zero sum. When I pay you, my account decreases by the same amount that yours increases.	Many possible formulas, including addition, multiplication, or any monotonic function. Some transactions are positive-sum, whereby wealth is generated by the transaction itself.
What gets measured?	Money has its own dynamic partially based on the mechanics of the medium and partly based on the history of human interactions. This dynamic guides behavior in ways not fully aligned with optimal well-being.	Genuine well-being of self and others is measured at each opportunity. Compounding return via multiple exchanges leads to more power and influence to do good (because the measurements promote what is actually valued).
Who initiates transactions?	The buyer.	Usually, the recipient or the recipient's well-being bot.
When and how is price determined?	At the time of the sale.	It starts at the beginning of a transaction or interaction of a transaction, but adjustments can continue forever.
What tendencies are promoted and reinforced?	Concentrating wealth.	Finding new niches where the least dollars and least effort can do the most good.

Where does innovation come from?	The finance industry.	Everyone.
What are the historical antecedents?	Cows, land, gold, cash, bank balance, credit, and data.	Everything in the other column, plus the improvements to money outlined in Chapter 9, and widespread cryptographic literacy to the point where enough people carry a general grasp of what is possible and expect good products and services built on crypto and operating in their interests.
What is currency created by?	Mutual agreement, centralized authority, and more recently, crypto.	Evolving agreement about what is important and what has value (enabled by crypto and bandwidth).
What is the legal and regulatory framework?	It already exists with complexity, nuance, and subtlety.	It doesn't exist yet, although GDPR in Europe is a good start.
INTERACTIONS BETWEEN THE TWO TYPES OF CURRENCY		
How will this currency interact with the currency in the other column?	You will be able to use this currency plus some effort or ingenuity to buy genuine safety, belonging, esteem, and self-actualization. You will probably want to do this with any dollars you have after you've provided for your physical needs.	If you can enhance others' genuine emotional well-being in measurable ways, they will probably be glad to pay you in the kind of money you need for physical items.

ACKNOWLEDGMENTS

I cannot possibly thank all the people without whom I would not have had the ideas that eventually gelled into this book. Like you I live in a sea of thoughts, conversations, ideas, memes, books, lectures, and all the other ways that thoughts take form. That said, the synthesis here is purely my own and as such all errors, mistakes, omissions, and incomplete conclusions are solely my responsibility. I would like to offer special thanks to Berit Anderson who helped me think through what to include, Jeff Bakeman who yelled "that's your title" when I first uttered the words "live forever and fix everything," Robin Brooks who helps me remain sane, John Cornichello for my author photo, Elizabeth Dimarco who helped me understand what it takes to write a book, Ray Freeman who created the CAD design of Figures 6 and 10–12, and Kelly Lyles who connected me with Ray. I cannot say enough good things about Scribe Media who signed up to help me through the technical details of publishing a book and became the bridge by which I become an author. I especially want to thank Hussein Al-Baiaty, Hal Clifford, Emily Gindlesparger, Chas Hoppe, and Meghan McCracken at Scribe. I'd also like to thank fellow authors Jane Bader, Mary Guirovich, Lisa Kaye, and Cori Lathan who each helped me overcome hurdles in the process. Finally, I'd like to thank the lovely Shelly, who has been supportive of this project, the truth, and me at every stage.

ENDNOTES

1   ...According to Abraham Maslow, we have a hierarchy of needs.

After listing the propositions that must be considered as basic,
the author formulates a theory of human motivation in line
with these propositions and with the known facts derived
from observation and experiment. There are five sets of goals
(basic needs) which are related to each other and are arranged
in a hierarchy of prepotency. When the most prepotent goal is
realized, the next higher need emerges. 'Thus man is a perpetually
wanting animal.' Thwarting, actual or imminent, of these basic
needs provides a psychological threat that leads to psychopathy.

Quoted from: Maslow, A. H. (1943). "A Theory of Human
Motivation," *Psychological Review*, 50(4), 370–396. Also described in
the book: *Motivation and Personality*, Maslow, Abraham, Harper 1954.

2   In nineteenth-century Manchester, England, over half of working-
class children died before reaching their fifth birthday, mostly from
infectious disease.

Frequently, the inspectors found two or more families
crowded into one small house and often one family lived in

a damp cellar where twelve or sixteen persons were crowded. Children are ill-fed, dirty, ill-clothed, exposed to cold and neglect; and in consequence, more than one-half of the offspring die before they have completed their fifth year.

Quoted from: *The Moral and Physical Condition of the Working Classes Employed in the Cotton Manufacture in Manchester*, Kay-Shuttleworth, James, 1832.

3   What is surprising is that the same brain sensors can detect activity before you decide to move. Or at least before you think you have decided to move.

> Contrary to what most of us would like to believe, decision-making may be a process handled to a large extent by unconscious mental activity. A team of scientists has unraveled how the brain actually unconsciously prepares our decisions. "Many processes in the brain occur automatically and without involvement of our consciousness. This prevents our mind from being overloaded by simple routine tasks. But when it comes to decisions we tend to assume they are made by our conscious mind. This is questioned by our current findings."

Quoted from: "Decision-making May Be Surprisingly Unconscious Activity," *Science Daily*, April 15, 2008 Source: Max-Planck-Gesellschaft.

4   *Homo Deus: A Brief History of Tomorrow*, Harari, Yuval Noah, HarperCollins, 2017.

5   These mechanisms pivot down from the ceiling to allow vehicles (with loads attached) to climb or descend to tracks oriented in a different direction on the next higher or next lower floor.

For an example of vehicles that move horizontally and then climb vertical tracks, see the SqUID autonomous warehouse robot from Israeli company Bionic HIVE.

6   Princeton scientists Angus Deaton and Daniel Kahneman published
     research in 2010 showing that happiness is the result of the
     fulfillment of two abstract psychological states: emotional well-being
     and life evaluation. Plus, an income of at least $75,000 a year.

     Based on: "High Income Improves Evaluation of Life but Not
     Emotional Well-Being," Daniel Kahneman and Angus Deaton,
     PNAS September 21, 2010, 107 (38) 16489-16493 (Proceedings of
     the National Academy of Sciences of the United States of America).

7   Pentland, Sandy, *Social Physics: How Social Networks Can Make Us
     Smarter*, Penguin Books, 2015.

8   A typical human brain has a bandwidth of several billion bits per
     second between the left and right hemispheres. That's about a
     million times the bandwidth of all our senses combined.

       Traditionally human central nervous systems (CNS) and
       electronic computation and communication devices have been
       linked via the bodily senses and musculature—an approach
       requiring only simple technology and incurring little medical
       risk. Unfortunately this straightforward avenue has very low
       information bandwidth: effectively a few kilohertz of sensory
       information (primarily vision) into the CNS, and a mere
       one-tenth of that figure out. Much higher transfer rates are
       observed within the CNS. In particular, the corpus callosum
       connects the right and left cerebral hemispheres with 500
       million fibers in the human. Each fiber signals on average at
       about ten hertz, for an aggregate rate of several gigahertz:
       about one million times the bandwidth of the senses.

     Quoted from: *An Invasive Approach to High-Bandwidth Neural-
     Electronic Interfaces*, by Dexter Wyckoff, Rajiv Kamar, and Fred
     Wright; IEEE Transactions on Medical Electronics v15 n3 July-
     September 1971, pp. 1175:1195.

9   Based on population numbers, humans have been a very successful species, accounting for about 36 percent of all mammals by mass. Our domesticated livestock and pets account for another 60 percent. Wild mammals account for the remaining 4 percent.

From Figure 1 and Table 1 of "The Biomass Distribution on Earth," Proceedings of the National Academy of Sciences of the United States of America; PNAS June 19, 2018 115 (25) 6506-6511; first published May 21, 2018.

Table shows 0.1 gigatons total biomass of livestock, 0.06 gigatons of humans and 0.007 gigatons of wild mammals.

10   *Ending Aging*, de Grey, Aubrey, St. Martin's Press, 2007.

11   But longevity has been increasing among people at all wealth levels in most countries. By a lot!

Gapminder.org has a series of visually compelling and highly informative interactive charts, none more so than the animated chart for income and life expectancy between the years 1800 and 2020. It shows the correlation between wealth and longevity, but what jumps out is how the effects of history are much more significant.

As you move the timeline slider from left (1800) to right (2020), the bubbles for each country almost leap toward the top of the chart, indicating longer life expectancy. As recently as 1960, even the richest countries were below today's world average life expectancy. Also interesting is the worldwide life expectancy dip during the pandemic of 1917–1919.

12   In the long run, the research toward longevity will lead to cost reduction in the delivery of healthcare in wealthy countries.

On May 7, 2019, Aging Analytics Agency presented a new analytical report at the All-Party Parliamentary Group for Longevity in the UK Parliament. The 315-page open-access report is entitled "National Longevity Development Plans: Global Overview 2019—First Edition."

Among the points made in the report:

- A global shift from treatment model to prevention model in medicine is necessary.
- As there are economic benefits to healthy longevity in the population, future development planning should pursue the longevity dividend.
- This dividend is attainable due to advancements in technologies that will extend healthy lifespan, including the science of aging, preventive medicine, and age tech.

13 *An Inquiry into the Nature and Causes of the Wealth of Nations*, Smith, Adam (1776), W. Strahan and T. Cadell.

14 Prestigious economics journals have published papers from Princeton and Harvard professors on why people brush their teeth and why Cinderella wasn't invited to the ball.

"The Economics of Brushing Teeth" by Alan S. Blinder, *Journal of Political Economy*. Vol. 82, No. 4 (Jul.–Aug., 1974), pp. 887–891 https://www.jstor.org/stable/1837155.

"The Cinderella Paradox Resolved" by Edward L. Glaeser, *Journal of Political Economy*. Vol. 100, No. 2 (Apr., 1992), pp. 430–432 https://www.jstor.org/stable/2138613.

15 At current annual growth rates of 3.5 percent to 4 percent a year, and with expected increases in population, fivefold economic growth would take approximately another fifty years.

To arrive at these figures, I took the latest (2019) figure of $133 trillion from the World Bank's International Comparison Program and population projections from Worldometers online. Worldometers is based on data from the United Nations Department of Economic and Social Affairs World Population Prospects 2019 report.

A spreadsheet of growth at 4 percent shows the $133 trillion growing to $777 trillion after forty-five years, when population is expected to be 10.32 billion. That works out to $75,300 each. At 3.4 percent annual growth, after fifty-two years the $133 trillion of 2019 has grown to $796 trillion, and world population is expected to be 10.51 billion. That works out to $75,700 each. (The numbers here are rounded.)

16 "A Mathematical Theory of Communication," by Shannon Claude, (1948), The Bell System Technical Journal, vol. 27, pp. 379–423, 623–656, July, October, 1948.

17 "Stabilized feed-back amplifiers," H.S. Black, Electrical Engineering, vol. 53, pp. 114–120, Jan. 1934.

INDEX

abundance
  fruits of, 169
  notions of, 36–37, 197
accordion construction, 24–25, 51–52,
  53*f*–54*f*
accounting systems, 207
actors, role-playing by, 81–82, 98
advertising, 85, 90
aging
  belief systems and, 129
  causes of, 119–122, 137
  death from, 220, 230
  mechanisms of, 126, 137*f*, 138
  process of, 124–126, 125*f*
  reversal of, 140–141, 239
  stalling, 33, 136
  threats of, 13–14
airflow
  contagion and, 26–27
  filtration and, 59
  friction and, 259, 264
  laminar, 60, 143
algorithms
  personalized data, 89

public, 164
unseen, 30
alternate realities, art and, 81–82
alternative currencies, 162
altruism, self-interest *versus*, 3–5, 4*f*,
  165, 224
ancestors, 76
animals
  cruelty to, 12
  farming of, 66, 74–75, 145
  genomic alteration of, 135–136
  quality of life for, 147
annihilation, threats of, ix, 3, 215, 227,
  239
artificial intelligence
  data sharing through, 84–85
  expectations and, 82
  learning and, 113–114
asymmetric crypto, 273
augmented reality, construction
  and, 62
autonomy, work and, 39

bacteria, replication of, 120–121

bandwidth
  human brain, 105, 111, 115, 293*n*8
  optical fibers and, 36
  outbound, 105–111, 116, 147, 235
  perception and, 35, 111
  public good as a, 35
  simplicity and, 106
  ubiquitous, 34–36
batteries, 46, 253–254
behavior
  curve, 158
  destructive, 154, 195, 277
  free choice and, 1
  human relationships and, 234
  marketplaces and, 157
  monitoring of, 154
  unconscious patterns and, 28–29
belonging, sense of, 87
  crypto and, 95
  importance of, xii
  rewards of, 197–198
biases, discrimination and, 158–159
birth rates, 11*f*, 123. *see also* population
  growth
Black, Harold, 271, 296*n*17
blockchain technology, 273–275
brain, human
  bandwidth of, 105, 111, 293*n*8
  communication, work and, 38–39
  communication as a tool, 22–23
  decision-making and, 28–29
  focusing of, 23–24
  movement and, 292*n*3
  psychoactive drugs and, 110
brain machines
  accomplishments and, 182, 183
  bandwidth of, 115, 147
  decision making with, 292*n*3

development of, 106–107
economics and, 180
empathy and, 104, 186
jobs and, 182
leveraging of, 193–194
making experiences with, 165
mechanisms of, 105
new senses through, 107–109
permissions set for, 112–113
as a tool, 22
branding, value and, 159
bribery, 270
business failures, 160–161

cancer, 129, 138, 147
capitalism, excesses of, 85–86
careers, 193
cattle, 34, 150
causality
  aging and, 137–138
  proximate, 119
cell division, 122*f*
central bank, 163
centralized authority, 151, 184
change
  expectations and, 80–81
  global problems and, 9–16
  inertia *versus*, 149–150
  phases of, 15–16
choices
  future outcomes and, 227–229, 228*f*
  individual *versus* collective, x, 152,
    220
  influences on, 80
  unconscious, 28
chronic diseases, 129
the city, 5–6, 43–77
  area required for, 225

cost of, 265–268
cross-section of, 68*f*, 69*f*
cutaway view of, 70*f*, 72*f*, 73*f*
energy requirements of, 249–255
floors of, 246, 247*f*–248*f*
layout of, 45–48, 47*f*, 49*f*
modules within, 47
space utilization in, 245–249,
    247*f*–248*f*
sports venue in, 72*f*
civilization
altruism *versus* self-interest, 3–5, 4*f*,
    165, 224
technological, 172
worldwide, 6
climate change, 10, 227
cognitive bias, 158
collaboration
achievement and, 172
brain machines and, 194
conversations and, xi
crypto and, 277–278
economy of, 173–174, 200
esteem and, 198
intersubjective reality and, 40
jobs and, 186
safety and, 197
successful, 196
well-being bots and, 31, 90
collective action, importance of, x, 240
communication
brain-based, 22–23
cellular, 137
choices in, 113
interrelatedness and, 15
symbolic, 115–116
theory of, 105
transmission of, 272–273

whale, 115
communications theory, 105, 271
competition
barriers to, 166
forces of, 173
money systems and, 165–166
motivation and, 209
product *versus* feature, 278
specialization and, 181–182
computing power, 267
concrete, 251
conflict resolution, 185
connectivity, infrastructure for, 34–35
consumer lust, 236
consumerism, 178–179
marketing and, 179
a world culture of, 229
consumption, creation *versus*, 153,
    179, 192
contagion, airborne, 26–27, 143–144
plant, 74
plumbing and, 143–144
containers for farming, 67, 74
convenience, logistics and, 194
cooling, energy requirements, 250
cooperation, money systems and, 152
corporations
collaboration and, 117
competition and, 209
corpus callosum, 105, 293*n*8
corruption, tracking of, 93–94, 234
costs of construction, 56, 266–267
costs of the city, 265–268
creation
consumption *versus*, 153, 192
of imagination, 104
of new services, 41
rewards from, 66

creativity
  consumerism *versus*, 192
  currency and, 175
  disequilibrium and, 236–237
  expression of, 107
  ownership and, 63
  sacrifice *versus*, 20
credit scores, 156–157, 160–161
crime, deterrence of, 93, 154, 195, 222, 234
crowding, sensory input and, 56–57
crypto, 269–279
  acceptance of, 220
  competing demands of, 91
  definition of, 18, 269–279
  encounters tracked by, 75–76, 144
  human relationships and, 94–96
  product creation and, 40–41
  public-key, 273
  relationships and, 85, 277
  society and, 39
cryptocurrencies, 164, 273–276
  control of, 274–275
  development of, 276
  limitations of, 274
  mining, 274–275
cryptographic literacy, 18, 39–41, 269, 276
cultural limitations
  aging and, 129
  expectations and, 82
currencies. *see also* money systems
  comparisons of, 282*f*–287*f*
  conventional, 202–203, 209
  crime and, 93
  democratizing creation of, 162–163
  design of, 174–175
  dimensions of, 202, 205

exchange rates, 157, 189
feedback from, 181
individual, 155–156, 200–201
new forms of, 196
sublinear, 207
super-linear, 203–204
transactions and, 203
well-being based, 201–202, 208–209, 236

de Grey, Aubrey, 33, 126, 136, 137*f*, 294*n*10
death
  causes of, 122
  cutoff age, 224–225
  immortality thinking and, 33–34
  impacts of thinking about, 131*f*
  problem of, 13–14
  psychology of, 130, 221, 238
  rate of, 124
death-row psychology, 130, 221
Deaton, Angus, 86, 176, 293*n*6
decision-making
  food choices and, 135
  relationships and, 101
  simulations and, 28–29
decryption, 273
dementia, 14, 221
democracy, progress in, 15
dental care, 295*n*14
detective, artificially intelligent, 84, 89
developmental inertia, 119–120, 126
digital currency, 93–94
discrimination, 156, 158, 223
diseases. *see also* infectious diseases
  aging and, 127–129, 141, 221
  animals and, 146
  causes of, 14

immune systems and, 25–26
plumbing and, 25–27, 291*n2*
problem of, 14
surface decontamination and, 60
transmission of, 142–145
distributed systems, 154
DNA
as computation, 146, 218
editing of, 126
encoded instructions in, 33
modification of, 138–139, 146–147,
218
repair of, 272
domineering, 24
dystopian alternatives, 228*f*

ears, processing by, 105
Earth, 232, 233*f. see also* natural world
economic growth, trends in, 176–177,
192, 292*n15*
economics
cost of the city, 265–268
interpersonal relationships and,
171–172
journals, 295*n14*
needs and, 191–192
transactions and, 196
well-being bots and, 90–91
economies
expanded, 34
of experiences, 104, 181–182
ownership and, 62–63
well-being and, 90
education, continuing, 193
ego, 198
electricity
functions of, 18, 269
limitations of, 18, 39, 270

elevators, 48, 50, 52, 259–260
in farms, 75
space for, 245
speed of, 256, 259
emotional health
money and, 174
relationships and, 79–80
emotional well-being, xii, 172
age of, 4
comparisons of currencies, 282*f*–287*f*
currencies of, 201, 204, 237
economics of, 198–200, 207–210
importance of, 21
investment in, 196
labor and, 213
life evaluation and, 293*n6*
measurement of, 172–176, 212
personal development and, 180–181
psychological state of, 86
empathy, 103–118
brain machines and, 186
enhancement of, 186
employment
brain machines and, 182–183
value of, 38
encryption, 273
Ending Aging (de Grey), 126, 136,
294*n10*
energy
blockchain mining and, 275
collection of, 46, 47*f,* 254–255
efficiency of, 254–255
lifespan and, xii
requirements for, 249–255
storage for the city, 46, 253
enough, 61
entertainment, 182
environment, 59

error correction, 272–276
escape velocity, 31–33, 123
escrow services, 155
esteem
    emotional well-being and, 174
    importance of, xii
    value of, 198, 212, 240
    well-being and, 87
evolution
    control of, 124–125
    species success and, 124
exchange rates
    currencies and, 155, 157, 162–163,
        200–201
    influence and, 189, 209
    risk and, 161
    transactions and, 159–160
expanded economy as a tool, 34
expectations
    altering, 29, 112
    cultural limitations and, 82
    limitations of, 80, 229–230
    power of, 213, 241
experiences
    communication of, 38, 103–104,
        180, 193–194
    influence of, 81, 189
    market for, 165, 182–183
    shared, 104, 114–115, 219
    value of, 104, 210
externalities, economic, 153
extinction, human, ix, 19, 227–230,
    239
eyes, processing by, 105

fairness
    privilege and, 29
    sense of, 2, 238–239

farming, 66–75
    animal husbandry and, 145
    area, 254
    granularity in, 66
    robot labor in, 74
    sunlight, 67
farms, vertical construction of, 66–67,
    68f, 69f
fears
    influence of, 221
    limitations and, 172–173
finance industry, 152
fissures in society, 216
food
    choices, 134
    conservatism, 135
    cost of, 151
    freshness of, 74–75
    health and, 142–146
    preparation areas, 74
fraud
    investments and, 195
    official documents and, 96
    recognition of, 154
free choice, behavior and, 1
friction
    economic, 194
    losses in air, 256, 264
fuel cells, 46, 253

gapminder.org, 294n11
garments, evolution of, 63–64
gene therapy, 138–139
germ cells, 122
gifts, 156
giving, 21–22, 90, 156, 175
gold, 34, 150, 162
Goldilocks Zone, 232, 233f

good behavior, 156–158, 163, 196
government policies, 88, 94, 96, 163
granularity in farming, 66
greenhouse effect, 232
growth hormones, 145–146

happiness, 86, 293*n*6
Harari, Yuval Noah, 40, 41, 213,
    292*n*4
haves and have-nots, 167, 215, 216*f*
health, 133–148
    animals and, 145, 147
    food and, 74
    immune exposure, 26
    improved, 194–195
    optimization of, 138
    poverty and, 216
    sanitation and, 14
healthcare
    costs of, 129, 194, 294*n*12
    participatory nature of, 135
    personalized nature of, 134
    predictive nature of, 134
heat pumps, 250–251
heating, energy requirements for, 250,
    264
heliostats, 251
hierarchy of needs, 20*f*, 172, 291*n*1
    crypto and, 94–96
    investment in levels of, 224
    Maslow's, xii
    satisfaction of, 196–199
Homo Deus (Harari), 40, 292*n*4
honesty, value of, 96, 195
housing
    construction of, 24, 53*f*, 54*f*
    flexibility of, 37
    ownership of, 62

human relationships
    crypto and, 94–96
    discrimination and, 158–159
    well-being bots and, 30–31
humanity
    death of, 13, 229–230
    future paths of, ix
    long-term future of, 218–219
hydra, 121*f*

ideas
    entrenched, 211
    memories *versus*, 111
    power of, 6
identity authentication, 207, 270
identity documents, 96
illnesses, life interruptions and,
    194–195
illusions
    simulations and, 29
    Zone Pods and, 23–24
imagination
    importance of, 3
    new senses through, 106–109
    psychological inertia and, 240
    sacrifice *versus*, 20
    status and, 62
    worlds generated by, 104–105, 116
immortality, 119–131, 217
    description of, 122–123
    embracing, 221–222
    expectations of, 217–219
    impacts of thinking about, 131*f*,
        237–238
    importance of, 123–124
    life extension and, 31–33
    misperceptions about, 122–123, 238
    research into, 127–128

immortality *(continued)*
    spirituality and, 241
immortality thinking, 33–34, 130–131
immune systems
    aging and, 141
    training of, 141
inaction
    causes of, 1–2
    costs of, 267
income
    distributed evenly, 266
    emotional well-being and, 86,
        293n11
    guaranteed minimum, 65
    life expectancy and, 294n11
    maximization of, 174–175
    satisfaction *versus*, 176
    well-being bot and, 209
inequity, 11
    addressing, xi
    economic growth and, 176–177
    problem of, 11
    wealth and, 153
inertia, xi
    annihilation and, 226
    inaction and, 2
    money and, 149–150, 178
    psychological, 240
infection, 14
    aging and, 141
    immune systems and, 25–26
    tracking, 144
infectious diseases. *see also* diseases
    avoiding, 14, 25
    crowding and, 291n2–292n2
    food and, 146
    immunity and, 141
    transmission of, 143

influence
    choices and, 80, 278
    crypto and, 270
    data and, 30–31
    evaluations and, 204
    human relationships and, 99–100,
        270, 278
    measures of, 100
    money and, 162
    personal data and, 83
    personal development and,
        208–209
    personal evaluations and, 187–189
    person-to-person, 189
    prioritization of, 222
    as a resource, 210
    simulations and, 98–99
    sources of, 113
    spreading, 99, 173
information
    business, 160, 162
    institutions *versus*, 154–155
    presentation of, 35
    private personal, 30
    sharing, 91–92
    transmission of, 272–273, 276–277
information theory, 235, 271
infrastructure
    accounting, 207–208
    energy-related, 252
    investment in, 66
    manufacturing, 62–64
    well-being bots for, 211
injustice, problem of, 11
innovation
    investment in, 195
    scaling with, 65
    successful, 153–154

inspiration
  importance of, 3
  social buy-in and, 19–20
intellectual property, 209
intelligent life, 230
interpersonal relationships
  behaving differently, 97
  crypto and, 75–76
  economics and, 174, 178
  emotional health and, 79–80
  experimentation within, 112
  problem of loneliness and, 12
intersubjective reality, creation of,
  40–41, 213
inventions, 1
  crypto-enabled, 269
  price curve of, 88
investment capital, 161, 193, 195, 224
investments, public policy and, 220

Jevon's paradox, 250
jobs. *see also* work
  automation of, 220
  the future of, 182–185

Kahneman, Daniel, 86, 176, 197, 293*n*6

labor. *see* work
laminar airflow, 60, 143
language
  learning of, 106, 114
  whales and, 115–116
LCD glass, 50–51
learning
  brain machine, 109–110
  human, 113–114
  machine, 113–114
  from mistakes, 225

leisure, value of, 38
life expectancy
  changes in, 31–32, 32*f*
  extension of, 31–33, 123, 231
  if not for aging, 125*f*
  multiplier as a, 193
  problems revealed by, 133
  technology and, 224
  trends in, 216–217
  wealth and, 216, 224, 294*n*11
lifespans
  approaches to extension of, xi,
    31–33, 127, 145
  engineering interventions in,
    136–137, 137*f*
  interventions to expand, 135–136
  length of, 193
  limited outlooks and, 15–16
  motivation and, 13–14
  quality of life and, 133
  rates of expansion of, 31–32, 32*f*
  technology and, 123
literacy, progress in, 15
living space requirements
  assumptions for, 51–52, 245, 249
  twenty-room house example,
    53*f*–54*f*
living standards, 212–213
loneliness, problem of, 12
longevity. *see also* immortality;
    lifespans
  healthcare costs and, 129, 294*n*12–
    295*n*12
  history of, 294*n*11
  increased rate of, 31
  research into, 127–129
long-term planning
  lifespans and, 34

long-term planning *(continued)*
  mindset, 186, 219
luxury, delivery of, 76

machine intelligence, 107
  bandwidth of, 110–112
  copying, 113
  learning and, 110–112
magnetism, sense for, 108
mammals, by weight, 124, 231, 294*n*9
manufactured items
  attitudes toward, 63–64
  history of, 44
manufacturing capacity, 4, 36–37
  the future of, 45, 267
  infrastructure for, 61, 64
  innovation and, 65
  on-demand production and, 64
  ownership of, 65–66
  standardization and, 64–65
marginal cost, 165, 167, 210
Mars, 233*f*
Maslow, Abraham, xii, 20*f*, 94, 151,
    172, 199, 291*n*1
materials, recycling of, 36, 59–60, 252
"A Mathematical Theory of
    Communication" (Shannon), 271
measures, new forms of, 21–22, 206
meat
  animal-free, 146
  cultured, 74–75
  engineered, 146
memories
  behavior and, 103
  ideas *versus*, 111
  stored, 219
misinformation, consequences of, 1
monetary monoculture, 163

monetary policies, 163, 274
money systems, 149–169. *see also*
    currencies
  companies and organizations, 159
  competition and, 165–166
  description of, 150
  digital currency and, 93–94
  dollar-based, 162
  exchange rates and, 156–157
  flaws in, 151–152
  influence and, 162
  measurement by, 80, 88
  mint your own, 155, 160–161
  monetary policies and, 163–164
  new forms of, 21–22
  ownership of, 236
  personal, 160
  purposes of, 174
  requirements of, 39
  successful, 152–153
Moore's Law, 267
motivations
  collaboration and, 117
  growth of, 38–39
  lifespan and, xii, 13–14
  source of, 181, 238
multipliers, 177, 191, 212

natural selection, 120, 123, 152
natural world
  damage to, x–xi, 2, 10–11, 19
  human relationship to, 54–55
  interspecies relationships and, 12–13
  restoration of, 185, 193
  wealth creation by, 37
near term future, xiii, 219, 239
negative feedback amplifiers, 271
network effect, 166

noise
    cancellation of, 57–58
    communication channel, 272
    control of, 58
    crowding and, 56–57
    neurological, 110
    reception of, 272
nudges, the science of, 99

objective reality, 40
obsolescence, 36, 184
octopus, 126, 147, 218
online trolls, 11–12
optical fibers, bandwidth and, 36
outbound bandwidth, 105–107,
    110–111, 115–116
ownership
    foundations of, 168
    mechanisms of, 184
    pride of, 64
    records of, 96
    rights of, 65–66
    types of, 62–63

p53 gene, 138–139
pathogens, 26, 60, 141
peace, desire for, 3
Pentland, Sandy, 99, 293*n*7
perception, bandwidth and, 35, 110
personal data
    anonymity of, 90–91
    commodification of, 83–85
    influences and, 30–31
    laws and, 88, 235
    ownership of, 89
    profiling and, 89–90
    relationships and, 88–89
    sharing of, 84–85

    surveillance capitalism and, 83
    trade in, 30–31
personal development, 90, 181, 208
personal space, 53*f*–54*f*, 56–57,
    245–249
perspiration, 3–4. *see also* work
pets, 145
physical needs, importance of, xii,
    20, 86
place, sense of, 54
planets, 230, 233*f*
plants. *see also* farming
    alteration of, 135
    breeding of, 67, 135
    in the city, 51
    containers for, 142
    pollinators for, 67
    tracking the health of, 74
plumbing
    drinking water and, 142
    waste removal and, 59
"plumbing," as a tool, 25–27
politicians, role-playing by, 81
pollinators, 67
pollution, solutions to, 58–59
population density
    crowding and, 56–57
    downsides of, 44, 56, 58
population growth, 294*n*9. *see also*
    birth rates
    history of, 231
    immortality and, 123, 221
    income and, 295*n*15
    peak, 249
    trends in, 11*f*
post-human existence, 218–219
poverty
    currency and, 284*f*

poverty *(continued)*
  dynamics of, 179–180
  elimination of, 167–168, 174, 193,
    208
  injustice, inequity and, 11
  unrest and, 229
prediction information, 205
price curves, 88, 157
price systems, 21, 150–152, 164
prices, setting of, 157, 166, 187,
    204–208
privacy
  in the city, 50–51
  crypto and, 181, 270, 276
  identity authentication and, 207
  infrastructure issues, 144
  loss of, 11–12
  personal data and, 30–31, 89, 95
  preservation of, 75–76
  surveillance capitalism *versus*, 153
  video encryption and, 93
privilege
  ancestors and, 199
  equality and, 29
  resistance to change and, 2
problems
  global, 9–16
  interrelated nature of, 9, 229
  predictability of, 1
  scale of, 19, 61, 219
product pricing, 166–167
proximate causes, 119
psychoactive drugs, 103, 110
psychological advantages, lifespan
    and, xii
psychological defenses
  fear and, 172–173
  usefulness of, 21

psychological diseases, 14
psychological health, 3
psychological inertia, 240
psychological limitations, 172
psychological needs, 61, 172–173
public policies, x, 127, 220
public-key crypto, 273

quality of life, lifespans and, 133, 221

racism, 11, 29, 158–159, 223
radio transmissions, 271–272
rail lines, 69f
  for the city, 48, 49f
  cut-away view of, 73f
  direction of, 256–258, 260–263, 263f
  extent of, 57, 74–75
  for farming, 75
  number of floors for, 261f, 262,
    263f, 264
  tracks, 258
  versatility of, 48
reality
  human relationship to, 54–55
  intersubjective, 40
  objective, 40
  simulations and, 29
  virtual, 55, 62, 82, 104
recycling, 36–37
  air, 60
  construction materials, 252
  materials, 59–60
Reed-Solomon encoding, 272
regeneration, 127f, 139
relationships, 79–110, 277–278
reputation, branding and, 159
resources
  increased use of, 250

influence as a, 210
limitation on, 175
money and, 152
scarce, 21, 165, 212
reverse aging, 140, 239
rich or young, 128, 216*f*
risks, 155, 160–161, 237
of extinction, 77
robots
farming functions of, 74
food preparation by, 74, 142
manufacturing roles of, 45

sacrifice, work and, 19–20
safety
crime deterrence and, 93
definition of, 197
DNA modification of, 139
emotional well-being and, 86–87, 174
importance of, xii
personal data privacy and, 89–90, 98
threats to self and, 2
trust and, 112
Sagan, Carl, 234
salamanders, 126, 127*f*, 139
sanitation, 25–27
satisfaction
correlation with, 99
evaluation of, 176, 270
inner development and, 181
measures of, 37–38, 205–206, 212
prediction of, 206, 211
prices and, 204
relationships and, 83
reporting of, 100
transactions and, 204–205

scientific breakthroughs, 240
search engines, data collection by, 84
self-acceptance, 201–202
self-actualization
definition of, 87, 198
importance of, xii
relationships and, 100–101
service and, 87, 198
well-being and, 87
self-knowledge, 207–208
self-reflection, 37, 100, 186
senses, 35, 103, 107, 109–111
sensory input
bandwidth of, 293*n*16
crowding and, 56–57
noise control and, 57–58
shadow self, 201
Shannon, Claude, 271, 296*n*16
short-term thinking, 34
simplicity, bandwidths and, 106
simulations
human relationships and, 97–99, 173
as a job, 182
learning and, 81
machines, 107
meeting environments, 62
as tools, 28–29
singularity, 240
slavery, lingering effects of, 16
Smith, Adam, 87–88, 151, 153, 172, 180, 295*n*13
social buy-in as a tool, 19–20
social media, 222, 234
collective action and, x
environment of, 11–12
online trolls, 11–12
ranking on, 85

social networks, 270
Social Physics (Pentland), 99, 293n7
society, institutions within, 39
software, development of, 222
solar power, 46, 47f, 68f, 251–254
solvency, measures of, 161–162
space telescopes, 231
space utilization, 245–249, 247f–248f
   per person needs, 51–52, 53f–54f,
     60, 245–249
specialization, competition and, 152,
   181–182
species
   relationships, 12–13
   successful, 124, 294
   unit of survival of, 120, 136
spirituality, 16, 241
spores, survival of, 121, 141
sports venues, 72f
stability, desire for, 3
storage
   in the city, 62
   energy, 46, 252–253
Strategies for Engineered Negligible
   Senescence (SENS), 33, 126, 136,
   137f, 138
stress, avoidance of, 130, 134
success, measures of, 152, 164–165, 173,
   181, 206
suffering, avoidance of, 130
sunlight for the city, 50
surveillance capitalism, 11–12, 222, 235
   future of, 86
   personal data and, 83–84
   privacy and, 153

taxes, 163
   administration of, 163, 270

anonymity of, 91
   management of, 91–92
technology
   connectivity infrastructure, 35
   disruptive, 153–154
   human relationships and, 80, 234
   impact on lifespans and, 13–14
   life extension-related, 217–218
   lifespans and, 123, 126, 140
   scenarios facilitated by, 82–83
   software development and, 222
   well-being bots and, 211
telepathy, machine-mediated, 104,
   235. *see also* brain machines
tipping point, climate, 2, 227
tools, 17–41
touch surfaces, decontamination of,
   60, 143
toxins, 122
   accumulation of, 133–134, 148
   removal of, 135
trade credit, 160
training
   brain machines, 22, 109
   machines, 113
transactions
   additive nature of, 203
   business-to-business, 159–160
   pricing of, 157
   satisfaction and, 203–205
   transparency in, 155
transportation
   for the city, 48, 49f
   energy requirements, 250
   friction loss and, 264
   space for, 247f–248f, 249
   travel times, 256–264
   versatility of, 48

of Zone Pods, 48, 256–259
traumatic events, effects of, 81, 122, 168
travel times, 256–264
trees, 67, 69f, 70f
trust
  behaviors and, 163
  building of, 95–96
  confidence and, 97
  information and, 154–155
  money and, 160–162, 270
  safety and, 112
  societal, 158

ubiquitous bandwidth, 34–36
unfairness, sense of, 2, 238
units of evolution, 124
urban density
  downsides of, 44, 56
  reasons for, 5, 43
urban dwelling, advantages of, 75
utopia, xiii

vaccine research, 141
value
  definition of, 192
  measures of, 167, 199–200
  predicting, 176
  storage of, 150
Venus, 232, 233f
video surveillance, 93, 222
virtual goods, 194
virtual layouts, design of, 55
virtual reality, 82
  empathy and, 104
  landscapes, 55
  material construction and, 62
viruses, transmission of, 26, 141–142

vision, learning through, 106
Visual Capitalist website, 265
vitals, 138
Voyager I, 233–234

warehouses, 292n5
waste
  elimination of, 178, 192
  pollution and, 25, 59
water
  capacity of, 61
  recycling for the city, 46
  safety of, 142, 144
wealth
  concentration of, 166, 203
  concepts of, 208
  creation of, 229
  definitions of, 34
  desire for, 3
  display and, 86
  distribution of, 216
  emotional well-being and, 86
  experiences and, 191
  generation of, 37
  inequity in, 153
  influence and, 80
  life expectancy and, 224, 294n11
  longevity and, 128–129
  marketing and, 178–179
  measures of, 208
  money versus, 150
  ownership and, 62–63, 184–185
  poverty and, 151, 167, 208, 216
  satisfaction versus, 176
  shifts in, 178
  sustainable, 237
  value and, 192
  world, 236–237, 265–266

Wealth of Nations (Smith), 151, 295*n*13
wear and tear, 14, 122–124
well-being
    collaboration and, 90
    currency, 175
    emotional, xii, 86
    hierarchy of needs and, xii
    income and, 86
    investment in, 220
    measures of, 100, 164–165
    optimization of, 211
well-being bots, 30–34, 90
    collaboration between, 201
    development of, 185
    discrimination and, 159
    feedback from, 206
    formation of, 201
    interactions mediated by, 270
    personal data and, 89
    technology and, 211
    technology requirements, 200
    tool as a, 30–31
    user interface, 211

whale communication, 115
wheeled platforms, 50
winner-take-all, 165–166, 210
withdrawal, limited outlooks and,
    15–16
work. *see also* perspiration
    compensation for, 38
    emotional well-being and, 213
    importance of context in, 18
    jobs, 181–182
    nature of, 38–39
    sacrifice and, 19–20
World Bank, 176

zero marginal cost, 165, 191, 210
Zone Pods
    human relationships and, 97–98
    perceived surroundings in, 62
    as a tool, 23–24
    transportation of, 48–50, 256–259